Black Mountain College
EXPERIMENT IN ART

Black Mountain College
EXPERIMENT IN ART

EDITED BY
Vincent Katz

WITH ESSAYS BY
Martin Brody
Robert Creeley
Vincent Katz
Kevin Power

THE MIT PRESS
CAMBRIDGE, MASSACHUSETTS
LONDON, ENGLAND

This book was designed by Gonzalo Armero, set in Futura by BruMa, and printed and bound in Spain.

Library of Congress Cataloging-in-Publication Data.

Black Mountain College: experiment in art / edited by Vincent Katz; with essays by Martin Brody, Robert Creeley, Vincent Katz & Kevin Power.
    p. cm.
  Includes bibliographical references and index.
  ISBN 0-262-11279-5 (hc.: alk. paper)
  1. Black Mountain College (Black Mountain, N.C.). 2. Arts-Study and teaching (Higher), North Carolina, Black Mountain. I. Katz, Vincent, 1960. II. Brody, Martin. III. Museo Nacional Centro de Arte Reina Sofía.

NX405.B55 B552 2003
707'.1'175688— dc21
2002032414

This publication accompanied the exhibition *Black Mountain College: Una Aventura Americana*, curated by Vincent Katz, which took place at the Museo Nacional Centro de Arte Reina Sofía of Madrid, Spain, from 28 October 2002 to 13 January 2003.

Production: Armero Ediciones (Lola Martínez de Albornoz; Carmen del Río)
Coordination Museo Nacional Centro de Arte Reina Sofía: Lucía Ybarra
DL: M-44702-2002

Contents

BLACK MOUNTAIN COLLEGE: AN AMERICAN EXPERIENCE

Our methods for teaching art are in need of oxygen. Between 1933 and 1956, Black Mountain College—and this is already apparent on the cover of the book the reader is holding—was exactly that: oxygen, open air and intelligence at work, aimed at creating an environment of living together in freedom which favored artistic dialogue and creation.

When I met Vincent Katz, it was not at Black Mountain College—which I have still not visited—but in another location where nature is equally to the fore, in the state of Maine. Right from the start, he seemed to me to be the right person to recreate the story that is told here: of the years that that institution came to represent for the American generation of abstract expressionism, something close to what, several years earlier, the Bauhaus school had represented in the Europe of international rationalism. Poet, art critic, and personal friend of Creeley and other leading figures of that movement, Vincent Katz has always been keen on dialogue between the arts, so much at the center of the school's concerns.

So here we have reconstructed that tremendous American adventure whose diverse participants, both teachers and pupils, were artists central to modern culture in America and around the world. Among the famous names remembered here are the poets Charles Olson (who became school rector), Paul Blackburn, Robert Creeley, Robert Duncan, Denise Levertov, Jonathan Williams, and Louis Zukofsky; the painters Josef Albers (one of the people responsible for giving the school its early direction), James Bishop, Ilya Bolotowsky, Jean Charlot, Robert De Niro, Lyonel Feininger, Joseph Fiore, Helen Frankenthaler, Ray Johnson, Franz Kline, Willem and Elaine de Kooning, Robert Motherwell, Kenneth Noland, Amédée Ozenfant, Robert Rauschenberg, Dorothea Rockburne, Xanti Schawinsky, Ben Shahn, Theodoros Stamos, Cy Twombly, Jack Tworkov, and Esteban Vicente; the sculptors John Chamberlain, José de Creeft, Richard Lippold, and Ossip Zadkine; the textile designer Anni Albers; the engineer Buckminster Fuller; the composers Stefan Wolpe, John Cage, Roger Sessions and David Tudor; the choreographer Merce Cunningham; the dancer Paul Taylor; the writer Anaïs Nin; the art critic Clement Greenberg; and the photographers Rudy Burckhardt, Harry Callahan, and Aaron Siskind. The list is truly fantastic and first-class. The presence of a German, or to be more exact Bauhausian, nucleus consisting of Albers, Wolpe, and Schawinsky, and a Spanish one made up of José de Creeft and Esteban Vicente—from whose lips, incidentally, I heard for the first time the name of Wolpe—in addition to the individual cases of Bolotowsky, Jean Charlot, Willem de Kooning, and Amédée Ozenfant, speak to us of something as crucial in the birth of American culture as the contribution of the European exile. Other names, meanwhile, speak to us of what was then the future, a future that had one of its birthplaces in that place both separate and at the same time absolutely central so that, to continue with the comparison, if it was something similar to Bauhaus, it was a Bauhaus much more open and spontaneous. Of particular interest is the joining together of art and music that came to fruition with events such as the performance in 1948 of *Le Piège de Méduse*, by Erik Satie, and in the setting up of joint projects between John Cage, Merce Cunningham and Robert Rauschenberg.

In Spain, unfortunately, there has never been anything like Black Mountain College. As I have just pointed out, two Spanish people were there: that very singular character for too long forgotten, José de Creeft, and Esteban Vicente, who by his own admission could be part of the adventure only following the departure of Albers, with whom he had clashed head-on right from the beginning. In addition, it should be stressed that the school magazine, like the majority of its books of poems—magnificent examples of modern typography—were printed in Palma de Mallorca because Creeley was living there at the time. I would like to express my special appreciation to the great American poet for his contribution to this volume— designed with his usual skill by Gonzalo Armero. Ever the pioneer, Armero some years ago dedicated part of an edition of his marvelous magazine *Poesía* to the subject we are dealing with today, under the responsibility of Kevin Power, who has also been collaborating with us.

JUAN MANUEL BONET
Director, Museo Nacional Centro de Arte Reina Sofía, Madrid

Vincent Katz

BLACK MOUNTAIN COLLEGE:
EXPERIMENT IN ART

I WOULD LIKE TO THANK the following people for their contributions to and advice on the exhibition and book:

Julie Amino, Gonzalo Armero, Bill Berkson, Robert J. Bertholf, Vivien Bittencourt, Juan Manuel Bonet, Peter Boris, Connie Bostic, Martin Brody, Barbara Cain, Trevor Carlson, Angelica Clark, Tom Clark, John W. Coffey, Roger Conover, Robert Creeley, Brenda Danilowitz, Susan Davidson, Fielding Dawson, Vincent Demeusoy, Steve Dickison, Charles Eubanks, Hermine Ford, Sabine Hartmann, Steven Harvey, Rhona Hoffman, Muffet Jones, Sam Jornlin, Peter Macgill, Mac McGinnes, Robert Mann, Lola Martinez de Albornoz, Bridget Moore, Gianni Morselli, Kevin Power, Carmen Del Rio, Kenneth Rosen, Nicola Del Roscio, Ellen Russotto, Amy Schichtel, Alice Sebrell, Kate M. Sellers, Stacy Supman, Adrian Turner, David Vaughan, Harriet Vicente, Barry Walker, Joan Washburn, Klaus Weber, Nicholas Fox Weber, David White, Jonathan Williams, Rutherford Witthus, Ashley Yandle, Lucía Ybarra.

It should be noted that there can be no definitive study of Black Mountain College. The exhibition I have curated represents my personal analysis, at the present time, of the situations that pertained at that institution. As to the artworks discussed, they too represent a personal choice, sometimes dictated by availability for exhibition. They certainly do not represent all the bodies of work done at Black Mountain, even by those artists discussed. Inevitably, some artists have been left out or slighted. For this I apologize. I leave it to future scholars to recognize more fully their achievement.

I was greatly aided in curating the Black Mountain exhibition and editing the accompanying book by being granted the John Guare Writer's Fund Rome Prize Fellowship by the American Academy in Rome for 2001–2002.

VINCENT KATZ
24 July 2002

This book is dedicated to the memories of Fielding Dawson, Richard Lippold, Peter Voulkos, and John Wieners—their visions will always shine.

V. K.

Perhaps, ultimately, it was more about seeing than about an idea. When one looks at the work of the diverse talents that at one time or another composed Black Mountain College, an underlying factor seems to have been the desire to see in a new way, free from previous restrictions. Looked at distinct from the rhetoric that bound and binds so much artistic endeavor, the art is free to be seen afresh. When there is a use of abstraction, as there so often was in those days, maybe now it can be seen less as an idea than a way of seeing.

•

During the twenty-three years of its existence, from 1933 to 1956, Black Mountain College, in southwestern North Carolina, was a magnet for artists establishing their professional identities. What was encouraged, what was engaged in at Black Mountain—both by student and by artist/teacher—was experimentation. People felt free there to undertake activities geared toward finding new ways of doing, rather than studying and repeating the past. For artists who taught there, Black Mountain was a sojourn of great fertility, and like the shaman who travels in quest of experience, these artists derived significant personal strength from their artistic voyages. Upon leaving Black Mountain, this personal power often translated into worldly power in an artist's career. At Black Mountain, relationships were forged or strengthened with fruitful and important repercussions. Artistic work initially dismissed as slight or casual ultimately achieved the support, sometimes verging on apotheosis, of museums, critics, galleries, collectors, and publishers. The transition from experimentation to power occurs regularly in the arts—a consequence of an artist discovering a way to do something that no one else has or can. What is rare is for one academic institution to have attracted such high numbers of students and faculty who effected this transition with such astounding frequency. It is sobering to reflect that the size of the College at any one time averaged fifty students. Part of the story reflects the link between Black Mountain and New York City. Artists exhibiting at the Museum of Modern Art, Peggy Guggenheim's Art of This Century, Charles Egan Gallery, Sam Kootz Gallery, and Betty Parsons Gallery were among those who taught at the College, which pursued and attracted artists with ambitious ideals. Why Black Mountain? The source of its nature can be found in its origin.

John Andrew Rice. Black Mountain College, 1930s.

I. The Beginning

A man who has almost vanished from public consciousness is the key to the Black Mountain story: John Andrew Rice. Raised in South Carolina, a Rhodes Scholar at Oxford, he became an innovative educational theorist and teacher, a colleague of John Dewey. Rice aspired to teach philosophy as Socrates might have, by promoting constant questioning among class participants, the teacher serving as discussion leader, and though more experienced in the dynamics of query and pursuit, not ultimately possessor of The Answer.

LEE HALL PORCH, BLUE RIDGE CAMPUS, BLACK
MOUNTAIN COLLEGE, 1930S.

JOHN ANDREW RICE WITH DAVID BAILEY.

For this approach—and for its concomitant slight to the pre-established syllabus—Rice was fired in early 1933 from his position at Rollins College in Florida. An independent review later exonerated him, but by that time Rice had gathered a group of educators and idealists who chafed at the rigid methods that were, and in many cases still are, universal at educational institutions. These teachers and students resolved to found their own school, with an array of pedagogic safeguards, the most important being that there would be no governing board. The school would be run solely by its teachers, with genuine input from its students, who in turn would be free to create independent patterns of study, their careers divided into two divisions, Junior and Senior. In the Junior division, teaching would be in small classes; in the Senior, largely on a tutorial basis. The new institution derived elements—a bipartite division and tutorials—from the Oxford University system. There would be no credits and no accreditation. When a student felt ready to graduate, he would request an examination, which would then be conducted by an outside examiner.

As Rice put it in an essay in 1935, ". . . those who are responsible for the founding of the College reverted to a form of government found in the older universities

of England and once fairly common in this country, namely, government by the faculty, or self-government. The proper function of a Board of Trustees is performed for the College by an Advisory Council, composed of men and women distinguished in the educational world and the world of affairs. But the legal responsibility for the conduct of the College rests in the faculty and the principal student officer. The idea of including a member of the student body on the Board was borrowed from the Middle Ages."[1]

In addition to regular meetings between student officers and the elected faculty's "Board of Fellows," matters of grave importance would be discussed by the entire faculty and student body. Everyone could speak at these meetings, the only restriction being there would be no voting. At the end of a discussion, the Rector would deliver a "sense of the meeting." Whenever this proved impossible, the issue was postponed for further discussion.

[1] John Andrew Rice, "Black Mountain College," unpublished typescript, 1935, North Carolina Museum of Art, Black Mountain College Research Project, North Carolina State Archives, Raleigh, p. 1.

WORK TEAM LEAVING LEE HALL FOR LAKE EDEN.

TED AND BOBBIE DREIER'S LIVING ROOM AT BLUE RIDGE, BLACK MOUNTAIN COLLEGE, 1930S.

LEE HALL, BLUE RIDGE CAMPUS, BLACK MOUNTAIN COLLEGE, 1933–1941.

VIEW OF LEE HALL WITH DOGWOOD BLOSSOMS. BLUE RIDGE CAMPUS, BLACK MOUNTAIN COLLEGE, 1930S.

These organizational principles were adhered to for the duration of the college's existence. They proved its great blessing, its difference, and its difficulty. Freedom of structure combined with a small, but devoted faculty (remuneration was minimal; the faculty served from personal desire), were the hallmarks that enticed a parade of figures—student and faculty—who would play significant roles in the history of twentieth-century art.

A major drawback to not having a board of trustees was the lack of a predictable financial base, and this would plague Black Mountain throughout its twenty-three year existence. The future of the institution was frequently in doubt, and its final years were ones of conspicuous material paucity. One of the founding teachers, along with Rice, was the physics instructor Ted Dreier, nephew of the collector Katherine Dreier. Ted was an indefatigable fund-raiser, and his connections to high-powered New York art circles proved crucial.

On September 25, 1933, Black Mountain College opened fifteen miles from Asheville, North Carolina, in the Blue Ridge Mountains, at a site used by the YMCA during the summer, but unused the rest of the year. The College's first years were spent at this Blue Ridge campus, most activities taking place in Robert E. Lee Hall, a building with a huge porch and massive wooden columns, which conferred an atmosphere of American classicism. Instead of physical education, the College had a required work program for students, which, with a 1,600 acre-property at their disposal, could be anything from vegetable farming and raising animals, to building and maintenance projects.

•

In a May 1937 article in *Harper's Magazine*, Rice responded to the philosophy of Robert Hutchins, president of the University of Chicago, famous for his promotion of a "great books" curriculum. Rice argued that theoretical habit, which is what institutions of higher learning then as now promote, should be integrated with rather than divorced from other forms of knowledge and experience. Language, Rice went so far as to say, could exist beyond thought. "If by any chance," he wrote, "you ever say what you think without thinking what you say, it is obviously often language that makes the choice, and there may be no thought discoverable in it anywhere. Here language calls for language as one tune calls for another."[2]

In 1936, Louis Adamic wrote an article, also published in *Harper's*, about his experiences spending two and a half months at Black Mountain. Some of his article is based on Rice's 1935 essay on the college. Through Adamic's article, Black Mountain's experiment became widely known, and it was because of this article that many students determined to attend Black Mountain College.

"BMC is one of the smallest colleges in existence," wrote Adamic, "at first inevitably, now deliberately so. It is not only a place where one can take most of the courses available in other colleges, but where one is obliged to live as an

[2] John Andrew Rice, "Fundamentalism and the Higher Learning," *Harper's Magazine*, May 1937, p. 4.

integral part of a close-knit social unit; so close-knit indeed that it has characteristics of a huge family—and this latter fact . . . is as important in the scheme as is class work."[3] Black Mountain's social structure—the proximity of the living situations—would fuel fierce acrimony and remarkable collaborations in the years ahead.

"Group Influence" was how people at the college described the collective effect of bringing people out of their shells—sometimes a painful process of dropping pretenses and defenses, other times a warmly welcomed experience of inclusion. "Also," Adamic wrote, ". . . one belongs, functions, is 'important' in BMC. One, too, is constantly *invited*, verbally and by implication, to be intelligent, to mature. . . . The BMC community, so to speak, psychologically strips the individual, and there he stands revealed to everyone, including himself—and finally likes it."[4]

As quoted in Adamic's article, Rice said his classes strove for "group thinking, cooperative intelligence," in which individual achievement was subordinated to collective effort, and this would have political as well as intellectual consequences. Adamic believed that Black Mountain would serve as a vehicle for social change, an antidote to the individualism that he saw sterilizing American society. He even thought, somewhat fantastically, that Black Mountain would send out offshoots, clone-institutions of self-determined education that by 1950 could number three hundred. Suffice to say, Adamic underestimated the difficulty of keeping just one experiment alive.

Rice also thought it essential that a college teach the works of its own time, as well as the classics. As he put it, "If you can stand a little bootleg stuff, Gertrude Stein's *Lectures in America* is headier than Aristotle's *Poetics* or Horace's *Ars Poetica*. And, if that will make it more palatable, harder reading."[5]

Rice was convinced that the arts should play a central role in a college education and for that reason determined that Black Mountain should find a significant artist to lead its art instruction. Though he did not want Black Mountain to be an art school, he felt that the arts should be at the center, not the periphery of a student's educational experience. As he wrote, "There is no expectation that many students will become artists; in fact, the College regards it as a sacred duty to discourage mere talent from thinking itself genius: but there is something of the artist in everyone, and the development of this talent, however small, carrying with it a severe discipline of its own, results in the student's becoming more sensitive to order in the world and within himself than he can ever be through intellectual effort alone."

The community life of the college was essential to Rice's vision: "But the individual, to be complete, must be aware of his relation to others. Here the whole community becomes his teacher."[6] As Adamic put it, "Let me be as explicit as I can in

[3] Louis Adamic, "Education on a Mountain," *Harper's Magazine*, April 1936, p. 520.

[4] Ibid., p. 524.

[5] John Andrew Rice, "Fundamentalism and the Higher Learning," *Harper's Magazine*, May 1937, pp. 6–7.

[6] John Andrew Rice, "Black Mountain College," unpublished typescript, 1935, North Carolina Museum of Art, Black Mountain College Research Project, North Carolina State Archives, Raleigh, p. 3.

saying that the place is a *process*, a way of education (which, in the BMC concept, is synonymous with life). . . ."[7]

II. Geometric Abstraction

The dominant spirit of our epoch is already recognizable although its form is not yet clearly defined.
—WALTER GROPIUS[8]

BAUHAUS 1919–1928. EXHIBITION AT THE MUSEUM OF MODERN ART, NEW YORK, 1938. INSTALLATION OF BLACK MOUNTAIN COLLEGE SECTION. PHOTOGRAPH BY HERBERT BAYER. Bauhaus-Archiv, Berlin.

With Black Mountain College hardly a month old, the search began for the artist who would manage and inform that central aspect of the college's activity. Ted Dreier recommended consulting Philip Johnson, director of the department of architecture at the Museum of Modern Art in New York, and Johnson knew just the man to lead the art department at Black Mountain College: Josef Albers of the recently closed-down Bauhaus. Indeed, Katherine Dreier's gallery, *Société Anonyme*, had shown various Bauhaus artists in the 1920s, including future Black Mountain instructor Lyonel Feininger.

From its earliest days, Black Mountain had established an important link with the Museum of Modern Art. As the leading modern art institution of its time, the Modern provided vital visibility and credibility to the artists it exhibited, and several Black Mountain teachers exhibited there: the Bauhaus exhibition of 1938 included work by Josef and Anni Albers, Lyonel Feininger, and Xanti Schawinsky; Feininger had a retrospective exhibition with Marsden Hartley in 1944; "Are Clothes Modern?" was curated by Bernhard Rudofsky in 1944–1945; "Modern Handmade Jewelry" included Anni Albers in 1946, who also had a solo exhibition in 1949.

Josef Albers possessed an outstanding artistic and pedagogic pedigree, having taught at the renowned Bauhaus in Germany since 1923, first in Weimar, then in Dessau and Berlin. The Bauhaus, founded by Walter Gropius, its first director, was a state-sponsored school with a strong social agenda. Primarily, it attacked the art academies which, in Gropius's view, had created a false division between craft and art, and fostered a false sense of superiority in the latter. It also attacked neo-classical and historicizing architecture.

The Bauhaus syllabus combined high and low arts, with students learning photography, typography, weaving, pottery, and furniture design, along with painting, architecture, and theater. Students were taught by artists and craftsmen, and had apprenticeships with industrial manufacturers, equipping the students to create in a way that was stylistically modern and socially democratic. Gropius advocated not a "Bauhaus style," the development of which he would have considered a fail-

[7] Louis Adamic, "Education on a Mountain," *Harper's Magazine*, April 1936, p. 529.

[8] Walter Gropius, *The Theory and Organization of The Bauhaus*, originally published as *Idee und Aufbau des Staatlichen Bauhauses Weimar* (Munich: Bauhausverlag, 1923), translation in *Bauhaus 1919–1928*, edited by Herbert Bayer, Walter Gropius, and Ilse Gropius (New York: Museum of Modern Art, 1938), pp. 20–29.

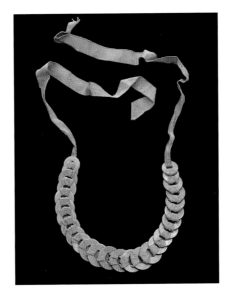
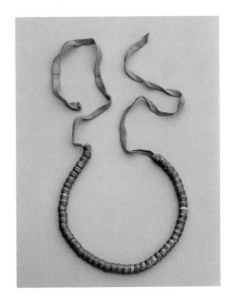

ANNI ALBERS

NECKLACE FROM HARDWARE, CA. 1940.
Drain strainer and paper clips.
The Josef and Anni Albers Foundation.
Photograph by Tim Nighswander.

HARDWARE NECKLACE, CA. 1940.
Washers and grosgrain ribbon.
The Josef and Anni Albers Foundation.
Photograph by Tim Nighswander.

NECKLACE FROM HARDWARE, CA. 1940.
Brass grommerts on lenght of chamois.
The Josef and Anni Albers Foundation.
Photograph by Tim Nighswander.

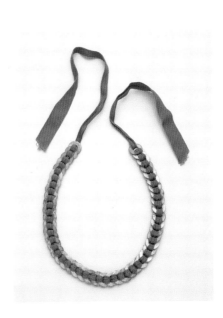

ANNI ALBERS Y ALEX REED
NECKPIECE, CA. 1940.
Aluminum washers and red grosgrain ribbon.
The Josef and Anni Albers Foundation.
Photograph by Tim Nighswander.

NECKPIECE, CA. 1940.
Bobby pins and chain.
The Josef and Anni Albers Foundation.
Photograph by Tim Nighswander.

ure, but rather a generation of individual designers who shared a desire for "simple and sharply modeled designs in which every part merges naturally into the comprehensive volume of the whole."[9]

From the outset, the Bauhaus itself was attacked—first by craftsmen, who feared Bauhaus teaching would contribute to a decline in crafts, then by those who thought traditional crafts had no place in a school devoted to modern architecture. Its ultimate success, despite its need to shift locations, was undeniable. In 1924, Theo van Doesburg wrote that when he first encountered the Bauhaus, it seemed to him the only school to be offering a stimulating art education. "Neither in France, nor England nor anywhere else was there an institution where the students themselves were encouraged to create, instead of being taught merely to repeat that which had already been created."[10]

Albers taught a preliminary course, which introduced students to the characteristics of various materials: clay, glass, wood, stone, textiles, metal, and paint. Traditional craft techniques formed the basis for developing design invention in specialized workshops, that formed the second phase of the Bauhaus curriculum. Materials were the basis, and they remained a constant as students moved from novice to apprentice to professional, with complementary instruction in crafts (*Werklehre*), formal problems (*Formlehre*), including the study of nature, descriptive geometry, the drawing of plans and construction of models, and theories of space, color and design.

After the Bauhaus moved to Dessau in 1925, Albers became a Bauhausmeister, professor of the elementary course in drawing. Later he was in charge of the furniture workshop and taught wallpaper design and typography. His own work during this period was primarily in colored glass. In 1928, Albers wrote,

> To experiment is at first more valuable than to produce; free play in the beginning develops courage. Therefore, we do not begin with a theoretical introduction; we start directly with the material. . . .

> The most familiar methods of using [materials] are summarized; and since they are already in use they are for the time being forbidden. For example: paper, in handicraft and industry, is generally used lying flat; the edge is rarely utilized. For this reason we try paper standing upright, or even as a building material; we reinforce it by complicated folding; we use both sides; we emphasize the edge. Paper is usually pasted: instead of pasting it we try to tie it, to pin it, to sew it, to rivet it. . . .

> Our aim is not so much to work differently as to work without copying or repeating others. We try to experiment, to train ourselves in "constructive thinking.". . .

> . . . an essential point in our teaching is *economy*. Economy is the

[9] Walter Gropius, *The New Architecture and the Bauhaus* (Cambridge: MIT Press, 1965), p. 44 (first published in 1936).

[10] Theo van Doesburg, quoted in *Bauhaus 1919–1928*, edited by Herbert Bayer, Walter Gropius, and Ilse Gropius (New York: Museum of Modern Art, 1938), p. 91.

sense of thriftiness in labor and material and in the best possible use of them to achieve the effect that is desired.[11]

Specific esthetic styles were not taught. Rather, students learned the nature of their materials and developed economic methods of using them. Later, an individual esthetic, based on knowledge of materials and bolstered by self-confidence built from experimentation, could develop. After 1928, when László Moholy-Nagy left the Bauhaus and Albers took complete charge of the preliminary course, he refined its plan as follows: the first month was devoted solely to glass, the second to paper, the third to combinations, and the fourth to a free choice of materials. A procedural pattern was thus built up based on fresh analysis of problems and situations, rather than on established recourses.

Although part of the drawing course was devoted to representation, it was only after 1929 that Albers allowed students to do freehand drawing. The reasons for this decision are not clear, but it foreshadows the free line Albers himself would employ, in addition to strictly geometric work, after his move to Black Mountain.

Gropius recommended to the Council of Masters that women should go from the preliminary course to the weaving workshop, or possibly bookbinding or pottery. No women were allowed to study architecture, which was considered the highest branch of study at the Bauhaus. Women students at the Bauhaus were encouraged to enter the textile workshop, to reserve spaces in the other workshops for men. As with the other workshops, weavers could secure commercial contracts for certain products, while making other works of purely esthetic appeal.

After the departure of Gropius, the Bauhaus became more focused on utilitarian and commercial aims. Anni Albers, who produced weavings of great esthetic merit at the Bauhaus, was keenly aware of the industrial potential for textiles. In this period, she designed a fabric which absorbed sound on one side, while the other refracted light.

In the last years of the Bauhaus, despite the efforts of its director, Mies van der Rohe, to de-politicize the school, it became associated with the Communist Party. Before the 1931 elections, the regional Nazi party had issued a flyer whose first demand was the Bauhaus closure: "Immediate stoppage of Bauhaus funding. Foreign teachers must be dismissed without notice, for it is irreconcilable with the responsibility of worthy municipal leadership towards its citizens that German comrades go hungry while foreigners are handsomely paid from the taxes of a starving nation."[12] The Nazis won enough votes in 1931 to force the Dessau Bauhaus to close. Josef Albers—along with Kandinsky, Mies van der Rohe, and others—had his state contractual rights directly violated, but an appeal by the Masters achieved only a settlement.[13]

[11] Josef Albers, "Concerning Fundamental Design," from "Werklicher Formunterricht," published in *bauhaus. zeitschrift für gestaltung*, nos. 2/3 (Dessau: 1928), pp. 3–7.

[12] *Wähler und Wählerinnen Dessaus!* 1931 election handbill from the Dessau branch of the National Socialist German Workers' Party, quoted in *bauhaus* by Magdalena Droste, Bauhaus-Archiv Museum für Gestaltung/Taschen, Berlin/Köln, 1998, p. 227.

[13] See Peter Hahn, "Die Schliessung des Bauhauses 1933 und seine amerikanischen Nachfolgeinstitutionen" in *100 Jahre Walter Gropius: Schliessung des Bauhauses 1933* (Berlin: 1983), p. 66.

ANNI ALBERS CARD WEAVING. WEAVING CLASS,
BLACK MOUNTAIN COLLEGE.

MIRIAM FRENCH, STUDENT, WEAVING. BLACK
MOUNTAIN COLLEGE.
PHOTOGRAPH BY CLAUDE STOLLER.

JOHN VIRGIL DEAVER, STUDENT, WEAVING. BLACK
MOUNTAIN COLLEGE, 1940–1943.
PHOTOGRAPH BY CLAUDE STOLLER.

Josef and Anni Albers arrived in New York on the S.S. *Europa* on November 24, 1933, just in time for Thanksgiving. An article in the *New York Times* stated, "The Coming of Professor Albers . . . is heralded by his sponsors at the Museum of Modern Art as the beginning of a new era here in the teaching of art." Those words were prescient. The Albers brought with them ideas from the Bauhaus, which they supplemented with their experience in America.

The Albers were connected with Black Mountain for the next sixteen years, both of them as teachers. Josef directed the art program and ultimately served briefly as rector. They departed when the college changed and took a direction they did not consider appropriate. Throughout this period, the Albers maintained contact with Gropius, who came to head the architecture department at Harvard, and Marcel Breuer, a former Bauhaus student and master, who became a professor of architecture at Harvard. While Josef taught occasionally at Harvard and received offers for permanent teaching positions, both the Albers were extremely attracted to the freedom they enjoyed at Black Mountain—not only personal freedom, and the freedom to establish methods of teaching, but also the freedom to choose the artists who made Black Mountain College what it became as an arts institution.

Josef and Anni Albers did some of their best and most experimental work at Black Mountain—and the sixteen years they spent there were central to their careers— but on their own they would have been incapable of making Black Mountain a symbol of artistic experimentation. From his experience at the Bauhaus—where painters such as Kandinsky and Klee taught alongside designers like Breuer and multi-talents like László Moholy-Nagy—Josef Albers decided that diversity would be the backbone of the experience to which he wished to expose Black Mountain students.

Given the associations most people have for Albers—the design-driven Bauhaus and geometric abstraction—it is noteworthy that he invited to teach at Black Mountain artists associated with Surrealism, Humanism, Abstract Expressionism, and Chance Operations. Many of the teachers came for the summer sessions, which became famous to artists and students alike. Usually, an exhibition of the instructor's work was organized.

In the early years of Black Mountain, artists involved with the attractions of geometry came to teach. In fact, until the summer of 1944, the arts were taught mainly by the Albers, with the addition of former Bauhaus student and teacher Xanti Schawinsky from 1936 to 1938. From 1946 to 1948, Ilya Bolotowsky was a full-time teacher, taking over in 1946–1947 when the Albers took the year off.

Anni Albers played an essential role at Black Mountain College. She established the weaving workshop, which became a principle area of study. Her career as an artist also flourished in this period, culminating in her 1949 solo exhibition at the Museum of Modern Art. The number of pieces she produced was never huge, and her output at Black Mountain was consistent with other periods in her career. *Untitled*, 1934, and *Monte Alban*, ca. 1936, are examples of two different approaches Albers took to weaving. The first piece, composed of stacked rectangles whose regularity is occasionally broken by the extension to a double length or by a diagonal edge, demonstrates a willingness to create from a geometric basis what some were calling a pure abstraction, not based on nature, despite the precise and suggestive interaction of form and color.

Monte Alban, on the other hand, with its rising and falling motifs that suggest mountains and clouds, as well as pre-Colombian designs, shows the impact that pre-Colombian art had on both the Albers. After their first trip to Mexico in 1935, they traveled to Mexico eleven more times, and motifs based on pre-Colombian art, usually geometric in nature, found their way into both artists' work. They began collecting, and put on an exhibition of Mayan art at Black Mountain in 1937. Their relationship with the Mayan was an example of their finding a connection between art of the past and the art they wished to produce.

Anni Albers was endlessly experimental in her weaves, combinations of material, and use of imagery. *Untitled*, 1934, uses rayon, linen, cotton, wool, and jute, while *La Luz 1*, 1947, is made from cotton, hemp, and metallic gimp. In *Cityscape*, 1949, Albers uses a gridded geometric format to form an abstracted image of a city, brilliantly using the continuities of cotton thread to form a skyline with its buildings reflected in a lake or river.

DON PAGE, STUDENT, WEAVING. BLACK MOUNTAIN COLLEGE, 1936–1942. PHOTOGRAPH BY CLAUDE STOLLER.

ALEXANDER REED WEAVING. BLACK MOUNTAIN COLLEGE, 1936–1940.

ALEXANDER REED WEAVING. BLACK MOUNTAIN COLLEGE, 1936–1940.

31 >

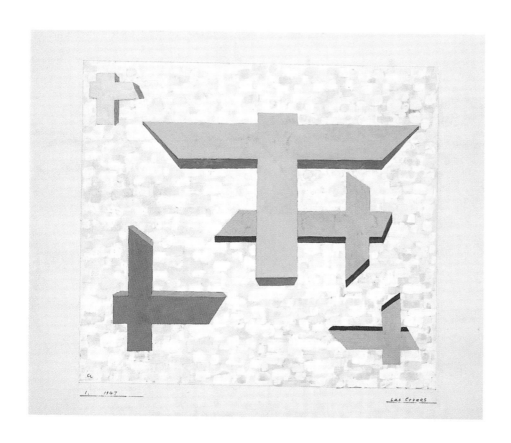

ANNI ALBERS
LAS CRUCES I, 1947.
Gouache on paper, 16 ½ x 19 ¹⁵⁄₁₆ inches.
The Josef and Anni Albers Foundation.

ANNI ALBERS
UNTITLED, 1948.
Gouache on paper, 13 ¾ x 10 ¾ inches.
The Josef and Anni Albers Foundation.
Photograph by Tim Nighswander.

ANNI ALBERS
DEVELOPMENT IN ROSE I, 1952.
Cotton and hemp, 22 ½ x 17 ¼ inches.
The Josef and Anni Albers Foundation.

ANNI ALBERS
TWO, 1952.
Linen, cotton and rayon, 18 x 41 inches.
The Josef and Anni Albers Foundation.
Photograph by Tim Nighswander.

ANNI ALBERS
MONTE ALBAN, CA. 1936.
Silk, linen, wool, 57 ½ x 44 inches.
Busch-Reisinger Museum, Harvard University Art Museums,
Gift of Mr. and Mrs. Richard G. Leahy.
Image © President and Fellows of Harvard College.
Photograph by Michael Nedzweski.

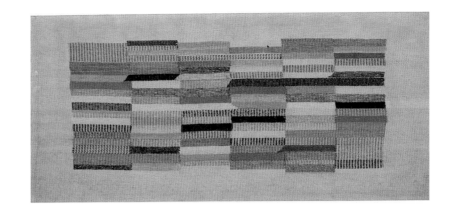

ANNI ALBERS
UNTITLED, 1934.
Rayon, linen, cotton, wool, and jute, 21 x 46 inches.
Collection of Mrs. John Wilkie.
Photograph by Peter Lauri, Bearn.

ANNI ALBERS
PICTOGRAPHIC, 1953.
Cotton with chenille, 18 x 40 inches.
The Detroit Institute of Arts. Founders Society Purchase,
Stanley and Madalyn Rosen Fund, Dr. and Mrs. George
Kamperman Fund, Octavia W. Bates Fund, Emma S.
Fechimer Fund, and William C. Yawkey Fund.
Photograph © 1989 The Detroit Institute of Arts.

ANNI ALBERS
LA LUZ I, 1947.
Cotton, hemp, and metallic gimp, 19 x 32 inches.
The Josef and Anni Albers Foundation.
Photograph by Tim Nighswander.

ANNI ALBERS
CITYSCAPE, 1949.
Bast and cotton, 17 ½ x 26 ½ inches.
The Josef and Anni Albers Foundation.
Formerly collection of the Agoos Family.
Photograph by Tim Nighswander.

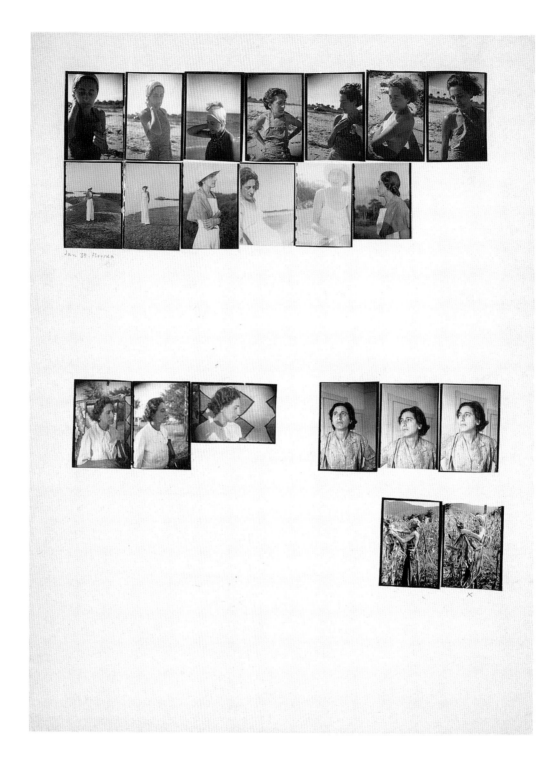

JOSEF ALBERS
JAN 39. FLORIDA (PORTRAITS OF ANNI ALBERS), 1939.
Photo collage of 21 images, 12 x 9 inches.
The Josef and Anni Albers Foundation.
Photograph by Tim Nighswander.

Albers was active as a designer of commercial textiles in her Black Mountain period and prolific as an author. Her texts, though not widely known, are some of the most perceptive from that period. Taking ideas from her mentor Gropius, she went beyond his rigid adherence to the idea that architecture was the queen of the arts, under which all the others must be subsumed. She argued that marginalized crafts (and here she makes a subtextual critique of the Bauhaus's relegation of women to "women's arts") had every chance of being great art in the right hands. Anni had an early training in English Josef lacked. When they first arrived, Anni was Josef's ears and voice, and many were enamored of her clear style and thought.

"Life today is very bewildering," she wrote in 1937 in "Work with Material," published as a *Black Mountain College Bulletin*. "We have no picture of it which is all-inclusive, such as former times may have had. We have to make a choice between concepts of great diversity. And as a common ground is wanting, we are baffled by them." She goes on to analyze the role materials can play in providing personal strength. "We use materials to satisfy our practical needs and our spiritual ones as well. We have useful things and beautiful things—equipment and works of art. In earlier civilizations there was no clear separation of this sort." By learning the qualities of and then experimenting with materials, one could create art:

> But most important to one's own growth is to see oneself leave the safe ground of accepted conventions and to find oneself alone and self-dependent. It is an adventure which can permeate one's whole being. Self-confidence can grow. And a longing for excitement can be satisfied without external means, within oneself; for creating is the most intense excitement one can come to know.[14]

By 1944, Albers's obervations, always marked by moral acuity, increasingly addressed the international situation, which included her own precarious position in Germany as someone of Jewish descent, though converted to Christianity. The opening to her "One Aspect of Art Work" is relevant today, and admirable for its insistence on individual creative effort:

> Our world goes to pieces; we have to rebuild our world. We investigate and worry and analyze and forget that the new comes about through exuberance and not through a defined deficiency. We have to find our strength rather than our weakness. Out of the chaos of collapse we can save the lasting: we still have our "right" or "wrong," the absolute of our inner voice—we still know beauty, freedom, happiness . . . unexplained and unquestioned.

Art can be more than therapy; it can improve the world. Yet, to be fully engaging, it should be based on the manual interaction with materials, not simply an idea:

---

[14] Anni Albers, "Work with Material," *Black Mountain College Bulletin*, no. 5, November 1938, reprinted in Anni Albers, *Selected Writings on Design* (Middletown: Wesleyan University Press, 2000), pp. 6–7.

Art work deals with the problem of a piece of art, but more, it teaches the process of all creating, the shaping out of the shapeless. We learn from it that no picture exists before it is done, no form before it is shaped. The conception of a work gives only its temper, not its consistency. Things take shape in material and in the process of working it, and no imagination is great enough to know before the works are done what they will be like.

Art is always a personal moral adventure:

We learn courage from art work. We have to go where no one was before us. We are alone and we are responsible for our actions. Our solitariness takes on religious character: this is a matter of my conscience and me.[15]

Josef Albers, in his writing and speeches, also engaged the moral and political issues of his day. On June 12, 1940, "three days before the evacuation of Paris," as the subtitle reads, Albers delivered an "Address for the Black Mountain College Meeting at New York," in which he calls on education to take a leading role in combating the moral calamity represented by Hitler. Following Rice's lead, Albers called for education in which "qualities of character are considered just as much as intellectual abilities, in which the development of critical thought, of creative ability and social adjustment, are more respected than mere acquisition of knowledge and skill. . . ." Education should be based in ethics and philosophy, and foster achievement for the non-intellectual intelligence: "If education would aim more at being something instead of at getting something, then our schools would be, maybe, less intellectualistic, but less unjust to the unintellectual types; I mean, for instance, the visual type, the manual type, which are just as important as intellectuals."[16]

Earlier, in "Concerning Art Instruction," published as *Black Mountain College Bulletin* No. 2 in June 1934, Albers made clear his basis in Bauhaus theory and also his divergence from it. He reiterated the need to have beginning students experiment freely in various materials to find those that best suited their abilities and to which they were most attracted. As for the structure of his course, there were to be three elements: Drawing, Basic Design (frequently referred to by its German name, *Werklehre*), and Color-Painting. "These are supplemented," Albers explained, "by exhibitions and discussions of old and modern art, of handicraft and industrial products, of typographic and photographic work."

When Albers first arrived at Black Mountain and could not yet speak fluent English, a student asked him his goal at Black Mountain. Albers was very pleased to have a response: "To open eyes." This became a slogan for Albers and his students, and retains its pithy validity. If a teacher could make a student see more clearly—

[15] Anni Albers, "One Aspect of Art Work," first published as "We Need the Crafts for Their Contact with Materials," *Design*, 1944, retitled and reprinted in Anni Albers, *Selected Writings on Design* (Middletown: Wesleyan University Press, 2000), pp. 25–26.

[16] Josef Albers, "Address for the Black Mountain College Meeting at New York," unpublished statement, 1940, North Carolina Museum of Art, Black Mountain College Research Project, North Carolina State Archives, Raleigh.

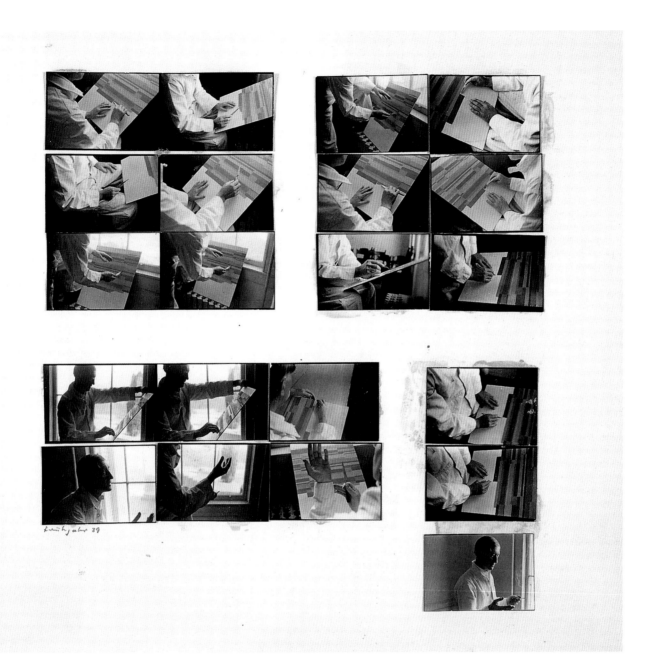

JOSEF ALBERS
SPRING 39 (JOSEF ALBERS PAINTING AT BLACK MOUNTAIN COLLEGE), 1939.
Photo collage of 21 images, 8 x 9 inches.
The Josef and Anni Albers Foundation.
Photograph by Tim Nighswander.

JOSEF ALBERS DRAWING CLASS (ALBERS AT RIGHT). LEE HALL PORCH, BLUE RIDGE CAMPUS, SPRING 1936. PHOTOGRAPH BY ANNE CHAPIN WESTON.

JOSEF ALBERS DRAWING CLASS (FRANCES GOLDMAN AND RUDOLPH HESSE LEARNING PROPORTION WITH DÜRER FRAME). CA. 1939–1940.

JOSEF ALBERS DRAWING CLASS (WITH JANE SLATER AND EVA ZHITLOWSKY). BLACK MOUNTAIN COLLEGE.

JOSEF ALBERS DESIGN CLASS. EXAMPLE OF PAPER FOLDING TO PRODUCE DRAMATIC SPATIAL MOVEMENTS.

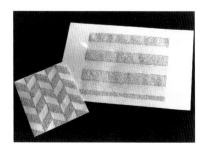

STUDY IN TEXTURE AND PATTERN. PHOTOGRAPH BY CLAUDE STOLLER.

color, form, texture—he would have bestowed an enormous artistic advantage. Seeing, in Albers's curriculum, developed from drawing:

> We cannot communicate graphically what we do not see. That which we see incorrectly we will report incorrectly. We recognize that although our optical vision is correct, our over-emphasis on the psychic vision often makes us see incorrectly. For this reason we learn to test our seeing, and systematically study foreshortening, overlapping as the main form problems of graphic articulation, and distinction between and the pronunciation of nearness and distance.

In the *Werklehre* section, Albers continued the Bauhaus's exercises with basic materials, such as paper, metal, and wire, avoiding the use of tools and testing unusual aspects of materials. Within the *Werklehre* section, there would be a distinction between *matière* studies and material studies, the former studying "the appearance, the surface (epidermis) of material," while the latter examined the properties of various materials. As in the Preliminary Course at the Bauhaus, Albers stated, "We stress economy of form, that is the ratio of effort to effect."

In the area of color experimentation and theory, Albers went beyond his Bauhaus experience. At Black Mountain, Albers developed the principles he later applied in his definitive series, "Homage to the Square." Part of the curriculum, the color course, began with a systematic exploration of "the tonal possibilites of colors, their relativity, their interaction and influence on each other, cold and warmth, light intensity, color intensity, psychical and spatial effects."[17]

In introducing the college seal and library bookplate he designed in 1935, Josef Albers published a brochure in which he quoted Plato:

[17] Josef Albers, "Concerning Art Instruction," published as *Black Mountain College Bulletin*, no. 2, Black Mountain College, June 1934.

By beauty of shapes I do not mean, as most people would suppose, the beauty of living figures or of pictures, but, to make my point clear, I mean straight lines and circles, and shapes, plane or solid, made from them by lathe, ruler and square. These are not, like other things, beautiful relatively, but always, and absolutely.[18]

In most people's minds, Albers is associated with the "Homage to the Square" series to which he devoted the last part of his life. These paintings represented a psychological shift into the effects of color combinations in a slightly varied formal framework. It is work based in theory, and as such has been easy to digest by the public. On the contrary, the work Albers did while at Black Mountain, which should be seen as the middle phase of his career, represents his greatest interest in experimentation. As a result, Albers's work from the Black Mountain period is full of surprises in terms of approach, technique and imagery. Living in the United States was a new experience, which the Albers gratefully enjoyed. It is natural for an artist's work to reflect a shift in lifestyle. Social expectations were less defined in the United States; so were expectations for art. Being isolated at Black Mountain, being the only painter there for many years, and being in an environment that encouraged openness of approach all contributed to the opening up of Albers's work. Albers's Black Mountain years were prolific, and he produced a great quantity of prints, drawing and paintings.

A painting like *Etude: red-violet*, 1935, immediately locates Albers's different artistic region. Unlike his Bauhaus glass pieces and his later Squares, this painting is cut loose from any geometric basis. It revels in the impastoed application of paint on board (most of his paintings during this period were on board). One would call it expressionistic but for Albers's notorious theoretical mode of approach. It could be termed, however, an essay in color relations. Albers was concerned

[18] Plato, *Philebus*, 51C, quoted by Josef Albers in *Leaflet Presenting BMC Seal and Library Bookplate*, designed by Josef Albers, Black Mountain College, March 1935.

with making dark colors recede and light colors come forward, part of the interest here. As his wife wrote nine years later, ". . . no picture exists before it is done, no form before it is shaped. . . . Things take shape in material and in the process of working it. . . ." The way *Etude: red-violet* was painted is essential to its existence, and that is equally if not more important than any theory it exemplifies.

In a series of works painted from the mid-1930s to the mid-1940s, Albers achieved the most crucial balance in his career between paint and form. In the works *Monument (of General Omega)*, 1936, *Open (B)*, December 1940, *Growing*, 1940, and *Memento*, 1943, Albers's shapes have geometric bases, but they are not rigidly defined. The edges in these paintings, the definitions between one form and another, one color and another, are delicately handled, visibly painted, so that the forms are not contained, but suggest a slight movement. In the earlier two pieces, Albers used diagonals and overlapping, creating illusions of depth which were not literal, and his colors are subdued. In the later two pieces, influenced of Paul Klee's flatly arrayed patterns, the colors are daringly provocative—pinks, purples, scarlets—and there is no overlapping of forms.

Other paintings from the Black Mountain period, such as *Repetition Against Blue*, 1943, and *Kinetic (III)*, 1945, works with sharply defined edges and complex geometric forms, were based in part on Albers's study of Mayan architecture and decoration, with a surprising use of hot pinks and deep reds, and an exciting formal inventiveness. Not content to contemplate primal shapes, Albers used straight lines to develop continually evolving complexities between thickness of bands, change of direction, and echoic patterning. A constant awareness of geometry's spatial requirements is put to artistic use. It is never employed as an optical trick, one reason Albers bristled when later called the father of Op Art.

In graphic work done at Black Mountain, even more than in his painting, Albers revealed willingness to experiment. Particularly surprising are the freehand drawings, some with fanciful decorative trills. Alongside starkly original geometric drawings such as *Untitled I: Linear Construction*, 1936, are drawings like *Untitled Abstraction*, ca. 1942, where the goal was to see the result of moving as far as possible from the straight line, while still refusing reference to the visible world. This was abstraction not based in nature, but on an idea about drawing—the curlicue. The conceptual basis behind this drawing was a precursor to ideas used years later by Sol LeWitt. Freely evolving curlicues appeared in Albers's prints as well, although the prints, perhaps due to their more richly evolved textures and imagery, displayed a more biomorphic aspect than the pencil drawings. The title of the drypoint *Girl/Maturity*, 1940, indicates the biomorphic nature of this image, while pieces like *Escape* and *Rondo*, drypoints from 1942, reference animal and human figures respectively.

Albers's more freely evolved forms exist side by side with brilliant works of geometric abstraction. One of the most significant bodies of work Albers produced at this time were his drawings and prints entitled Graphic Tectonics. Based on his observations of pre-Columbian art and its determining use of parallels, Albers drew dense series of geometric outlines in horizontal and vertical lines that vary in thickness and sometimes in length and separation, creating powerful illusions of space which retain their mystery through a stubborn refusal to be reduced to any

46 >

JOSEF ALBERS
ETUDE: RED-VIOLET, 1935.
Oil on panel, 15 3/8 x 14 inches.
The Josef and Anni Albers Foundation.

JOSEF ALBERS
MONUMENT (OF GENERAL OMEGA), 1936.
Oil on masonite, 16 x 11 ⅞ inches.
The Josef and Anni Albers Foundation.
Photograph by Tim Nighswander.

JOSEF ALBERS
OPEN (B), DECEMBER 1940.
Oil on masonite, 19 ⅞ x 19 ⅝ inches.
Solomon R. Guggenheim Museum, New York.
Photograph: Carmelo Guadagno © The Solomon R.
Guggenheim Foundation, New York.

JOSEF ALBERS
GROWING, 1940.
Oil on masonite, 24 x 26 ¾ inches.
San Francisco Museum of Modern Art.
Gift of Charlotte Mack.
Photograph by Ben Blackwell.

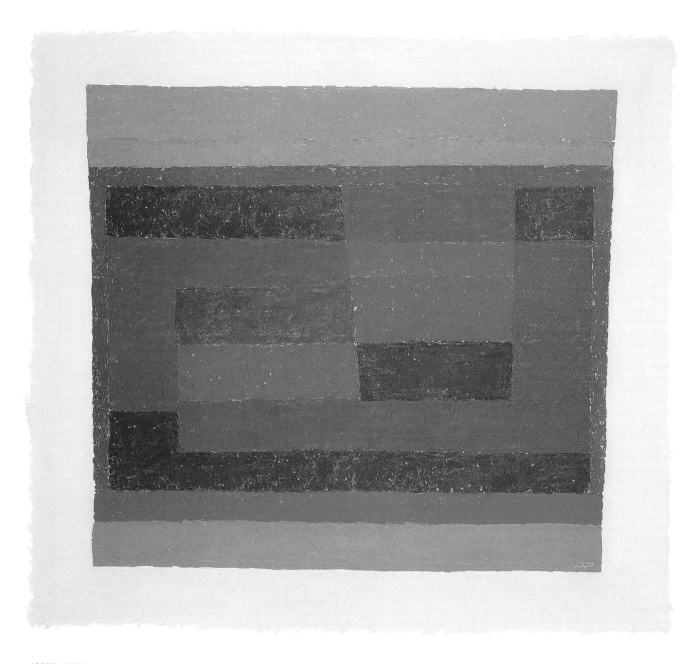

JOSEF ALBERS
MEMENTO, 1943.
Oil on masonite, 18 ½ x 20 ⅝ inches.
Solomon R. Guggenheim Museum, New York.
Photograph: Carmelo Guadagno © The Solomon R. Guggenheim Foundation, New York.

JOSEF ALBERS
REPETITION AGAINST BLUE, 1943.
Oil on masonite, 15 ¾ x 31 inches.
The Josef and Anni Albers Foundation.
Photograph by Tim Nighswander.

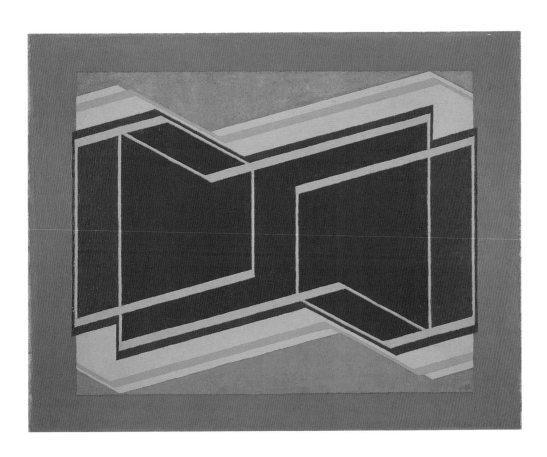

JOSEF ALBERS
KINETIC III, 1945.
Oil on masonite, 24 ¼ x 30 ⅝ inches.
The Josef and Anni Albers Foundation.
Photograph by Tim Nighswander.

JOSEF ALBERS
UNTITLED ABSTRACTION, CA 1940.
Oil on Victor Talking Machine, "Victrola" cover, 14 ½ x 12 ½ inches.
The Josef and Anni Albers Foundation.
Photograph by Tim Nighswander.

JOSEF ALBERS
RELATED I (RED), 1943.
Oil on masonite, 24 ½ x 18 ½ inches.
The Josef and Anni Albers Foundation.
Photograph by Tim Nighswander.

JOSEF ALBERS
OSCILLATING (A), 1940.
Oil on masonite, 36 ½ x 28 inches.
The Josef and Anni Albers Foundation.
Photograph by Tim Nighswander.

JOSEF ALBERS
STUDY FOR «DIPTYCH», 1934.
Pencil, ink, wash and watercolor on heavy wove paper,
15 ¾ x 11 ¾ inches.
The Josef and Anni Albers Foundation.
Photograph by Tim Nighswander.

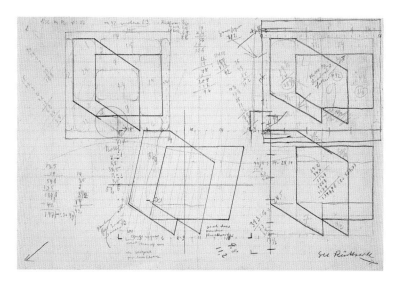

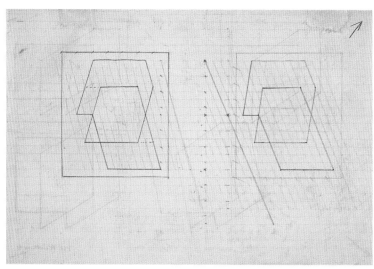

JOSEF ALBERS
STUDIES FOR ABSTRACT PAINTINGS, CA 1937.
Pencil and red pencil on wove paper
ruled in pencil, 9 ¼ x 13 ¾ inches.
The Josef and Anni Albers Foundation. Photograph by Tim Nighswander.

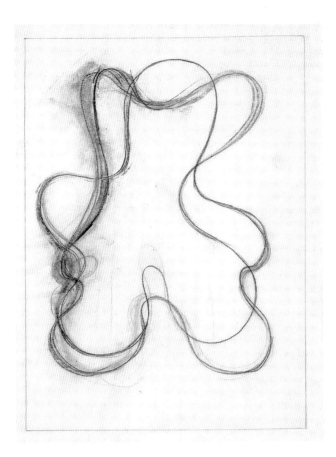

JOSEF ALBERS
STUDY FOR MATURITY, 1942.
Pencil and red pencil on paper, 13 15/16 x 10 ½ inches.
The Josef and Anni Albers Foundation.
Photograph by Tim Nighswander.

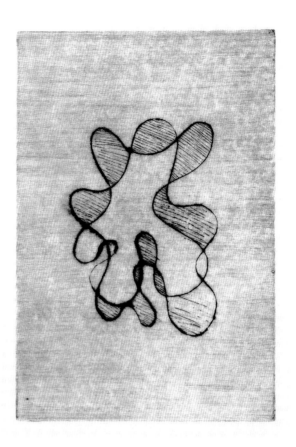

JOSEF ALBERS
MATURITY I, 1940.
Drypoint, image size: 4 5/8 x 3 ¼ inches. Sheet size: 10 ¾ x 8 ¼ inches.
The Josef and Anni Albers Foundation.
Photograph by Tim Nighswander / Katherine Newbegin.

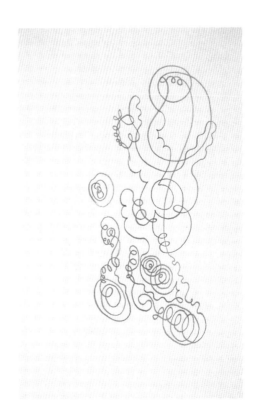

JOSEF ALBERS
UNTITLED ABSTRACTION, CA 1942.
Pencil on Strathmore bond paper, 8 ½ x 5 ½ inches.
The Josef and Anni Albers Foundation. Photograph by Tim Nighswander.

literal depiction. Even when they look like receding or projecting spaces, they do not resemble an actual structure. Albers was interested, too, in subverting the usual expectations of modulation in drawing and in lithography, relying instead on simple, unmodulated line-color. A series of relief prints done at the Biltmore Press in Asheville used geometry on a non-overlapping, Mayan model (the woodcut *Contra*, 1944) or to create subtle illusion (the lineoleum cut *Fenced*, 1944, and woodcut *Multiplex D*, 1948).

Albers's paintings on paper paralleled his interests in paintings on board and drawings. At the end of his Black Mountain period, Albers moved away from liberal experimentation, and towards his "Homage to the Square" series. A precursor to this was his series, "Variants," which he began while still at Black Mountain and continued afterwards. Particularly in the studies, such as *Study for a Variant (I)*, ca. 1947, and *Study for a Variant (II)*, ca. 1947, the edges separating the geometric forms are like the trembling, non-rigid ones of his earlier Black Mountain paintings. Combined with Albers's intricate play of shape and color, those edges make these works intensely alive.

Albers exhibited widely while at Black Mountain. His first United States exhibition, of woodcuts, took place at the Addison Gallery in Andover, Massachusetts in January 1935. He showed at J. B. Neumann's New Art Circle gallery in New York in 1936, and in the same year organized a show of his Bauhaus and Black Mountain work to be shown for ten days at Lee Hall and then to travel as part of an exhibition of the work of four artists, including Katherine Dreier, to the Wadsworth Athenaeum, the Addison Gallery, the San Francisco Museum of Art, and the Chicago Arts Club. In 1937, Albers was included in an "Exhibition of Abstract Artists" at the Squibb Building in New York with Bolotowsky, George Cavallon, Burgoyne Diller, Balcomb Greene, Alice Mason, George L. K. Morris, Vaclav Vytlacil, and others. Also in 1937, Albers began exhibiting with Katharine Kuh Gallery in Chicago. In 1942, he participated in a group show at Kuh, alongside Jawlensky, Kandinsky, Léger, Mondrian, and Ozenfant. In 1943, Albers was included in the 7th Annual Exhibition of American Abstract Artists, at the Riverside Museum, with Bolotowsky, Fritz Glarner, Morris, and others. In 1944, he participated in the important traveling show, "Abstract And Surrealist Art In The United States," curated by Sidney Janis, which appeared at five museums. In 1949, he had two concurrent solo exhibitions at two of New York's most prominent galleries, Charles Egan and Sidney Janis. While Clement Greenberg, writing in the *Nation*, felt that Albers's coloristic acuity was hampered by his adherence to geometric restrictions, the reviewer in *Time* magazine was much more favorable, citing the experimental nature of Albers's work.[19]

Overall, while at Black Mountain, Albers showed interest in a multiplicity of approaches, for example, demonstrating that the geometric could be as free as freehand, and freehand as abstract as the geometric. Albers's conclusion to a text on the Graphic Tectonics summed up his attitude at the time: ". . . we cannot remain in a single viewpoint, we need more for the sake of free vision." He was

[19] Clement Greenberg review in the *Nation*, February 19, 1949, pp. 221–222, and review in *Time*, January 31, 1949, p. 26.

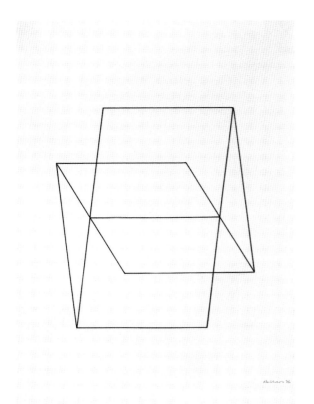

JOSEF ALBERS
UNTITLED I: LINEAR CONSTRUCTION, 1936.
Pen and ink on heavy wove paper, 14 ½ x 11 inches.
The Josef and Anni Albers Foundation.

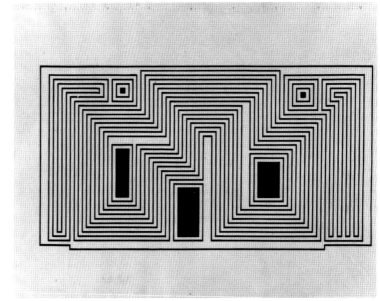

JOSEF ALBERS
STUDY FOR SANCTUARY I, CA 1941–1942.
Pen and ink on wove graph paper ruled in blue, 17 x 22 ⅛ inches.
The Josef and Anni Albers Foundation.

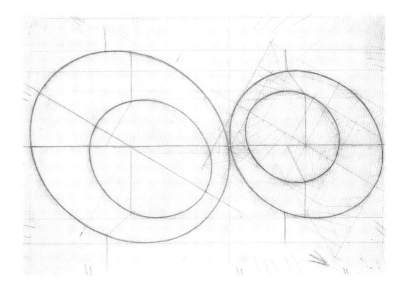

JOSEF ALBERS
UNTITLED ABSTRACTION, CA 1930.
Pencil and red pencil on wove paper
torn from a tablet, 10 ¹⁴⁄₁₆ x 15 ¾ inches.
The Josef and Anni Albers Foundation.
Photograph by Tim Nighswander.

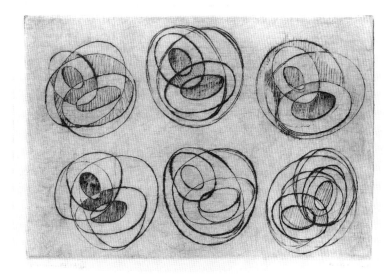

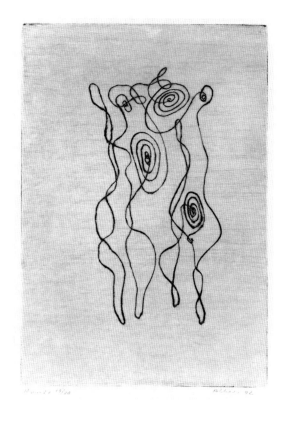

JOSEF ALBERS
ESCAPE, 1942.
Drypoint, edition 20, 5 ½ x 8 inches.
The Josef and Anni Albers Foundation.
Photograph by Tim Nighswander / Katherine Newbegin.

JOSEF ALBERS
VARIANTS, 1942.
Drypoint, edition 20, printed at Swan Press,
Chicago, 6 x 8 ⅞ inches.
The Josef and Anni Albers Foundation.

JOSEF ALBERS
RONDO, 1942.
Drypoint, edition 20, 8 x 5 ½ inches.
The Josef and Anni Albers Foundation.

a meticulous planner and organizer, entirely devoted to his task as pedagogue, determined to provide the most varied and stimulating environment for the students—all this while being equally devoted and prolific in experimentation and achievement in his own art in various media. Albers painstakingly arranged for traveling exhibitions to come to Black Mountain, to borrow glass slides for presentations on ancient and modern art, and, at least from 1944 on, made sure that the students were exposed to a variety of artistic viewpoints in the form of the artists invited to teach at Black Mountain.

It is remarkable to think that Albers would invite artists and critics who were not necessarily in his camp. Certainly, they were all modernists, but coming from all over the map and from both sides of the geometric/nongeometric divide. The parties ranged from Neoplasticism and the Bauhaus, to Abstract Expressionism, to Surrealism and Social Humanism. With the era of John Cage, particularly when Cage became involved with Chance Operations, modernism moved beyond abstraction into concept. This occurred shortly after Albers's departure, but the principle of inclusiveness he established continued to be felt.

It is worth noting that Albers's ideas, or at least his expression of them, developed after he left the Bauhaus. In a 1946 issue of *design* magazine devoted to Black Mountain College, a subtle difference of opinion is noticeable in the statements of Albers and Gropius. The founder of the Bauhaus compares two buildings—the conservative and generic National Gallery of Art in Washington, designed by John Russell Pope, and the adventurous Bear Run House by Frank Lloyd Wright: "The [National Gallery] is 'art for art's sake,' denying man's genuine creative power for expression of form, using ever so skillfuly the morphology of dead styles; it is a piece of archaeology. The [Bear Run House] shows a creative conception of present-day life representing a piece of living American architecture."[20] Albers would not have argued with Gropius's assessment of the two pieces of architecture. By this time, however, and perhaps as a result of living in a more open American society, Albers believed that art need not, indeed should not, be subordinated to any loftier aim. As he wrote in the same issue of *design*, "Art, therefore, can be considered as an end instead of a means. So 'l'art pour l'art' can be justified. To restrict art to a means of propaganda, for instance, proves only a psychological, and so a fundamental error."[21] Albers believed more than he was willing to say, in deference to his friend and former mentor. Not only should art not be propaganda, but it need not be subordinated to architecture, as though architecture were a more important endeavor.

To give an idea of Albers's efforts on behalf of Black Mountain's art students, in February 1943, he wrote Barbara Morgan requesting photographs for a Morgan exhibition at Black Mountain to coincide with a talk he would give on photography. Morgan agreed to send a group of new prints and offered to give six prints to the College. Ultimately, she sent twenty-four prints for the exhibition, a combination of dance and non-dance pictures. Morgan also taught in the 1944 Summer Art Institute. Periodically, Albers appealed to alumuni and friends to donate art

[20] Walter Gropius, "Living Architecture or 'International Style'?" in *design* 47, no. 8 (April 1946):10.

[21] Josef Albers, "Present and/or Past," in *design* 47, no. 8 (April 1946):17.

52 >

JOSEF ALBERS
GRAPHIC TECTONIC, CA 1942.
Pen and ink on wove graph paper ruled in blue, 22 ⅛ x 17 inches.
The Josef and Anni Albers Foundation.
OF HIS *GRAPHIC TECTONIC* LITHOGRAPHS, ALBERS WROTE "THESE RESULTS
REQUIRE THE USE OF RULER AND DRAFTING PEN AND ESTABLISH UNMODULATED LINE
AS A LEGITIMATE ARTISTIC MEANS. IN THIS WAY THEY OPPOSE A BELIEF THAT THE
HANDMADE IS BETTER THAN THE MACHINE-MADE, OR THAT MECHANICAL
CONSTRUCTION IS ANTIGRAPHIC OR UNABLE TO AROUSE EMOTION." THE SAME
APPLIES TO THE *GRAPHIC TECTONIC* DRAWINGS.

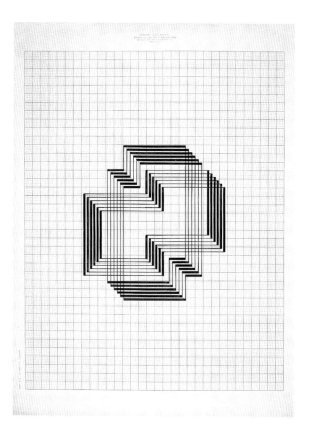

JOSEF ALBERS
UNTITLED GRAPHIC TECTONIC VI, CA 1941–1942.
Pen and ink on wove graph paper ruled in orange, 23 ½ x 18 inches.
The Josef and Anni Albers Foundation.
Photograph by Tim Nighswander.

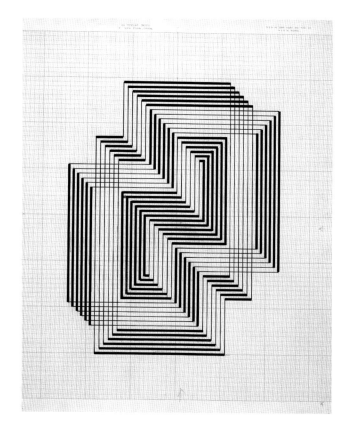

JOSEF ALBERS
UNTITLED GRAPHIC TECTONIC IV, CA 1941–1942.
Pencil, pen and ink on wove graph paper ruled in orange, 22 x 17 ½ inches.
The Josef and Anni Albers Foundation.
Photograph by Tim Nighswander.

JOSEF ALBERS
CONTRA, 1944.
Woodcut, edition 25, Biltmore Press,
Asheville, 9 ¼ x 13 ⅛ inches.
The Josef and Anni Albers Foundation.
Photograph by Tim Nighswander / Katherine Newbegin.

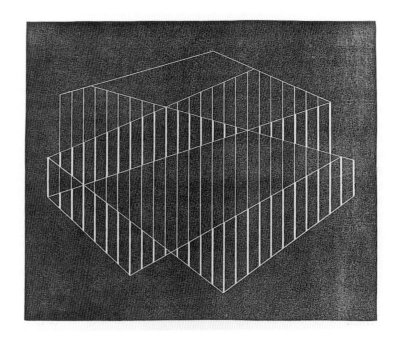

JOSEF ALBERS
FENCED, 1944.
Linoleum cut, Biltmore Press, Asheville,
10 x 12 ¼ inches.
The Josef and Anni Albers Foundation.
Photograph by Tim Nighswander / Katherine Newbegin.

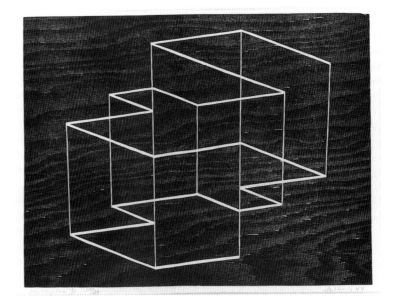

JOSEF ALBERS
MULTIPLEX D, 1948.
Woodcut, edition 30, Biltmore Press, Asheville,
9 x 12 inches.
The Josef and Anni Albers Foundation.
Photograph by Tim Nighswander / Katherine Newbegin.

"BLACK MOUNTAIN COLLEGE. VIEW OF STUDIES BUILDING NORTH OF LAKE. ERECTED WITH STUDENT AND FACULTY LABOR IN 1940–1941. CONTAINS STUDENT AND FACULTY STUDIES AND CLASSROOMS. BACKGROUND, BLACK MOUNTAINS (6000 FEET) NEAR MT. MITCHELL" (POSTCARD).

books to the library. He wrote in a 1943 circular, "Our new course, 'Seeing Art,' has an unusual enrollment: two thirds of the student body participates. It is for this course in particular that we need books and reproductions and slides. We have no color reproductions and no slides at all." To this he added a special plea: "It may interest you to know that most of the members of the faculty receive no cash salary, only room and board. Therefore we dare to ask our friends to look over the books in their libraries for books which might be particularly useful here."[22] One person to respond was Alfred H. Barr, Jr., Director of The Museum of Modern Art, who offered to send books on Miró, Klee, Indian Art, and Walker Evans. In 1948, Black Mountain students participated in an exhibition, "Art Schools, U.S.A.," organized by the Addison Gallery of American Art, that examined the state of art education and included the major art schools of the time. Black Mountain sent work by six students, including Ruth Asawa, Joseph Fiore, and Kenneth Noland.

In 1941, the college moved from the rented Blue Ridge campus to a property, bought by the college, at nearby Lake Eden. The 667-acre property came with sixteen buildings and an artificial lake, but the buildings were not winterized, and the college needed to construct residential and educational facilities. Marcel Breuer and Walter Gropius were asked to design the new campus, which they did, brilliantly utilizing the Lake Eden waterfront in a series of modern buildings. After fund-raising efforts and many meetings, it was decided that the Breuer-Gropius plan could not be afforded, and a more restrained plan was designed by future faculty member A. Lawrence Kocher. Even Kocher's plan was not fully executed. In typical Black Mountain fashion, with students and faculty sweating it out in the trenches of the foundation, one wing of Kocher's plan was built in 1940–1941, henceforth known as the Studies Building. Divorced from its balancing counterparts, it looks a little odd, projecting out from the woods towards the

[22] Josef Albers, "Black Mountain College, to our alumni and friends," 1943, North Carolina Museum of Art, Black Mountain College Research Project, North Carolina State Archives, Raleigh.

JOSEF ALBERS
STUDY FOR MANTIC, CA 1940.
Oil on paper, 12 ⅝ x 13 ¾ inches.
The Josef and Anni Albers Foundation.

lake, but it certainly served its purposes, forming a base for some of the most exciting experiments at Black Mountain College.

In May 1940, Breuer was also involved with the college in a different way, as the outside examiner for the first four students to graduate Black Mountain College in the field of art. As reported in a college newsletter, "The examination consisted of judging the class work and free studies of each student, reading their papers on three assigned subjects, discussing their work, papers and notebooks, and testing their familiarity with past periods of art. According to Mr. Breuer, the standard of achievement was unusually high."[23] Although Black Mountain did not confer degrees, its graduates were accepted by the graduate schools of Columbia, Harvard, and other universities.

In February 1941, Fernand Léger visited the college for about two weeks. While there, he gave a lecture and met individually with students. In these discussions, he stressed what he called "Truth" in color and form, the use of strong, unmodulated tones and "design that reinforces color." As he put it, "pure tone in painting is reality." Whether the form be "objective or invented," Léger believed in simplicity, based on geometric principles, with a minimum of painterly obfuscation. "Education, religion, the 'decorative life' are three inventions," he said, "three envelopes created to conceal truth."[24]

The Summer Art Institute at Black Mountain College was initiated in 1944. The invited artists were Jean Charlot, José de Creeft, and Amédée Ozenfant, as well as Albers and Walter Gropius, who came to lecture. There was also a Music Institute that included Roger Sessions, among others; Barbara Morgan, who visited, took a photograph of the music faculty. The Summer Art Institute for 1945 included three prominent painters as faculty—Lyonel Feininger, Fannie Hillsmith, and Robert Motherwell—along with sculptor Ossip Zadkine.

Lyonel Feininger was one of three artists sought and hired by the Bauhaus when it first opened in 1919. His woodcut was used to help proclaim the ambitions and ideals of Gropius's *Bauhaus Manifesto and Program*, published the same year. Feininger was well-known as an Expressionist painter whose work had a strongly geometricizing tendency. Like Kandinsky and Klee, who also taught at the Bauhaus, Feininger did not easily fit into a particular esthetic, but rather repre-

MARCEL BREUER AND WALTER GROPIUS MODEL OF DESIGN FOR BLACK MOUNTAIN COLLEGE COLLEGE CAMPUS, LAKE EDEN. DESIGNED 1939, NOT CONSTRUCTED.

ROBERT HAAS PRINTING CLASS: GETTING OUT PROGRAMS FOR VISITOR'S WEEK, MAY 3–7, 1940.

[23] "First Graduation in the Art Field," in *Black Mountain College Newsletter*, no. 8, May 1940, p. 1.

[24] Fernand Léger, quoted in "Visiting Speakers Provoke Discussions," *Black Mountain College Newsletter*, no. 12, March 1941, pp. 2–3.

Students on the pier at Lake Eden, Studies Building in background. Photograph by Stuart Atkinson.

People walking to Dining Hall. Lake Eden Campus, Black Mountain College.

"Lake Eden dining room / kitchen building, from the Studies Building, early in the morning, I think. Probably, spring 1942." Photograph and caption by Will Hamlin.

Lake Eden Campus, winter, late 1940s. Photograph by Trude Guermonprez.

sented an independent, analytic approach to painting. These three painters were chosen to join the Bauhaus faculty partly because they would contribute to the esthetic diversity.

Feininger was born on St. Mark's Place in New York in 1871. He studied art at the Kunstakademie in Berlin and also in Paris, where he saw the work of the Cubists in 1911. In 1913, he was invited by Franz Marc to exhibit with the Blaue Reiter group, which also included Kandinsky and Klee. In 1919, he was chosen by Gropius to be the first painting Form Master in charge of the graphic workshop at the Bauhaus. Feininger was influenced by Cubism, and his paintings relied more on rectilinear and planar depiction that did the other Blaue Reiter or Expressionist painters. In his geometric transformation of the visible world—often, in Feininger's case, seascapes or buildings—there is something similar to Mondrian's pier paintings, where the lines start to break away from depiction. Feininger maintained a closer relation to the observed world; the work he was doing in the 1940s was a powerful response to the linear valences of the modern city.

"DODY HARRISON LOOKING OUT OF HER STUDY WINDOW, LAKE EDEN, PROBABLY 1942." PHOTOGRAPH AND CAPTION BY WILLIAM HAMLIN.

Feininger was included in the inaugural exhibition of the Museum of Modern Art in New York and enjoyed a retrospective exhibition at the Modern in 1944, in conjunction with an exhibition by Marsden Hartley. In the summer of 1945, he was invited by Albers to teach at Black Mountain. In a piece written for *design* magazine in 1946, Feininger and his wife, Julia, also a painter, recall:

> The location of the college was in itself of importance to us: pretty high up in the mountains, on the shores of a small lake in a wide valley (about 15 miles from the nearest town, Asheville), and encircled yet by higher ranges, intensely wooded. . . . The mornings especially, were fraught with magic. Vapors steaming from the lake, mists enveloping the world around, and when slowly rising revealing the contours of trees and the mountains, the very element of light appearing as something mysterious and new, effects reminiscent of Chinese landscape paintings. Later in the day colors becoming strong and rich, distant ranges at times of a blue which, for its singleness has acquired a name of its own, connecting it with the region: Asheville Blue. The wonderfully quiet nights and the stars above more brilliant and seeming bigger than anywhere else.[25]

JULIA AND LYONEL FEININGER, BLACK MOUNTAIN COLLEGE, SUMMER, 1945. PHOTOGRAPH BY MARGARET WILLIAMSON.

Feininger worked in a methodical, cumulative manner, as noted by Thomas B. Hess in a 1949 article: "In comparing the oils with the charcoal drawings and watercolors and also with photographs of unfinished works, it is obvious that Feininger's creative method is one of addition, of increasing complexities and implications."[26] A work such as *Mid-Manhattan III*, 1943, shows an intermediate stage in Feininger's process, between a pencil sketch and an oil painting. Precise pen and ink lines, elaborated by the rubbing with charcoal, allow Feininger to

[25] Julia and Lyonel Feininger, "Perception and Trust," *design* 47, no. 8 (April 1946):7.

[26] Thomas B. Hess, "Feininger Paints a Picture," *Artnews*, Summer 1949, pp. 48, 50, 60–61.

play intimations of depth off carefully chosen linear rhythms. In the 1940s, Feininger was moving away from structures dominated by straight lines. As in *Manhattan Dawn*, 1944, he often took a more playful approach to the city—the buildings wavering uncertainly, like animated beings, in a manner reminiscent of the work of Feininger's artistic comrade Klee.

Feininger's stay at Black Mountain was part of his re-acclimatization to being in America and to claiming status as an experimental American painter. As the artist recalled, "Coming back after so many years of absence has been a strange experience. I went away as a musician; I came back as a painter. People I had known before were most of them dead. Of the conditions and surroundings I had been familiar with, nothing was left. I . . . sometimes felt my identity had shriveled within me. But I was met with kindness and good-will. . . . That helped me a great deal. . . ."[27]

Fannie Hillsmith was born and raised in Boston and had a grandfather, Frank Hillsmith, who was a painter. After studies at the Art School of Museum of Fine Arts, Boston, Fannie moved to New York in 1934, where she studied at the Art Students League with Alexander Brook, Yasuo Kuniyoshi, John Sloan, and William Zorach. Another teacher there, Vaclav Vytlacil, would later be instrumental in getting Ossip Zadkine to Black Mountain. Two 1936 exhibitions at the Museum of Modern Art had a big impact on Hillsmith—"Cubism And Abstract Art" and "Fantastic Art, Dada, Surrealism." She was also influenced by Albert Gallatin's Museum of Living Art, then at New York University, and by Solomon R. Guggenheim's Museum of Non-Objective Painting, as it was then called.

PORTRAIT OF FANNIE HILLSMITH WITH CHARLES EGAN BY AARON SISKIND. NEW YORK, LATE 1940S.

Hillsmith's first exhibition was in 1943 at the Norlyst Gallery, run by Eleanor Lust and Jimmy Ernst, an exhibition arranged through the Museum of Modern Art. After that, Hillsmith's career blossomed, and she was included in Peggy Guggenheim's Spring Salon at her Art of This Century Gallery, along with Robert Motherwell and Jackson Pollock, and in Sidney Janis's touring exhibition of "Abstract And Surrealist Art in the United States." She joined American Abstract Artists and found her work favorably reviewed by Clement Greenberg. By 1945, she was exhibiting at the prestigious Charles Egan Gallery, which also showed Albers, Willem de Kooning, and Franz Kline, and it was through this connection that Albers invited Hillsmith to teach at Black Mountain.

At the time she was at Black Mountain, Hillsmith was interested in Paul Klee's use of forms that were not strictly geometric. After her return to New York and studies at S.W. Hayter's renowned print studio, Atelier 17, Hillsmith worked with a Cubist vocabulary of overlapping planes and spaces, as in the engraving *Victorian Piece*, 1948. In the late 1950s and early 1960s, after a trip to Europe in 1958, the Cubist influence became more pronounced, and in works such as *Table With Ball Feet*, 1958, and *Honfleur Remembered*, 1961, she produced work firmly in that tradition, while proclaiming a distinct identity. *Table With Ball Feet* emphasized

27 Lyonel Feininger, quoted in "Lyonel Feininger—American Artist," by Alfred H. Barr, Jr., from the catalogue to the Feininger/Hartley exhibtion held at the Museum of Modern Art, New York, October 24, 1944, to January 14, 1945, p. 13.

LYONEL FEININGER
MANHATTAN SKYSCRAPERS, 1942.
Ink on paper, 21 ⅜ x 15 ¼ inches.
Whitney Museum of American Art, New York. Exchange.
Photograph by Matt Flynn.

LYONEL FEININGER
MID-MANHATTAN III, 1943.
Charcoal with stumping, outlined in pen and black ink, on cream laid
paper, 12 ⅝ x 9 ⅜ inches. Anonymous gift in honor of Harold Joachim,
1973.65. Image © The Art Institute of Chicago.

LYONEL FEININGER
MANHATTAN DAWN, 1944.
Oil on canvas, 34 ¹¹⁄₁₆ x 27 ⅜ inches.
Gift of Mr. and Mrs. Andreas Feininger, 1972.1208.
Image © The Art Institute of Chicago.

undifferentiated planes of color, reflecting Hillsmith's association with American abstract artists.

Russian-born Ilya Bolotowsky taught at Black Mountain right after the war, from 1946 to 1948. In an interview, Bolotowsky described an early art class, from a period when his family lived in Constantinople:

> They had an art class which I thought was preposterous because the teacher could not draw. He made us do geometric shapes free hand and model them. . . . So I could do freehand circles and other shapes. And it's funny that years later I became a geometric painter. Maybe this affected me more than I realize.[28]

Bolotowsky moved to New York in September 1923, and began studying at the National Academy of Design, where "color was known to be something rather evil . . ." as Bolotowsky remembered, ". . . was known to be not a very solid way of working in a culture where a gentleman would use very subdued silvery and brown tones."[29] Bolotowsky spent ten months in Europe in 1932, then returned to the States, working in textile design for the Works Progress Administration project. In Europe, Bolotowsky was influenced by an African-American painter named William Henry Johnson, who had also studied at the National Academy and was, according to Bolotowsky, a "fantastic colorist."

Bolotowsky had seen the work of the Russian Suprematists and Constructivists, as well as the Cubists, in New York in 1930, and he first saw the work of Mondrian in 1933 in the Gallatin Collection at New York University. This was a pivotal experience for Bolotowsky, who became one of Mondrian's most astute followers in the Neoplasticist movement. While often adopting Mondrian's thick black vertical and horizontal dividers of varying thicknesses and intervals, Bolotowsky allowed more illusion of depth than Mondrian, and more frequent recourse to a palette of softer lavenders, purples, and pinks.

In 1936, Bolotowsky and others formed American Abstract Artists. According to Bolotowsky, there was a division within this group from the beginning, the students of Hans Hofmann preferring abstraction derived from nature, while others sought to paint abstraction without reference to nature. Bolotowsky, with his striving after Platonic forms, belonged to this latter group. Mondrian's influence on Bolotowsky became more pronounced in the mid-1940s, when Bolotowsky made some of most successful paintings. Bolotowsky once observed that "Léger . . . never achieved pure abstraction for long. He painted a few paintings which were geometric and some which were almost Mondrian-like, but eventually he quit in disgust, and said, 'That's for saints and I am a man.'"[30]

[28] Ilya Bolotowsky, interview by Louise Averill Svendsen with Mimi Poser in *Ilya Bolotowsky* (New York: Solomon R. Guggenheim Foundation, 1974), p. 13.

[29] Ibid., pp. 14–15.

[30] Ibid., p. 18.

FANNIE HILLSMITH
THE HOUSE, 1946.
Oil on canvas, 50 x 28 inches.
Courtesy of Susan Teller Gallery, New York.

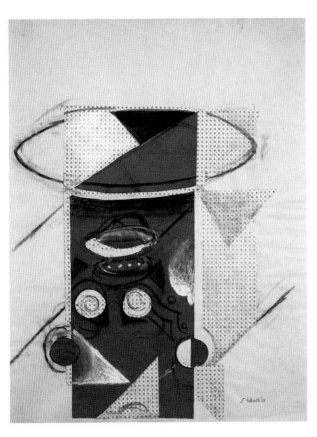

FANNIE HILLSMITH
TABLE WITH BALL FEET, 1958.
Collage with charcoal and pastel on paper, 25 x 19 inches.
Courtesy of Susan Teller Gallery, New York.

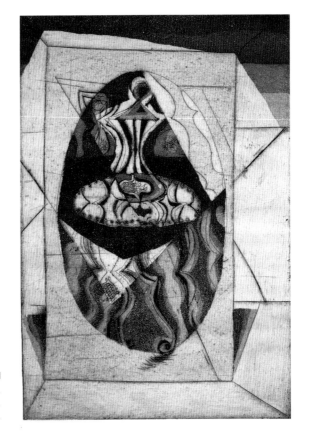

FANNIE HILLSMITH
VICTORIAN PIECE, 1945.
Intaglio, edition 30 ca., 8 ¾ x 6 inches (image size).
Courtesy of Susan Teller Gallery, New York.

FANNIE HILLSMITH
HONFLEUR REMEMBERED, 1961.
Collage with charcoal and pastel on paper, 20 x 14 inches.
Courtesy of Susan Teller Gallery, New York.

Upright in Gold and Violet, 1945, displays elements of Bolotowsky's most inter-esting work—oil paint brushed to a minimum of texture (less than in Malevich or Mondrian), color delicately balanced in fugitive tones, and spatial illusion in sub-tle bands or areas of color that appear to continue behind black grid lines of varying thicknesses. An illusion of superimposition is introduced by a diamond shape that changes hue depending upon which color it appears to be behind. The use of diagonals also contributes to the feeling of an extension in depth. Bolo-towsky expertly combined these elements in a work of satisfying and original pro-portions for the vertical format he selected. *Somber Key*, 1949, is notable for its inclusion of curved edges, along with more common rectilinear ones. As often in this period, Bolotowsky worked with purples and lavenders.

While Bolotowsky was showing at J. B. Neumann's New Art Circle in 1946, he met Albers, who invited him to teach at Black Mountain. Bolotowsky took over the art department while Josef and Anni Albers went on a leave of absence for 1946–1947. He also stayed for the following year, so that Albers and Bolotowsky overlapped as teachers. The art students divided into two camps, preferring the method of one or the other. Bolotowsky enjoyed teaching, but he found Black Mountain too isolated: "Altogether it was a very lively place, but very much inbred. And that finally became stifling, like living in a small room with mirrors; nothing else exists, except endless reflections."[31]

Bolotowsky's painting class for the summer 1947 session, was for all levels. Instruc-tion was given in oils, watercolor, tempera, and gouache, but "there is no stan-dard approach to the students [sic] problems." No class assignments were given. Students simply worked in whatever medium they chose, and Bolotowsky guided them. One photograph showed Bolotowsky's class on a porch, each student paint-ing the same view, but in a distinct style. For his course description, Bolotowsky wrote, "An art class that might superficially appear as a tower of Babel will on closer scrutiny be seen as a free movement towards a universal plastic language with sufficient room for the individual differences."[32] This approach was quite dif-ferent from Albers', and some students preferred it.

One such student attracted to Bolotowsky's style of teaching was Kenneth Noland, from nearby Asheville. Today Noland marvels at how, at a little college twenty miles from his home, one could study with artists of international renown.[33] At the time, a student could not find this environment even in New York. While at Black Mountain, Noland studied with Albers, Bolotowsky, Cage, Clement Greenberg, Willem de Kooning, and Buckminster Fuller. When Noland first arrived, the Albers were on sabbatical, and Noland right away became attracted to painting under Bolowtosky's tutelage. Noland was at Black Mountain from 1946 to 1948, after which he studied in Paris with Ossip Zadkine in 1948–1949. On his return to the

STUDENTS IN CLASS OF ILYA BOLOTOWSKY. BLACK MOUNTAIN COLLEGE, 1947 SUMMER SESSION. PHOTOGRAPH BY BEAUMONT NEWHALL. Copyright 1947, Beaumont Newhall, © 2002, The Estate of Beaumont Newhall and Nancy Newhall. Coutesy of Scheinbaum and Russek Ltd., Santa Fe, NM.

[31] Ibid., p. 21.

[32] Ilya Bolotowsky, *Summer Semester 1947*, North Carolina Museum of Art, Black Mountain College Research Project, North Carolina State Archives, Raleigh.

[33] This and other observations by Noland in this section are from an interview with Vincent Katz, 29 July 2001.

66 >

ILYA BOLOTOWSKY
UPRIGHT IN GOLD AND VIOLET, 1945.
Oil on canvas, 41 x 21 ⅞ inches.
Solomon R. Guggenheim Museum, New York.
Photograph: Carmelo Guadagno © The Solomon R. Guggenheim
Foundation, New York.

ILYA BOLOTOWSKY
UNTITLED, 1946.
Oil on canvas, 21 x 33 inches.
Joan T. Washburn Gallery, New York.

ILYA BOLOTOWSKY
SOMBER KEY, 1949.
Oil on canvas, 34 x 42 inches.
Joan T. Washburn Gallery, New York.

ILYA BOLOTOWSKY
CITY RECTANGLE, 1948.
Oil on canvas, 34 x 26 inches.
Joan T. Washburn Gallery, New York.

KENNETH NOLAND
UNTITLED, 1947.
Oil on pressed board, 34 x 24 inches.
Collection of the artist.

KENNETH NOLAND
UNTITLED, 1947.
Oil on masonite, 17 ¼ x 24 ½ inches.
Collection of the artist.

KENNETH NOLAND
TWO, 1950.
Oil on canvas, 52 x 34 inches.
Collection of the artist.

BLACK MOUNTAIN COLLEGE SEAL,
DESIGNED BY JOSEF ALBERS, 1935.
State Archives at North Carolina, Raleigh.

KENNETH NOLAND'S STUDY AT
BLACK MOUNTAIN COLLEGE, WITH *UNTITLED* (1947)
HANGING ON THE WALL.
PHOTOGRAPH BY JERROLD LEVY.

COLOR STUDY BY KENNETH NOLAND, BLACK
MOUNTAIN COLLEGE, (1946–1948). PHOTOGRAPH
BY JERROLD LEVY.

by the frame of the small-scale painting. After he left Black Mountain, Noland got more involved in the painterly aspect of craft, as one can see in a painting such as *Two*, 1950. By the end of the 1950s, when freely brushed all-over abstraction become the rule, rather than the exception, Greenberg wanted a more expansive, less expressionistic, technique, which he saw in Color Field painters. Noland nonetheless retained his strong connection to centralized form.

LIBRARY BOOKPLATE,
DESIGNED BY JOSEF ALBERS, 1935.
State Archives at North Carolina, Raleigh.

III. Biomorphs: Humanism/Surrealism

After return from Italy once by boat, we both felt so happy to be returning to this country, that was now ours, America, and there was the Statue of Liberty, and she was waving, and we felt this is something that really belongs to representational art. It meant something to see the waving of an arm, and I was always impressed. We didn't turn to representational art, but we felt there is something to it when you can identify like that with a person or an idea.

ANNI ALBERS[34]

To his credit, as can not be asserted too often, Josef Albers chose artists of diverse leanings to teach at Black Mountain. In keeping with Bauhaus philosophy, which emphasized technique and materials, not style, Albers believed exposing students to good artists was central, even when they worked in ways he did not promote. Most of the teachers Albers chose were modernists, to use the term broadly. Artists at Black Mountain who depicted the human form were generally interested in expressing humanistic concerns, in some cases influenced by the art of the Mexican muralists. That Albers shared these concerns can be seen from his quotes and comments, such as "To distribute material possessions is to divide them, to distribute spiritual possessions is to multiply them."[35]

Xanti Schawinsky was someone the Albers knew from the Bauhaus. He was a notable figure there, featured in photographs playing the saxophone, leading groups of revelers, a theatrical man who learned from a master, Oskar Schlemmer. Schawinsky did paintings, set design and commercial art with equal facility. At the Bauhaus, he first studied and then taught stage design and put on "colored light plays," in which the theatrical elements—sound, music, light, color, and form—were treated as forces, distinct from any narrative or descriptive task.

In the 1930s, after the Bauhaus closure, Schawinsky, who was Jewish, moved to Milan, where he worked for the Studio Boggeri advertising firm. There, he produced some classic works of commercial art, such as his posters for Olivetti typewriters and the Princeps line of the haberdasher Cervo. His poster for Illy Caffé is still in use in Roman cafes today. In his best designs, Schawinsky elevates commercial art to the level of fine art. He exhibited his paintings at the Galleria Del Milione in Milan and organized exhibitions there for Josef Albers, Kandinsky, Klee, and László Moholy-Nagy during 1934 and 1935. He also introduced Walter Gropius to a group of modern Milanese architects, which resulted in a number

ADVERTISEMENT BY "CINZANO," CA. 1934. Bauhaus-Archiv, Berlin.

[34] Anni Albers, from an interview for *Bauhaus in America*, produced and directed by Judith Pearlman for Cliofilm, New York, 1994.

[35] Josef Albers, in reprint from the book *American Abstract Artists*.

HERBERT BAYER, XANTI SCHAWINSKY, WALTER
GROPIUS. ASCONA, 1933.
Bauhaus-Archiv, Berlin.

of the periodical *Domus* devoted to Gropius's work. Schawinsky's paintings, such as *Untitled*, 1935, often reveal a Surrealist desire to juxtapose alien objects and settings. He liked to set biomorphic forms or architectural conglomerations in spatially ambiguous settings.

In 1936, as the political situation in Italy grew more grim, Schawinsky received an invitation from Albers to come to Black Mountain, where he began teaching in 1936. Shortly after his arrival, he gave a talk on Albers paintings, which were hanging in Lee Hall. Schawinsky later remembered, "i compared albers' work with the transparence of the venetians, penetrating space in layers and dissolving volume into components."[36] Schawinsky was given freedom by Albers to design his own courses. Observing the scope of the liberal arts environment at Black Mountain, something he had never seen in Europe, he decided to attack his old interest in the theater as a "laboratory":

> realizing that the atmosphere at black mountain was favorable to experimentation, i thought why not get at 'total experience'? [underlining by Schawinsky] had not my slumbering plans from eleven years before, at the bauhaus in dessau, laid a foundation for this undertaking?[37]

[36] Xanti Schawinsky, "My 2 years at Black Mountain College, N.C." unpublished essay, 1973, North Carolina Museum of Art, Black Mountain College Research Project, North Carolina State Archives, Raleigh. Note: I have preserved Schawinsky's orthography.

[37] Ibid.

XANTI SCHAWINSKY
POSTER FOR OLIVETTI, 1934.
Color lithography, 20 1/16 x 13 3/8 inches.
Bauhaus-Archiv, Berlin. © Gisela Schawinky.

XANTI SCHAWINSKY
UNTITLED, CA 1960.
Lithograph, 9 x 68 inches.
Black Mountain College Museum and Arts Center, Asheville.
© Gisela Schawinsky.

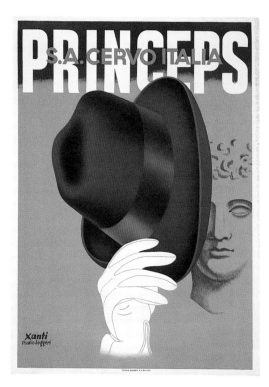

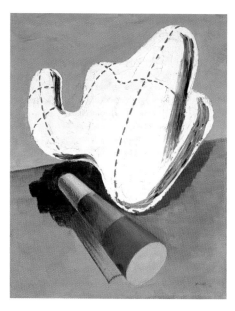

XANTI SCHAWINSKY
POSTER "PRINCEPS S. A. CERVO ITALIA," 1934.
Color lithography, 13 ⅔ x 9 ⅗ inches.
Bauhaus-Archiv, Berlin. © Gisela Schawinsky.

XANTI SCHAWINSKY
UNTITLED, 1937.
Oil on board, 17 ⅗ x 13 ¹⁵⁄₁₆ inches.
Bauhaus-Archiv, Berlin. © Gisela Schawinsky.
Photograph by Markus Hawlik.

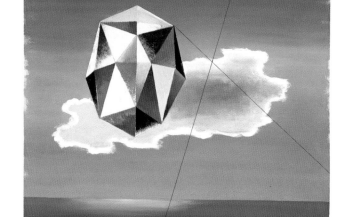

XANTI SCHAWINSKY
UNTITLED, 1935.
Gouache on paper, 14 x 17 ¹⁵⁄₁₆ inches.
Bauhaus-Archiv, Berlin. © Gisela Schawinky.
Photograph by Markus Hawlik.

Thus began Schawinsky's "Stage Studies" class, in which he would enlist students as set designers, musicians, actors, writers, speakers in multi-media performances that in a real way prefigure John Cage's famous *Theater Piece No. 1* (1952), enacted some fifteen years later at Black Mountain and universally acclaimed as "the first Happening" or performance with simultaneous, uncoordinated actions. As Schawinsky put it:

> my purpose was to use the stage for demonstrations in which all media and all branches of knowledge and artistic endeavor found an expression, with the collaboration of specialists (faculty members, students of various departments, etc.) . . . "stage studies" was actually an unfortunate title of the course, as . . . the subjects of the studies consisted of space concepts, color, form, motion, time, space-time, communication, sound, rhythm, poetry, language, music, architecture, physics principles, anatomy, economic principles, social aspects . . . and metaphysical phenomena, illusion, etc.[38]

Schawinsky collaborated with composer John Evarts at Black Mountain on *Spectodrama: Play, Life, Illusion* (1924–1937) and *Danse Macabre* (1938). The first piece, as can be seen from the dates, was a continuation of Schawinsky's Bauhaus work; the latter was a new piece, based on a medieval morality play. In the 1960s, Schawinsky published a script for *Spectodrama*. His descriptions make clear his visionary ideas for music and theater and establish a clear basis for such experimentation at Black Mountain. The English design magazine, *Form*, in which the script was published, as part of a series on Black Mountain, included this quote from Schawinsky: "While the work at the Bauhaus Theatre aimed at the modernisation of theatrical means and concepts, and had a definte professional and artistic scope, at Black Mountain College an educational crack at the whole man seemed to be in order."[39]

In other words, at Black Mountain, Schawinsky took his formal experiments to a different level: the investigation of the interaction of man and his environment, including man-made aspects of it. In the script, Schawinsky lays out a visual presentation in which the senses are symbolized by projections of ears or eyes, and anthropomorphic animation is used on inanimate elements. In 1938, Schawinsky became aware of a movement to oust John Rice from the faculty. Schawinsky felt that Albers was behind it, but could not find out why: "although i could never doubt the idealistic motives in albers, i could not understand why two different minds should not exist in this academic forum . . . i abhorred political makeshift for attaining power, and whatever the reasons were, my observations caused me suffering and dissatisfaction . . . as it looked to me, the founder of the college was kicked out! the tragedy played secretly, there was no open action among the community." That year was Schawinsky's last at Black Mountain. He was offered a position by Moholy-Nagy in Chicago at the New Bauhaus, or Institute of Design as it became known, but ultimately moved to New York instead. He was invited

SPECTODRAMA: PLAY, LIFE, ILLUSION (1924–1937) BY XANTI SCHAWINSKY. PRESENTATION AT BLACK MOUNTAIN COLLEGE 1936–1937, DIRECTED BY SCHAWINSKY, MUSIC BY JOHN EVARTS, PART IV, SCENE 1. PHOTOCOLLAGES BY XANTI SCHAWINSKY.

[38] Xanti Schawinsky, questionnaire, 1970, North Carolina Museum of Art, Black Mountain College Research Project, North Carolina State Archives, Raleigh.

[39] Xanti Schawinsky, "Spectodrama" in *Form*, Cambridge, England, no. 8, September 1968, p. 16.

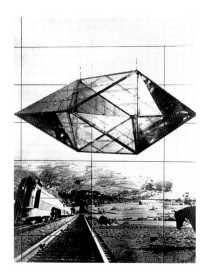

PHOTOMURAL AND CRYSTAL BY XANTI SCHAWINSKY
IN COLLABORATION WITH MARCEL BREUER AND
WALTER GROPIUS, FROM 1939 PENNSYLVANIA
WORLD'S FAIR EXHIBIT.

SUMMER FACULTY, 1944. JAMES PRESTINI, J. B.
NEUMANN, WALTER GROPIUS, JOSÉ DE CREEFT, JEAN
CHARLOT, JOSEF ALBERS (SEATED). PHOTOGRAPH BY
TOM MILIUS.

by Gropius and Breuer to collaborate on a competition for the Pennsylvania World Fair Pavilion of 1939, which they won. On his own, Schawinsky won the competition for the North Carolina Pavilion.

In 1944, for the first time, Black Mountain offered two Summer Institutes—one in music and one in art. It was the first time Black Mountain branched out so decisively, in music and art, to include many prominent figures who were not members of the Black Mountain faculty. In the visual arts, summer sessions would become a hallmark of the Black Mountain experience. "For a long time, we have left the care and publication of works of art, as well as judgement and criticism, mainly to the historian," reads a text, undoubtedly written by Josef Albers, which appeared in the *Black Mountain College Bulletin* advertising the Summer Art Institute. "This is one reason why old art stands in the foreground of interest, why we lose relationship with contemporary art and living artists."[40] Among those invited to teach that summer were photographer Joseph Breitenbach, Jean Charlot, José de Creeft, Walter Gropius, Barbara Morgan, gallerist J. B. Neumann, Amédée Ozenfant, designer James Prestini, Bernhard Rudofsky, and architect José Luis Sert.

Jean Charlot, born in France, had worked with the Mexican muralists. He went to Mexico in 1921 and seems to have played a role as a European cohort to the Mexican painters. In his autobiography, José Clemente Orozco, states that Charlot "tempered our youthful violence with his culture and equanimity and illuminated our problems with his lucid vision."[41] Charlot had also done archaeological studies in the Yucatan. He had taught at the Art Students League in New York and showed at Neumann's New Art Circle, as had Albers. He painted three murals in Mexico City in 1923 and did many in the United States from 1939 to the 1970s. Complementing the social messages of his work, Charlot was a formalist, closely linked to the ideas of modern abstract art. Albers had already asked Charlot to teach at Black Mountain, full-time, in 1939, indicating how highly he thought of him. Charlot visited Black Mountain in 1943, giving a lecture on Mexican art, before returning to teach at the 1944 institute.

At the institute, Charlot lectured on modern abstraction and praised Albers's work, saying "If he finds in his artistic endeavors that one area does not cooperate with another area, he tirelessly and painstakingly tries other techniques, other pigments. In this artist is the true spirit of purification."[42] He taught a drawing/painting class and one on composition. The course description for the latter reads, "In two dimensions, harmonious with regard to area covered. In three dimensions, creation of limited space in which solids are defined by three co-ordinates as opposed to unlimited spatial sensation with its romantic or impressionistic connotations."[43]

[40] *Black Mountain College Bulletin* 2, no. 6 (April 1944).

[41] José Clemente Orozco, *An Autobiography*, translated by Robert C. Stephenson (Austin: University of Texas Press, 1962), p. 87.

[42] "College Group Hears Charlot," *Asheville Citizen*, September 2, 1944.

[43] Course description in *Black Mountain College Bulletin* 2, no. 6 (April 1944).

While teaching and in between painting two frescoes—"Inspiration" and "Learning"—on the pylons underneath the Studies Building, Charlot kept a journal, which provides useful information as to how a visiting teacher at Black Mountain might pass his day: "August 1. Drawing class. p.m. I write synopsis Mexican murals book for Knopf. Evening at Albers. See his paintings. New ones beautiful. We speak of an exchange. Schnapps."[44] On the 9th, Ozenfant lectures and "illustrates with beautifully chosen pebbles and shells." On the 16th, Charlot shows the cartoons for his frescoes to Ozenfant. "His criticism: not enough space for the volumes. Evening. Ozenfant lectures on pre-forms. After, party at the Albers', with Gropius present."[45]

Amédée Ozenfant was linked with Léger and Le Corbusier in a post-Cubist modern movement called Purism, which advocated a reliance on pure form. This form could be based on depiction, of a still life say, and emphasized planar substantiality, giving more autonomy to the planes, instead of having them battle each other to create spatial tension, as in Cubism. The interests of the Purists in architecture and the proper positioning of man in modern, mechanical society connect them to Gropius's ideals for the Bauhaus, as well as to de Stijl. In 1939, Ozenfant moved to the United States and opened the Ozenfant School of Fine Arts in New York, which would remain a well-known modernist art school for years.

Ozenfant's own painting can look Precisionist in its hard-edged abstraction of landscape. In the 1930s, he did works that depict naked figures swimming or enjoying revels in a *joie de vivre* mode. In the mid-1940s, in such works as *Crazy Rocks*, 1945, and *The Sleeping Canyon*, 1945–1946, one can see a biomorphic element that is almost Surrealist becoming stronger, and in fact Sidney Janis showed Ozenfant's 1940s work with that of Yves Tanguy.

Also for the Summer Art Institute of 1944, José de Creeft was invited to teach sculpture, on the advice of José Luis Sert, an architect who had worked with Le Corbusier. De Creeft taught "Direct Carving In Wood And Stone." Albers liked to have as many artistic techniques and materials as possible presented to students, and de Creeft's formal, planar, approach to the figure would have recommended itself. Born in Guadalajara, Spain, de Creeft studied in Barcelona and in Madrid, at the workshop of Augustín Querol. He moved to Paris, where he met Gris and Picasso and, at the advice of Rodin, studied at the Academie Julian in 1906. De Creeft would later become a leading proponent of a revival of direct carving. In 1927, he did a commission of 200 carved stone sculptures for the fortress of Ramonje in Mallorca. He moved to the United States in 1929 and became a citizen in 1940. In 1959, he did one of his most famous commissions, the bronze group of figures from *Alice in Wonderland* in Central Park, New York. It should be noted that this piece is in an academic style he reserved for certain commissions and that he considered distinct from his noncommissioned work. Overall, de Creeft exhibited a spontaneous approach to material and form, letting the shape and substance of the rock or wood with which he was working lead him to vari-

JEAN CHARLOT POSTCARD.
Archives and Special Collections at the Thomas J. Dodd Research Center, University of Connecticut Libraries.

JEAN CHARLOT WORKING ON FRESCO ON PYLON. BLACK MOUNTAIN COLLEGE, 1944.

KNOWLEDGE BY JEAN CHARLOT (DETAIL), FRESCO ON PYLON OF STUDIES BUILDING. BLACK MOUNTAIN COLLEGE SUMMER, 1944. PHOTOGRAPH BY MARY HARRIS.
North Carolina Museum of Art, Black Mountain College Research Project, Raleigh, North Carolina.

44 Jean Charlot, "Black Mountain College: A Diary," 23 June–4 September 2002, *Form*, no. 6, December 1967, Cambridge, England, pp. 26–28.

45 Ibid.

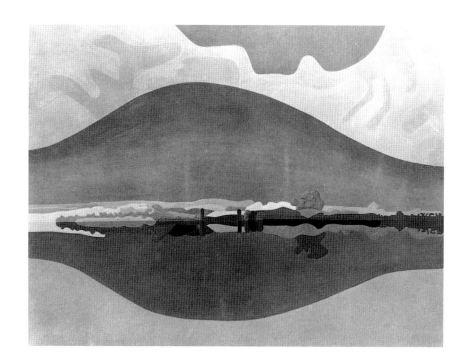

AMÉDÉE OZENFANT
BLACK MOUNTAIN, 1945.
Location unknown.
Photograph by John D. Schiff.
The Josef and Anni Albers Foundation.

AMÉDÉE OZENFANT
THE SLEEPING CANYON, 1945-1946.
Oil on canvas on masonite, 52 x 39 inches.
Walker Art Center, Minneapolis.
Gift of the T. B. Walker Foundation, Gilbert M. Walker Fund, 1946.

AMÉDÉE OZENFANT
CRAZY ROCKS, 1945.
Oil on canvas, 50 ⅘ x 26 inches.
Collection Galerie Larock-Granoff, Paris.

JOSÉ DE CREEFT
THE CLOUD, 1939.
Greenstone, 16 ¾ x 12 ⅜ x 10 inches.
Whitney Museum of American Art, New York. Purchase.
Photograph by Jerry L. Thompson.

JOSÉ DE CREEFT
RIVIERA, 1969.
Green pudding stone, 24 x 24 x 30 inches.
Collection of Lorrie Goulet, New York.

LORRIE GOULET
ALLEGRA, 1993.
Acrylic on canvas, 60 x 40 inches.
Collection of Lorrie Goulet, New York.

LORRIE GOULET
MIRADOR, 1994.
Black walnut, 38 x 16 x 13 inches.
Collection of Lorrie Goulet, New York.

ous imagery. His first exhibition was at El Círculo de Bellas Artes in Madrid in 1903, and in 1960 he was honored by a retrospective at the Whitney Museum of American Art.

Finding the right material was key to de Creeft, as one can see from a list of his pieces, which include clay, terra cotta, granite from the Vosges, beaten lead, Tennessee marble, wood from Indo-China, porhyry, pink quartz, bull's horn, pink marble from Mallorca, onyx from Morocco, green stone, Vermont marble, red pumice stone, limestone, apple tree root, olive tree, etc. In both *The Cloud*, 1939, and *Riviera*, 1969, separated by thirty years, we see the same respect for humanity's nurturing, life-giving potential. The way the human limbs combine to compose one curving form, cloudlike, suggests a harmony, which since it is at odds with political events, represents a necessary ideal.

Lorrie Goulet read about Black Mountain in Adamic's article and went to study art in 1943, staying for the 1944 Summer Art Institute. During that time, she studied with Albers and de Creeft. Although she learned from both, she was immediately drawn to the latter. The two ultimately married, and Goulet's mature sculpture bears the mark of what she absorbed from the Spanish master. Goulet too does direct carving in stone and wood, and her work also evinces a love of the human, particularly the female form. In *Mirador*, 1994, her respect for the black walnut wood seems to dictate the swelling forms of hair and countenance.

The 1944 Summer Art Institute having been a success, the idea was repeated in 1945, the participants being architect Paul Beidler, sculptor Mary Callery, Hillsmith, Feininger, Gropius, the designer Alvin Lustig, Motherwell, the art historian Karl With, the designers Bernhard and Berta Rudofsky, and Ossip Zadkine. Born in Vitebsk, Russia, Zadkine studied in London and at the École des Beaux Arts in Paris. He showed his work in the Salon d'Automne, Salon des Independents, and the Salon des Tuilleries. He worked in wood, terra cotta, marble, stone, and bronze. Fleeing the war, Zadkine moved from Paris to New York, where he remained until 1945.

Zadkine quickly became part of the New York art world, meeting de Creeft, Hélion, Lipchitz, Noguchi, Charles Sheeler, and Tchelitchew. In 1942, Zadkine was invited by Pierre Matisse to participate in the exhibition "Artists in Exile" at his gallery. The other artists, each represented by one piece, included Breton, Chagall, Ernst, Léger, Masson, Matta, Mondrian, Ozenfant, and Tanguy. Zadkine had solo exhibitions while in New York at the Wildenstein and Kurt Valentin galleries.

Zadkine's sculpture followed a familiar path, moving from Cubism to Neo-Classicism. While some works tended toward abstraction and others, such as *La Prisonnière*, 1943, and his Rotterdam commission, *Monument à la ville détruite*, dedicated in 1953, directly reflect the horrors of war, some of Zadkine's most affecting works are his torsoes of women. *Torse de Femme*, 1944, which is quite similar to the piece he showed in "Artists in Exile," exhibits Zadkine's mastery of the graceful lines of the human body, the delicate indication of bone structure below the surface. His decision to crop the figure at the chest and knees paradoxically establishes its continuous, flowing energy.

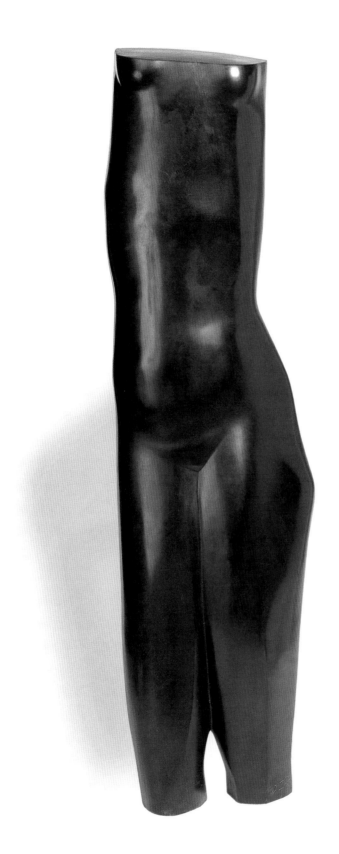

OSSIP ZADKINE
TORSE DE FEMME, 1944.
Bronze, edition number 2/8, 42 ⅛ x 12 ⅜ x 10 ⅝ inches.
Musée Zadkine, Paris.
Photograph: Pierrain © Photothèque des Musées de la Ville de Paris.

FACULTY PORTRAIT. BLACK MOUNTAIN COLLEGE, SUMMER 1946.

Zadkine declined an offer from László Moholy-Nagy to teach at the Institute of Design in Chicago, and instead accepted Albers's offer to teach at Black Mountain. Being an exile during the war, as well as being separated from his wife, who remained in Paris, understandably made Zadkine anxious during these years. As soon as the Summer Institute ended, in September of 1945, Zadkine returned to France.

OSSIP ZADKINE SCULPTURE CLASS (ZADKINE AT CENTER IN TIE). BLACK MOUNTAIN COLLEGE, 1945. PHOTOGRAPH BY ELAINE SCHMITT.

In 1946, the *Black Mountain College Bulletin* announced the "Third Art Institute," which would include sculptor Leo Amino, designer Will Burtin, painter Balcomb Greene, Gropius, Jacob Lawrence, who came with his wife, the painter Gwendolyn Knight, designer Leonard Lionni, photographer and curator Beaumont Newhall, sculptor Concetta Scaravaglione, and painter Jean Varda. Greene, who had been the first chairman of American Abstract Artists and would show at J. B. Neumann's New Art Circle in 1947 and 1950, had begun to reintroduce the human figure to his work. He gave a series of lectures on new realist art, with titles that included "Social Usages of Realist Techniques" and "The Theory of Attenuation in Modern Painting." Perhaps the most exciting development was the inclusion of Lawrence, whose work, for all its formal rigor, was firmly rooted in depicting subject matter, often narrative in nature, of African-American experience.

One would think that Black Mountain, founded on the principle of freedom of choice, would not think twice about openness regarding homosexuality, or its inclusion of African-Americans. In fact, on both counts, Black Mountain was slow to arrive at a publicly open position. As for gay issues, it could be argued that Black Mountain never really came to terms with them. Regarding African-American students and faculty, Black Mountain's progress was halting at best. The first black student was admitted only in 1944, and it was not until the following summer that two African-Americans, Carol Brice and Roland Hayes, were invited as music teachers.

JACK LIPSEY, THE COOK, CUTTING BEEF. BLACK MOUNTAIN COLLEGE.

RUBY LIPSEY. BLACK MOUNTAIN COLLEGE KITCHEN, 1930s.

Jacob Lawrence was born in Atlantic City in 1917 and grew up in Harlem, where he was encouraged by Charles Alston, whom he met at Utopia Children's House. Later, under the W.P.A., he studied with Alston again, as well as with Henry Bannarn. In the late 1930s, Lawrence became interested in the work of Mexican muralist Orozco. In 1938, he joined the Federal Art Project in the easel division. He was making many gouaches and some oil paintings. He won a fellowship, which enabled him to further hone his skills, and began exhibiting his work. At that time, Lawrence researched and painted what would become one of most famous works, *The Migration of the Negro During World War I*, sixty paintings now owned by the Museum of Modern Art and the Phillips Collection. At its exhibition in the Downtown Gallery in 1941, Lawrence's first solo show, this work made an impact beyond the art world. With their stark forms and rich colors, these pieces tell a dramatic story of African-Americans fleeing untenable situations in the hope of better opportunities. Lawrence also made works based on the lives of John Brown, Frederick Douglass, Touissaint L'Ouverture, and Harriet Tubman.

In a letter to Albers, sent before his arrival at Black Mountain, Lawrence included a short statement, "My Ideas on Art (Painting) and the Artist," in which he writes, "My belief is that it is most important for an artist to develop an approach and philosoophy about life—If he has developed this philosophy he does not put paint on canvas, <u>he puts himself on canvas</u>" [underlining by Lawrence].[46] In some ways this could seem diametrically opposed to Albers's philosophy, at least his teaching philosophy, which aimed to dissaude students from attempting to express themselves. However, both artists share a reluctance to impart technique. When Lawrence writes that "the technique will come if the subject the artist is painting is

[46] Jacob Lawrence, "My Ideas on Art (Painting) and the Artist," letter to Josef Albers, n.d. [April 1946], North Carolina Museum of Art, Black Mountain College Research Project, North Carolina State Archives, Raleigh.

important to him,"[47] there is a parallel emphasis, except that Albers would replace "subject" by "material." In a sense, Lawrence's emphasis on subject links him to his contemporaries, the abstract expressionists, who also believed they "put themselves" on canvas.

By the mid-1940s, Lawrence's work was getting more complex, in that he was lavishing more attention on tiny details and patterns in his depictions of African-American work. A piece from a slightly later period, *Prophesy*, 1954, shows that Lawrence could depict universal situations, that his cultural background was not a limitation but a springboard. There is an overarching emotion of fear, as the figure carrying a bayonet points to the blood-streaked darkness.

Gwendolyn Knight, like Lawrence, painted many gouache and tempera works in the 1940s. Her art could have a lyrical side, quite different from her husband's, as in *The Boudoir*, 1945. Knight grew up in Barbados, and moved to New York while still a girl. An exhibition of the work of John Singer Sargent fixed in her the desire to become an artist. In New York, Knight met the sculptor Augusta Savage, who would become a mentor. Savage had a gallery, the Salon of Contemporary Negro Art on 125th Street, at which Beauford Delaney and others, including Knight, exhibited. At the Harlem Community Art Center, Knight met Lawrence. Shortly after, the two were married.[48]

Leo Amino, another teacher at the 1946 Summer Art Institute, worked mainly with biomorphic abstraction. His work in the 1940s featured carving and finishing of

LEFT: JACOB LAWRENCE AND GWENDOLYN KNIGHT LAWRENCE. *RIGHT*: NANCY NEWHALL, GWENDOLYN KNIGHT LAWRENCE AND JACOB LAWRENCE. 1946 SUMMER ART INSTITUTE. BOTH PHOTOGRAPHS BY BEAUMONT NEWHALL.
Copyright 1946, Beaumont Newhall, © 2002, The Estate of Beaumont Newhall and Nancy Newhall. Courtesy of Scheinbaum and Russek Ltd., Santa Fe, NM.

[47] Ibid.

[48] Information on Gwendolyn Knight's life has been gleaned from *Black Mountain College Dossiers*, no. 7 (Gwendolyn Knight), by Glenis Redmond, Black Mountain College Museum and Arts Center, Asheville, 2001.

JACOB LAWRENCE
PROPHESY, 1954.
Tempera on board, 12 x 16 inches.
Collection of Susan and Alan Patricof.

GWENDOLYN KNIGHT
THE BOUDOIR, 1945.
Tempera on board, 18 x 12 inches.
Courtesy of the artist and Francine Seders Gallery, Seattle.
Artwork copyright Gwendolyn Knight Lawrence, courtesy of Jacob and
Gwendolyn Lawrence Foundation.

smoothly curved forms. He also made a series of insect-like beings with metal appendages forming antennae, arms, and legs. Amino was a dedicated experimenter in the uses of plastic as a sculptural material, first carving it, later making complex combinations of cast forms in colors. Born on the island of Formosa in 1911 to Japanese parents, Amino studied at Hosei University in Tokyo. He moved to New York in 1935 and studied briefly at New York University. While working for a Japanese wood importer, Amino began taking home samples of ebony and carving them. That he was largely self-taught is remarkable when one observes the technical sophistication of his work. He did study for three months at the American Artists School with Chaim Gross, a proponent of direct carving, in 1937. Amino had his first show at the Montross Gallery in 1940, and in 1949 the Addison Gallery of American Art became the first museum to own his work. He also taught at Black Mountain in the summer of 1950.

LEO AMINO. BLACK MOUNTAIN COLLEGE, 1950.
PHOTOGRAPH BY JULIE AMINO.

Amino began working with polystyrene in 1946, the same year he went to teach at Black Mountain. After that point, while continuing to work in wood, he became more and more interested in transparent and translucent plastics and the formal effects those materials allowed. As he wrote in 1955, ". . . transparent form displaces space just as any other, yet the distinction between its physical aspect and surrounding space is less conspicuous. . . . However, refraction and optical illusions created by light on transparent form . . . actually intensify the difference, thus creating a greater sense of three-dimensionality."[49]

It is often credited to Constructivist and Bauhaus theory that in the 1930s and 1940s sculptors experimented with non-traditional materials, such as metals and plastics. Thought of in this way, we can see a relationship to one aspect of Amino's work, his attitude toward material. Amino's actual results usually, at least in the 1940s, have a biomorphic base, sometimes echoing the abstracted figures of Henry Moore. As time goes on, Amino moves from a somewhat Surrealist biomorphism to a geometric use of color. *Head with Horn*, 1946, done at Black Mountain, is an unusual example of the artist's ability to transform a found piece. *Insect God*, 1954, and *Two-Piece Unit*, 1970, are more typical of Amino's output.

Richard Lippold, like Amino, was self-taught as a sculptor, although he received a B.F.A. in industrial design from the Art Institute of Chicago. Not long after he began, in 1942, making his sculptures of thin wires, arrayed to form geometric forms that glitter under light, his work was being prominently displayed in major museums, and he was regularly gaining significant commissions for large-scale works. Much of his work has a humanist strain to it, sometimes intimating a human figure, sometimes more a soaring life spirit, as in the signal work he created at Black Mountain, *Devotion I*, 1948. *Devotion II*, January 1949, is a larger version of the same image.

In 1944, Lippold had moved to New York, and his wife, Louise Lippold, began studying dance with Martha Graham and Merce Cunningham. Lippold had his first solo exhibition at the Willard Gallery in New York in 1947. That year he also began a series of works entitled *Variation within a Sphere*, some of which were

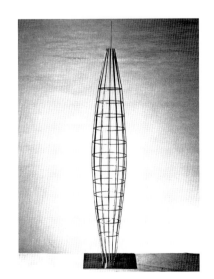

RICHARD LIPPOLD: *DEVOTION I*, 1948.
Stainless steel, bronze, 20" high brass.
Photograph by Richard Lippold.

[49] Leo Amino, statement in "The New Decade," Whitney Museum of American Art, New York, 1955, pp. 8–9.

91 >

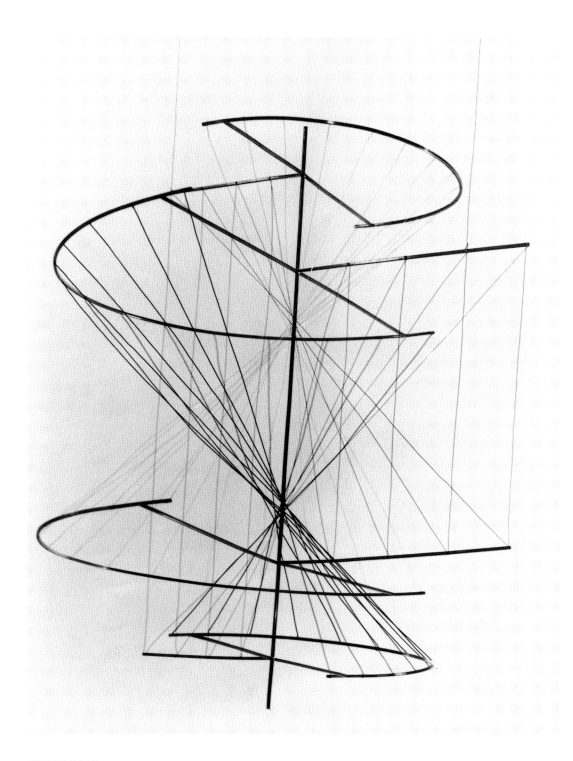

RICHARD LIPPOLD

VARIATION WITHIN A SPHERE Nº 6, 1948.

Stainless steel, brass and enameled wire, 8 x 8 x 8 inches.

Estate of Richard Lippold. Photograph by Richard Lippold, New York.

dedicated to John Cage. "I've always been very interested in music," remembers Lippold, "and that was one relationship I had with John. We had evenings together at his place or my place, playing the piano or doing whatever we could musically."[50] In the summer of 1948, Lippold visited Black Mountain, as an artist in residence, with his wife and two children, while Cage and Cunningham were there. Apparently there was a shortage of housing that summer as, in a letter to Josef Albers, dated May 24, 1948, Lippold writes:

> John Cage and Merce Cunningham bring back tales of wonder and delight from North Carolina which are the more tempting after the rush of a New York winter. I have bought an old hearse which I hope will get us to Black Mountain whenever you wish us to come. . . . I have arranged our old car for sleeping, and in discussing the summer with John and Merce last night, including plans for the collaboration on an opera for the coming year, we agreed that they might lend us their plumbing at Black Mountain while we sleep in the car.[51]

RAY JOHNSON AND RICHARD LIPPOLD AT MONROE ST. STUDIO, 1953.

Louise Lippold performed with Cunningham at Black Mountain, and Richard Lippold, while creating *Devotion I*, met Ray Johnson, with whom he would later share a studio. In October 1948, Lippold agreed to return to Black Mountain to perform the graduation examination for Vera Williams. In a letter of September 23, Josef Albers asked Lippold to propose six topics from which Williams might choose three to write about. In a telegram dated October 4, 1948, Lippold simply put:

> A blade of grass.
> On Herbert Read or Satie.
> What children see.
> Time in painting.
> Criticism of Hazel's work.
> Use of two dimensions in Egypt and the Middle Ages.
>
> Arrive in Black Mountain 7:45 a.m. Friday. Richard.[52]

Lippold made *Variation within a Sphere no. 6*, 1948, in November, after returning to New York, for Anni Albers. She reciprocated by giving him her weaving *La Luz 1*, 1947. One of Lippold's earliest commissions was done for Harvard at the request of Walter Gropius in 1950. In 1953, *Variation within a Sphere no. 10* was commissioned by the Metropolitan Museum of Art, New York. Another commission from Gropius came in 1963, when Lippold made *Flight* for the lobby of the Pan-Am Building, New York.

In 1951, Ben Shahn taught the summer session at Black Mountain. Shahn was another unlikely Black Mountain figure, although by this time Albers was gone, so

[50] Richard Lippold, in an interview with Vincent Katz, 2 October 2001.

[51] Richard Lippold, letter to Josef Albers, 24 May 2002, North Carolina Museum of Art, Black Mountain College Research Project, North Carolina State Archives, Raleigh.

[52] Letter and telegram, North Carolina Museum of Art, Black Mountain College Research Project, North Carolina State Archives, Raleigh.

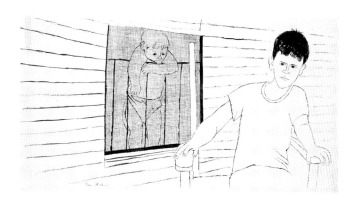

BEN SHAHN
PORCH #2, 1946. Ink on paper, 16 x 23 inches.
Walker Art Center, Minneapolis. John T. Baxter Memorial
Collection of American Drawings, 1949.

BEN SHAHN
MYTHICAL BIRD, JULY 1951.
Ink on paper, 18 x 23 inches.
Estate of Fielding Dawson.

BEN SHAHN
EVERYMAN, 1954.
Tempera on composition board, 72 x 24 inches.
Whitney Museum of American Art, New York. Purchase.
Photograph by Sheldan C. Collins, N.J. © 1998 Whitney
Museum of American Art, New York.

interests had shifted. Shahn knew Charles Olson, who was taking an increasingly dominant role at the College by that time and would be its final Rector. Shahn was born in Lithuania in 1898 and studied in Paris and New York, where he eventually settled. He had a retropsective at the Museum of Modern Art in 1947. Shahn's work had to do with the social connotations of a simple image from everyday life. Sometimes, the political tendentiousness of Shahn's images can be overbearing; other times, as in *Porch #2*, 1946, when the narrative is left ambiguous, his images can be provocative. Elsewhere, as in the tempera on board *Everyman*, 1954, the formal elements of composition play a central role, as in Jacob Lawrence's paintings.

While at Black Mountain, Shahn made *Mythical Bird*, July 1951, for Fielding Dawson's birthday, and he delivered a lecture entitled "Aspects Of Realism." In it, he attacked the solidity of the notion of "realism," the belief that there is one definition of that term. Beginning with the Cubist attack on one-point perspective, Shahn imagines his paintings critcized by a psychologist for not delving into the subconscious, as do those of the Surrealists, and by a philosopher, who says of his paintings, "I see in them no search for <u>ultimate</u> truth" [underlining by Shahn]. Another painter tells Shahn,". . . the only reality anyone can achieve is visual—that is, shapes and forms and colors. There's your realism. No matter what else you have, if you haven't got that, you haven't got anything, and you might as well say in words what you have to say." Finally, Shahn reveals his own preoccupations:

> So far as I personally am concerned, my frame of reference is a highly humanistic one. I am unwilling to regard man as of use value. To me the human being is ultimate value; the arts, its prime manifestation. . . . As to the wave of non-objective art that is presently sweeping the country, I do not feel—and neither do its leading practitioners—that it is anti-humanistic.

Ultimately, Shahn attempts to achieve with his images the power of symbols, and he does that by paying careful attention to detail: ". . . the clothing, the houses, furniture, people, are always particular ones, never generalities."[53] In his interest in symbol, Shahn reveals himself to be of his time, in much the same way, although using a different approach, as many abstract artists. Shahn was outspoken in his belief that art should be used to promote social justice, and he was not averse to attacking those artists he felt had social potential but were content to make merely formalist statements. Among those he chastised were Aaron Siskind and Robert Motherwell.

Motherwell, who taught at Black Mountain in the summers of 1945 and 1951, is usually grouped with the abstract expressionist painters, and certainly his sympathies, and most of his artistic friendships, lay there. However, his roots are so strongly based in Surrealism, and his use of the figure so predominant in his work

---

[53] Ben Shahn, "Aspects of Realism," lecture delivered at Black Mountain College, 29 July 1951, North Carolina Museum of Art, Black Mountain College Research Project, North Carolina State Archives, Raleigh.

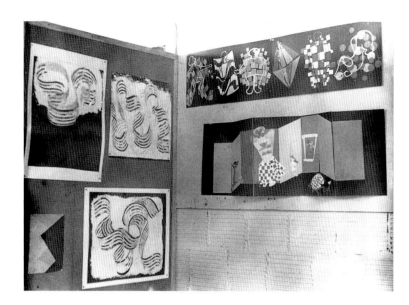

JANE SLATER GRADUATION EXHIBITION. BLACK
MOUNTAIN COLLEGE, MARCH, 1945. PHOTOGRAPH
BY JANE SLATER.

STUDENT STUDY OF JERROLD LEVY. LAKE EDEN
CAMPUS, BLACK MOUNTAIN COLLEGE, LATE 1940S.
PHOTOGRAPH BY JERROLD LEVY.

of the 1940s, that it useful to remember him also as a humanist, someone at pains to do justice to a shared human experience. Motherwell was influential in the modern art world from an early age. Although he knew he wanted to be an artist, he studied philosophy at Stanford as a way of satisfying his banker father, and from that education he gained resources that would steadily nourish his creative thought. Motherwell gained power from the equilibrium of his character's two aspects: the painter and the writer. Power accrued to him as it does to any perceptive critic but retained a special edge due to his status as an artist.

A prolific writer, Motherwell was perhaps even more ambitious as an editor, and his publishing efforts had a direct impact on mid-twentieth century literature and art. First there was the series *Documents of Modern Art*, which Motherwell directed, as well as editing many of its thirteen volumes. Writings by Apollinaire, Mondrian, Moholy-Nagy, Kandinsky, and others were made available in English for the first time. Gropius wrote the introduction to the Moholy-Nagy volume, and Julia and Lyonel Feininger wrote a preface to the Kandinsky. Perhaps the most influential of all was the Motherwell-edited *Dada Painters and Poets* volume, published in 1951. Coinciding with the *Documents* series was the *Problems of Contemporary Art* series, which included publications by Herbert Read and Albert Dorner, and *possibilities 1: An Occasional Review*, 1947–1948, edited by John Cage (music), Pierre Chareau (architecture), Robert Motherwell (art), and Harold Rosenberg (writing). This volume contained detailed listings of recordings of contemporary music, and commentaries on, among others, Lou Harrison and Stefan Wolpe. Another key document was *Modern Artists in America: First Series*, 1951, edited by Robert Motherwell and Ad Reinhardt, with photography by Aaron Siskind. This volume contained a roundtable discussion, "Artists' Sessions at Studio 35," with, among others, Willem de Kooning and Richard Lippold, and a fas-

cinating list of exhibitions in New York galleries for 1949–1950 at the critical moment when Abstract Expressionism was in the act of becoming.

In one of his earliest published writings, a review of the first two exhibitions in New York of Mondrian, Motherwell reveals his humanist roots: "[Mondrian] has spent his life in the creation of a clinical art in a time when men were ravenous for the *human* . . ."[54] Against an art such as Mondrian's, or Albers's, which placed a premium on not being self-expression, Motherwell set the Surrealists' limitless abandon to the self's mysteries:

> The power of [the formalist] position must not be underestimated. It has produced some of the greatest creations of modern art. But the fundamental criticism of the purely formalist position is how it reduces the individual's ego, how much he must renounce. No wonder there is such insistence among formalists on perfection. Such limited material is capable of perfection, and with perfection it must replace so much else.[55]

Yet, for all his admiration of "the dada strand in the fabric of surrealism," Motherwell could not completely align himself with its complete arrogation of authority.

[54] Robert Motherwell, "Notes on Mondrian and Chirico," orinigally published in *VVV*, New York, June 1942, reprinted in *The Collected Writings of Robert Motherwell*, edited by Stephanie Terenzio (Berkeley and Los Angeles: University of California Press, 1999), p. 20 ff.

[55] Robert Motherwell, "The Modern Painter's World," originally given as a talk in a forum that included José Luis Sert and Ossip Zadkine, 10 August1944, and published in *DYN*, 1944, reprinted in *The Collected Writings of Robert Motherwell*, p. 27 ff.

ROBERT MOTHERWELL
ABSTRACT COMPOSITION, CA. 1945.
Watercolor & graphite on paper, 12 ⅜ x 10 ⅜ inches.
Photography Courtesy the Museum of Fine Arts, Houston. Collection of
Isabel B. Wilson. Photograph © Museum of Fine Arts, Houston.

ROBERT MOTHERWELL
PERSONAGE, 1944.
Burin engraving on paper, 13 ¹⁄₁₆ x 9 ¹⁵⁄₁₆ inches.
San Francisco Museum of Modern Art. Gift of the Dedalus
Foundation, Inc., in honor of Phyllis Wattis.

ROBERT MOTHERWELL
ILE DE FRANCE, 1945.
Watercolor on paper, 7 ½ x 10 ⅝ inches.
North Carolina Museum of Art. Gift of W. R. Valentiner.
Image © North Carolina Museum of Art.

ROBERT MOTHERWELL
MÁLAGA, 1950.
Oil on board, 14 x 18 inches.
Gift of Mr. and Mrs. James W. Alsdorf, 1970.1038.
Image © The Art Institute of Chicago.

He would have to find a different path forward. This he did first in his many Personages of the 1940s. Many of these were done in direct response to the Spanish Civil War, and one of his lifetime projects would later be the *Elegy to the Spanish Republic*.

In 1944, Motherwell had his first solo exhibition, at Art of This Century, and the following year he began a relationship with the Kootz Gallery in New York. After teaching at Black Mountain in 1945, Motherwell contributed a statement to the issue of *design* magazine devoted to the college. In it, he affirmed his emphasis on the human: ". . . the artist stands for the human against society . . ." In an odd way, he seems to stake out a kind of realism against a colder formalism, when he writes:

> The "pure" red of which certain abstractionists speak does not exist, no matter how one shifts its physical contexts. Any red is rooted in blood, glass, wine, hunters' caps, and a thousand other concrete phenomena. Otherwise we should have no feeling toward red or its relations, and it would be useless as an artistic element.[56]

Around 1945, Motherwell started to go beyond the figure, at least literally. After 1950, there would be no more personages. There would be figures on grounds, but they would be abstract and could be read as landscapes, or nothing, as much as figures. *Ile de France*, 1945, shows what would become a recognizable pattern of strong verticals, upon or against which are played irregularly formed shapes. These may come from figures or landscape, they may have biomorphic elements to them, but ultimately they are irreducible as content. By 1950, and a work such as *Malaga*, 1950, there is an even flatter relationship, in that there is less of a desire for the overlapping of forms. Motherwell had long been striving to distance himself from Cubism, and here he achieved his desire. There is a palpable movement retained in the forms from the way they are painted; they breathe with the unconscious thoughts of the hand. There is space, but depth is ambiguous.

Ultimately, Motherwell was saved by paint. By recusing himself from the world of theory, he found an answer to his quandary. In the *design* essay, he wrote, "What an inspiration the medium is! Colors on the palette or mixed in jars on the floor, assorted papers, or a canvas of a certain concrete space—no matter what, the painting mind is put into motion, probing, finding, completing."[57] He amplified these thoughts in a statement for his second exhibition at Kootz:

> For me the medium of oil painting resists, more strongly than others, content cut off from external relations. It continually threatens, because of its motility and subtlety, to complicate a work beyond the simplicity inherent in a high order of abstraction. I attribute my increasing devotion to oil lately, as against the constructionalism of collage, to a

---

[56] Robert Motherwell, "Beyond the Aesthetic," originally published in *design*, April 1946, reprinted in *The Collected Writings of Robert Motherwell*, p. 35 ff.

[57] Ibid.

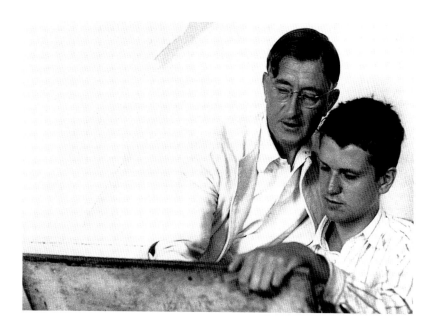 

JOSEF ALBERS DRAWING CLASS (*LEFT*: ALBERS WITH ROBERT DE NIRO; *RIGHT*: ROBERT DE NIRO WITH EDDIE DREIER). CA. 1939–1940

with the two Germans. De Niro's willful use of the figure, however, marks him as someone not willing to adhere to modernist dogma, and indeed he remained in that sense independent, wilfully availing himself of representative imagery—sometimes figurative, others with paint-patterned interiors in reference to Vuillard.

De Niro's first solo exhibition was at Peggy Guggenheim's Art of This Century in New York in 1946, and he had three exhibitions with Charles Egan Gallery in the early 1950s. In the 1950s, De Niro developed into a gestural painter, one with a remarkably fluid line in paint, capable of subtle atmospheric effects, as in *Still Life with Portrait Bust*, 1956. His work is hard to categorize as it falls between abstraction and representation, between expressionism and color field.

In Greenberg's opinion, 1947 and 1948 were watershed years for abstract expressionism. In general, there was a shift away from what Greenberg calls "easel painting," with its reliance on the verticals and horizontals of the frame for guidance in the deployment of similar vertical and horizontal formats, towards large-scale composition, abetted in part by experience in the W.P.A. Mural Project, in which the artist could lose sight of the geometric configuration within which he worked. 1948 was the year de Kooning had his first show, at the Egan Gallery, and shortly afterward, Mark Tobey being unavailable, Albers invited him to teach the summer session at Black Mountain. Franz Kline appeared on the New York scene two years later, also showing at Egan, and 1950 is noted by Greenberg as a high point: ". . . it was only in 1950 that 'abstract expressionism' jelled as a general manifestation. And only then did two of its henceforth conspicuous features, the huge canvas and the black and white oil, become ratified."[65]

[65] Greenberg, "'American-Type' Painting," published in *Art and Culture: Critical Essays* (Boston: Beacon Press, 1961), p. 219.

ROBERT DE NIRO
VENICE AT NIGHT, 1942–1943.
Oil on canvas, 38 x 44 inches.
Courtesy of Salander O'Reilly Galleries, New York.

ROBERT DE NIRO
STILL LIFE WITH PORTRAIT BUST, 1956.
Oil on canvas, 37 ½ x 35 ½ inches.
Courtesy of Salander O'Reilly Galleries, New York.

Elaine de Kooning described what drew so many important artists to teach with little remuneration at the same tiny school in a remote corner of North Carolina:

> Bill had his first one-man show at the Egan Gallery in April of 1948, the month I began writing reviews for *Artnews*. Nothing sold from Bill's show, and my reviews brought in only two dollars apiece. We were looking forward to the summer with trepidation. We were penniless with no prospects. The previous four summers of our married life spent in the city had taught us that living hand-to-mouth, at which we were expert, was more difficult in July and August than during the rest of the year when 'something would happen.'[66]

Egan kept the show up through June, when finally, owing to a favorable review in *Artnews*, "a letter from a stranger changed all." Albers had read the review and on its merits invited de Kooning to teach the summer session at Black Mountain. He would receive $200, in addition to room and board, studios, and round-trip trainfare for both Bill and Elaine. During that summer, Elaine painted a remarkable series of enamel paintings on wrapping paper, and Bill painted a major work, *Asheville*, in addition to several works on paper.

It was a key period for Willem de Kooning, in the midst of his black and white abstract enamel paintings. It was a period of pushing, to break through to something new. Pollock's appearance in *Life* magazine in 1949 announced American art's arrival. Just previously, with Greenberg cheering or giving commands from the sidelines, artists had striven to get beyond the European line. For de Kooning, this meant moving from works using contained forms, which he had made in the early 1940s, and which revealed him to be a sublime colorist, to those uncontained, gestural forms in which color was reduced to essentials.

Already, in the summer of 1948, at Black Mountain, de Kooning was moving beyond black and white. *Asheville* was painted in what become an accustomed manner for de Kooning, of working all day, then scraping the canvas down at day's end, to begin again the next day with only the previous day's residue present. De Kooning also did pastel drawings, which he may have ripped into sections and used to compose the painting.[67] Primarily by his reintroduction of color, de Kooning was able to consolidate elements that carried him to a new level of painting. The complex and irregular formal rhythms, developed in the black and white paintings, combined here with what would become a typically de Kooningesque palette of "weak" or "offbeat" colors, mark the emergence of a new phase or style, although the artist would not have used that term. In succeeding years, with paintings like *Gansevoort Street*, c. 1949, *Painting*, c. 1950, and *Abstraction*, 1949–1950, de Kooning moved toward active color rhythms in compressed space, though still relying on the linear definition of partially bounded areas.

[66] Elaine de Kooning, "De Kooning Memories," *Vogue*, December 1983, reprinted in *The Spirit of Abstract Expressionism: Selected Writings* (New York: George Braziller, 1994, p. 207 ff.

[67] See Marla Prather in *Willem de Kooning Paintings*, National Gallery of Art, Washington/Yale University Press (New Haven:1994), p. 97, and accompanying footnote 33.

110 >

WILLEM DE KOONING
UNTITLED, 1941.
Gouache on paper, 5 x 6 ¾ inches.
Estate of Rudy Burckhardt.

WILLEM DE KOONING
UNTITLED, CA. 1954 (recto).
Black ink on paper, 27 9/16 x 39 3/8 inches.
Collection of Nicola del Roscio, Rome.
Photograph by Mimmo Capone.

WILLEM DE KOONING
UNTITLED, CA. 1954 (verso).
Black ink on paper, 27 9/16 x 39 3/8 inches.
Collection of Nicola del Roscio, Rome.
Photograph by Mimmo Capone.

WILLEM DE KOONING
ASHEVILLE, 1948.
Oil and enamel on cardboard, 25 9/16 x 31 7/8 inches.
The Phillips Collection, Washington D. C. Acquired 1952.
Photograph by Edward Owen.

WILLEM DE KOONING
ABSTRACTION, 1949–1950.
Mixed media on board, 14 ½ x 18 ¼ inches.
Madrid, Museo Thyssen-Bornemisza.

ELAINE DE KOONING
UNTITLED 11, 1948.
Enamel on paper mounted to canvas, 21 ½ x 33 inches.
Courtesy of Salander O'Reilly Galleries, New York.

ELAINE DE KOONING
UNTITLED 12, 1948.
Enamel on paper mounted to canvas, 32 x 37 inches.
Courtesy of Salander O'Reilly Galleries, New York.

ELAINE DE KOONING
UNTITLED NUMBER 15, 1948.
Enamel on paper mounted on canvas, 32 x 44 inches.
Metropolitan Museum of Art, New York.
Purchase, Iris Cantor Gift, 1992.
Photograph © 1992 Metropolitan Museum of Art.

ELAINE DE KOONING
BLACK MOUNTAIN NUMBER 6, 1948.
Enamel on paper mounted on canvas, 13 ½ x 16 ¼ inches.
Collection of The Heckscher Museum of Art, Huntington, New York.
Museum Purchase, 1991.20. Courtesy of Salander O'Reilly Galleries, LLC, New York.

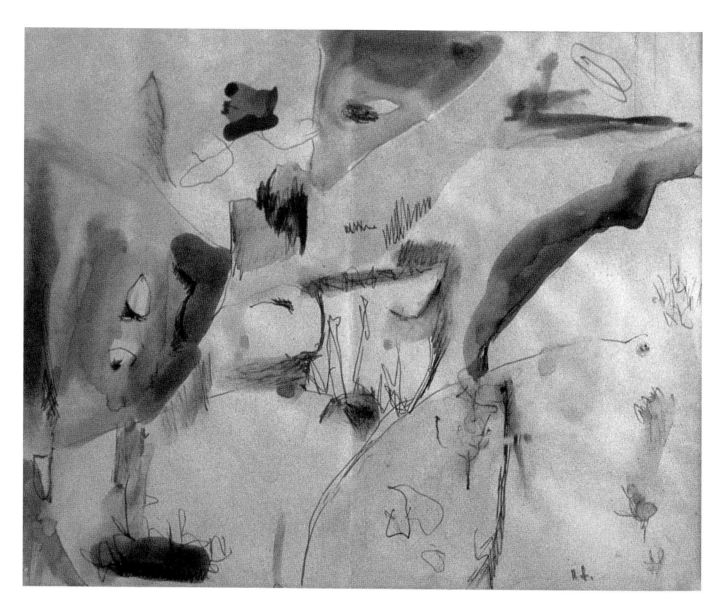

HELEN FRANKENTHALER
AT BLACK MOUNTAIN, 1950.
Ink on paper, 8 ½ x 11 inches.
Private Collection.
© Helen Frankenthaler.

creation and myth. His paintings in this period typically featured mysterious figures and shapes clearly delineated in somber atmospheres.

Stamos was selected for the Whitney Annual exhibition in 1945, and in 1946 the Museum of Modern Art bought his painting *Sounds in the Rock*. Travels to the Northwest, where he met Tobey, and to Paris, where he met Brancusi, Giacometti, and others, as well as a first trip to Greece, were for Stamos ultimate formative experiences. Combining an interest in Japanese painting with his studies of Greek myth and natural history, Stamos arrived at his signature style. A switch from board to canvas also contributed to this development, allowing him to soak lines and textures into the canvas, giving his forms an evanescent, floating quality that combined so effectively with his use of calligraphic line.

In 1950, Stamos was one of the artists among the Irascible Eighteen, who protested a juried exhibition at the Metropolitan Museum and ended up on the front page of the *New York Times*, thus bringing increased recognition to the abstract expressionist movement. That summer Stamos was chosen to teach at Black Mountain. After Albers's departure, Joe Fiore took part in the invitation process, and in the early 1950s, Fiore invited Philip Guston to teach. Guston replied that he was unavailable, but would like to teach at Black Mountain another summer; although he did visit for a few days, he never taught.

1950 was a key year for Stamos: inclusion with the Irascibles, a solo exhibition at the Phillips Collection in Washington, an exhibition at Parsons, participation in the Whitney Annual, and Black Mountain. At Black Mountain, Stamos painted two paintings, *Beyond the Mountains, No. 1*, and *The Emperor Ploughs the Fields*, that are signal examples of Stamos's mature efforts. In both paintings vertical and horizontal areas, roughly rectangular, float in relation to one another on light grounds. These forms' softened edges and their delicate balance gives them the air of hovering. In both paintings, these shapes are connected by long, curving lines that serve as phrasing markers in musical notation, tying the sequence of utterance together into unified statements. The muted earth tones are typical of Stamos's work in this period. Stamos later acknowledged the landscape at Black Mountain as the inspiration for these two paintings.[72]

Regarding *The Emperor Ploughs the Fields*, Betty Parsons wrote in 1957, "I know [Stamos] considers this one of his turning point pictures."[73] Apparently, the museum that purchased the picture, the Detroit Institute of Arts, was interested in what lay behind the title, and Stamos later wrote an explanation:

> This painting was done during the summer of 1950 while I was teaching painting at Black Mt. College. My studio looked over some beautiful farmland and mountains that were almost always shrouded in veils of mists that somehow gave me the feeling that the mts. in China must be similar and as ominous. The farmlands, which were inciden-

LEO AMINO AND THEODOROS STAMOS. BLACK MOUNTAIN COLLEGE, 1950. PHOTOGRAPH BY JULIE AMINO.

[72] Theodoros Stamos, questionnaire, North Carolina Museum of Art, Black Mountain College Research Project, North Carolina State Archives, Raleigh.

[73] Betty Parsons, letter to Franklin Page, Detroit Institute of Arts, April 4, 1957, North Carolina Museum of Art, Black Mountain College Research Project, North Carolina State Archives, Raleigh.

124 >

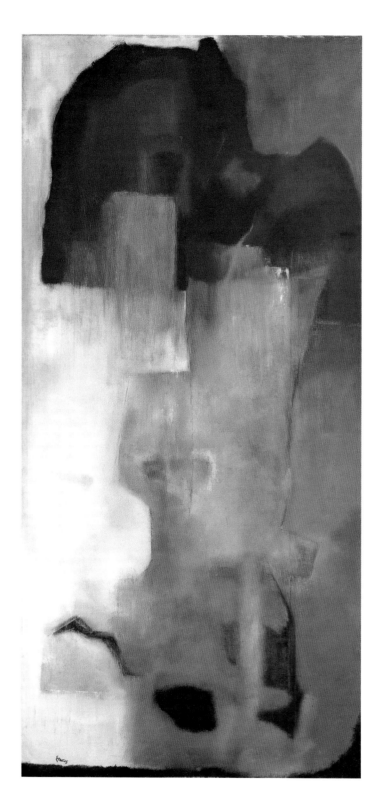

THEODOROS STAMOS
GREEK ORISON, 1952.
Oil on canvas, 67 x 27 inches.
Whitney Museum of American Art, New York. Purchase.
Photograph: Geoffrey Clements © 1996 Whitney Museum of American Art, New York.

THEODOROS STAMOS
BEYOND THE MOUNTAINS, NUMBER 1, 1950.
Oil on canvas, 86 ¼ x 41 inches.
Metropolitan Museum of Art, New York.
Gift of Miss Katherine Ordway, 1956.
Photograph © 1997 Metropolitan Museum of Art.

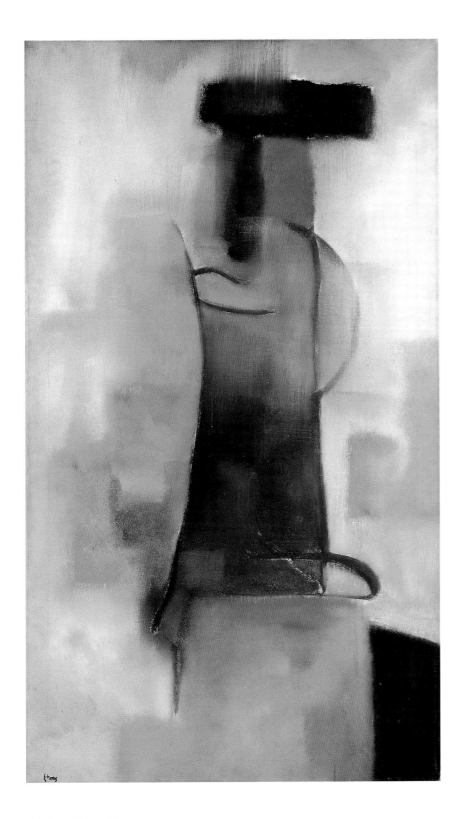

THEODOROS STAMOS
THE EMPEROR PLOUGHS THE FIELDS, 1950.
Oil on canvas, 54 x 31 inches.
The Detroit Institute of Arts. Founders Society Purchase, Friends of Modern Art Fund.
Photograph © 1997 The Detroit Institute of Arts.

tal in the mind's eye, became, strangely enough, *The Emperor Ploughs the Fields.*[74]

By 1952, the year Franz Kline taught the summer session at Black Mountain, Greenberg regarded him as one of New York's most important artists, despite Kline's having had only two exhibitions at Egan's. "His originality lies in the way in which he maintains a Cubist contact with the edges of his canvas while opening up a seemingly un-Cubist or post-Cubist ambiguity of plane and depth elsewhere."[75] Greenberg also offered a fascinating analysis of Kline's reliance on a polar black-and-white scheme:

> Value contrast, the opposition of the lightness and darkness of colors, has been Western pictorial art's chief means, far more important than perspective, to that convincing illusion of three-dimensionality which distinguishes it most from other traditions of pictorial art. . . . What is at stake in the new American emphasis on black and white is the preservation of something—a main pictorial resource—that is suspected of being near exhaustion; and the effort at preservation is undertaken, in this as in other cases, by isolating and exaggerating that which one wants to preserve.[76]

Robert Creeley, in "A Note on Franz Kline," published in 1954 in the *Black Mountain Review*, no. 4, along with reproductions of eight of Kline's paintings, put a different spin on the painter's obsession with the massive interaction of primal forms:

> There are women who will undress only in the dark, and men who will only surprise them there. One imagines such a context uneasily, having no wish either to be rude or presumptuous. Darkness, in effect, is the ground for light, which seems an old and also sturdy principle . . . Picasso? Much a way of being *about* something, minus night, etc. There are some men for whom it seems never to get dark. As, for example, for Klee it never quite seems to be sun, etc. . . . With Kline's work . . . it has to be black on white, because there he is, New York, etc. He has no wish to fight senses and all. But he is a savagely exact laugher, call it . . . What is "funnier" than forms which will not go away. If you say this to someone, they will laugh at you, but all the time, right behind them, there is a skyscraper! It's incredible how they can notice it, if they do, and still talk to anyone.[77]

Kline has always been notoriously mysterious. Certainly, the sequence of his paintings is known, how he began in the early 1950s to paint works of exquisite and

[74] Theodoros Stamos letter to Franklin Page, 1957, North Carolina Museum of Art, Black Mountain College Research Project, North Carolina State Archives, Raleigh.

[75] Clement Greenberg, *Partisan Review* "Art Chronicle": 1952, reprinted in *Art And Culture: Critical Essays* (Boston: Beacon Press, 1961), p. 151.

[76] Greenberg, "'American-Type' Painting," reprinted in *Art And Culture: Critical Essays* (Boston: Beacon Press, 1961), pp. 220–221.

[77] Robert Creeley, "A Note on Franz Kline," *Black Mountain Review*, no. 4, winter 1954, p. 23.

WILLIAM MCGEE AND FRANZ KLINE, 1952.
PHOTOGRAPH BY WILLIAM MCGEE.
Black Mountain College Museum and Arts Center,
Asheville.

unequaled force. Many people were shocked to learn that his large-scale paintings were frequently precise translations developed from delicate paper studies. How he could paint so precisely, on the large canvas, communicating such unleashed energy, remains a mystery. The myth of the "action painter" is often exaggerated. There were certainly painters for whom painting quickly, without time for conscious analysis was the key factor. De Kooning, on the other hand, was known to paint a stroke quickly, then sit down and look at the painting for a while before painting another.[78]

Kline, for all his myth and fame, rarely spoke for the record. Perhaps because he declined to mythologize himself, his myth grew greater. His painting retains the vivacity with which it was painted—and often the white is painted on top of the black. The exacting measure of scale and rhythm, even when one notes their peculiar tinkered-with quality, remains fresh, in movement. In some works, such as *Untitled*, 1952, Kline retained a starkly geometric approach, yet his rectilinears convey the same vitality of breath as his freer forms. *Painting*, 1952, the one piece Kline painted at Black Mountain, shows geometry just beginning to go haywire. The broad black swaths by and large maintain defined edges, yet odd interventions, broadenings, and slight curvings subtly throw the rectilinear impulse off course. The primary division is a horizontal white section, equal to about three black bands in width, that separates the top from the bottom of the canvas. This division can suggest many interpretations—conscious/unconscious, rich/poor, etc.—but what may be more to the point is Kline's fondness for the railroads among which he grew up in Pennsylvania, and for which he named several of paintings. Here, the two forceful parallels can serve to indicate a no-nonsense approach that Kline appreciated in life and in painting.

The other artist selected to teach in 1952 was also a formidable painter and later a figure on the New York art scene, often speaking at the Artists' Club and arranging discussions of various aesthetic topics. Jack Tworkov spent the summer of

[78] Observation by Rudy Burckhardt in interview with Vincent Katz published in the *Print Collector's Newsletter* 25, no. 5 (1994):197.

128 >

FRANZ KLINE
PAINTING, 1952.
Oil on canvas, 65 x 41 ¾ inches.
Wadsworth Atheneum Museum, Hartford. Gift of Walter K. Gutman.
Photograph © Wadsworth Atheneum.

FRANZ KLINE
UNTITLED, 1952.
Oil on paper, mounted on canvas, mounted on aluminum honeycomb panel, 32 x 44 inches.
Solomon R. Guggenheim Museum, New York. Gift, American Art Foundation, 1980.
Photograph: David Heald © The Solomon R. Guggenheim Foundation, New York.

JACK TWORKOV. NEW YORK, 1953.
PHOTOGRAPH BY RUDY BURCKHARDT.

1952 at Black Mountain with his wife and two daughters, one of whom, Hermine Ford, is a painter today. Tworkov was born in Poland in 1900 and moved to the States at 13. After studying English at Columbia University, Tworkov studied painting at the National Academy and The Art Students' League. He began showing with the Egan Gallery in 1947 and later moved to the Stable Gallery.

Ford remembers that Tworkov drew alot and that his drawings could generate ideas for paintings, but that drawings could also come from paintings, so that drawing and painting were always spurring each other on.[79] As Ford puts it, "In the studio, he was constantly experimenting, and doing work that was not directly related." He would make collages, draw from a model, at the same time as he was making his abstract work. In a 1953 *Artnews* feature, photographed by Rudy Burckhardt, the painter Fairfield Porter wrote of Tworkov's *House of the Sun* series:

> The subject here first appeared in a drawing made at Black Mountain last summer. He did not choose the subject but he came to know it. In mode it derived from a series of paintings he made a year before . . . where he, partly influenced by Futurism, showed figures in definitely ambiguous space—from more than one point of view at once. As the figures began to develop, the subject tended to become erotic. This is the internal origin of the subject and also the origin of the turbulence of the form. There then begins a pull between this origin on the one hand and aesthetic considerations on the other, which set a direction toward non-objectivity.[80]

Porter distinguishes between Tworkov's brand of expressionism and that of other painters, who let their unconscious dominate the painting process. "His painting is neither spontaneous nor automatic," concludes Porter, and he quotes Tworkov as saying, "It is in the nature of painting that it sometimes takes its own bent. . . . But still, painting is not to be considered a technique of exploiting accidents."[81]

Tworkov was a consummate draftsman, and a painting such as *House of Rocks*, 1952, reveals the artist's unique sensibility in being able to achieve great impact and intimation of density and space with the most minimal and evanescent linear painting. *House of the Sun Sketch*, 1953, part of the series that Porter examined, offers a look, unusual for the time, at Tworkov's ability with harmonies of bright reds, oranges, and yellows, the thickly painted lines here both evincing the liquid power of the sun's light and traces of its effects on objects. With *Untitled*, 1954, a large charcoal drawing, one can already see Tworkov moving towards a more conceptual approach to line, here by reducing its presence with understood hiatuses, that would take a different turn, more layered and with a more monolithic effect, in the 1960s.

In 1953, Esteban Vicente was invited by Charles Olson to teach the summer session. Vicente was born in 1903 in Turégano, a small town in Segovia, Spain. He grew up in Madrid, studied at the Royal Academy of Fine Arts of San Fernando and

[79] This and other observations by Ford in this section are from an interview with Vincent Katz, 1 March 2002.

[80] Fairfield Porter, "Tworkov Paints a Picture," *Artnews*, May 1953, p. 31.

[81] Ibid., pp. 31–32.

133 >

JACK TWORKOV
HOUSE OF ROCKS, 1952.
Oil on canvas, 50 x 45 inches.
Solomon R. Guggenheim Museum, New York. Gift, David A. Prager, 1981.
Photograph: Robert E. Mates © The Solomon R. Guggenheim Foundation, New York.

JACK TWORKOV
UNTITLED, 1952.
Oil, charcoal, crayon on paper, 24 1/4 x 38 1/4 inches.
The Museum of Fine Arts, Houston. Museum purchase with funds provided
by the Caroline Wiess Law Accessions Endowment Fund.
Photograph © Museum of Fine Arts, Houston.

JACK TWORKOV
UNTITLED, 1954.
Charcoal on paper, 25 3/4 x 19 7/8 inches.
Whitney Museum of American Art, New York.
Gift of Mr. and Mrs. Arthur Wiesenberger.
Photograph by Matt Flynn.

JACK TWORKOV:
HOUSE OF THE SUN SKETCH, 1953.
Oil on Upson board, 28 ¼ x 25 ⅜ inches.
Private Collection.

ESTEBAN VICENTE
BLACK MOUNTAIN, 1976.
Collage of charcoal on paper mounted on
cardboard, 11 x 8 ¼ inches.
Estate of Esteban Vicente.

ESTEBAN VICENTE
NUMBER 5, 1950.
Oil on canvas, 35 ⅛ x 45 ¼ inches.
Museo de Arte Contemporáneo Esteban Vicente, Segovia.

ESTEBAN VICENTE
MIDWEST, 1953.
Oil on canvas, 48 x 36 inches.
Museo Nacional Centro de Arte Reina Sofía, Madrid. Photograph by Joaquín Cortés.

in 1929 moved to Paris. In 1936, he moved to New York. By 1950, Vicente was painting abstractly and was part of the first generation of New York School painters. While in later years, Vicente would paint using a Color Field technique, in the 1950s the use of gesture and line, of drawing, was important to him. A painting such as *Number 5*, 1950, has a connection to how de Kooning was dividing space in his black and white paintings of the late 1940s, although Vicente's forms were more open, his use of line less declarative. By 1953, in a painting such as *Midwest*, Vicente was employing a more inventive palette, and structures of incident, particularly their spatial components, had become more complex.

MERCE CUNNINGHAM AND COMPANY: *SEPTET*, 1953. PHOTOGRAPH BY ARA IGNATIUS. Cunningham Dance Foundation Inc.

V. Chance Operations

Any experimental musician in the twentieth century has had to rely on painters.

—JOHN CAGE[82]

John Cage had thought about Black Mountain long before he finally made it there. He contacted the college in the late 1930s to see about studying there. In 1942, he had the idea to start a Center For Experimental Music there. Neither proposal was acted upon.[83] In the spring of 1948, Cage and Cunningham were touring the country, performing piano and dance where ever they could arrange it. They contacted Black Mountain, which this time agreed to a performance, after making it clear they would have no money to pay the performers.

[82] John Cage, in an interview with Irving Sandler, 1966, quoted in *Conversing with Cage*, edited by Richard Kostelanetz (New York: Limelight Editions, 1988), p. 190.

[83] From an interview with John Cage by Martin Duberman, 26 April 1969, referred to in Duberman's *Black Mountain: An Exploration in Community* (New York: Dutton, 1972), p. 288 (footnote 18).

At that time, there was common ground between Albers and Cage, who had met Mark Tobey in the 1930s and was impressed by the Bauhaus, Mondrian, and Malevich's white on white paintings. Cage had a professed leaning toward geometric abstraction and was less fond of the symbolism and psychology at the heart of Surrealist art. When he first moved to New York, in the mid-1940s, he stayed at the apartment of Peggy Guggenheim and Max Ernst, having been hired to perform a concert at the opening of Guggenheim's Art of This Century gallery. As Cage put it, "It was a marvelous place to land because . . . it was the whole gamut of the world of painting . . . in one fell swoop or series of evenings at Peggy Guggenheim's you met an entire world of both American and European artists."[84] Elsewhere, Cage spoke of having been "brought up on the twenties" and being "very impressed by geometrical abstract art," as well as Dada.[85]

The work Cage and Cunningham collaborated on grew from a desire to break free from traditional modern approaches to dance, primarily narrative and emotional, with music supplementing the emotions portrayed in the dance. They began their approach by determining a "rhythmic structure" within which both dance and music could be composed independently and then brought together.

A "Campus News" note in the *Black Mountain College Bulletin* of May 1948, described the first, brief, visit to Black Mountain of Cage and Cunningham:

> John Cage and Merce Cunningham visited Black Mountain College in April. . . . John Cage composes music . . . music for the piano transformed into a combination of percussive sound and tone. This transformation is brought about by the insertion of a certain number of bolts, screws, and leather scraps into the piano. He played for the college community a program of sixteen sonatas and four interludes, the work largely of the last two years. After the program, and after coffee in the community house, John Cage answered . . . questions. . . . He suggested that he was interested more in time than in harmonics. His music is structured according to duration in time, every smaller unit of a large composition reflecting as a microcosm the features of the whole. . . . Cunningham and Cage work together, or perhaps one should say separately . . . they work out the dance and music separately after having agreed upon a rhythmic structure. . . . Merce Cunningham gave for the community a program of dance exercises and dance compositions. . . . The current of creative energy since their visit has illuminated the college both in creation and in response.[86]

Due to the enthusiastic response all around, Cage and Cunningham were invited back for what was billed as Summer Session 1948, along with Willem de Kooning, Buckminster Fuller, Peter Grippe, Beaumont Newhall, and others. Cage decided to devote his efforts that summer to presenting the work of composer Erik Satie.

[84] John Cage, in an interview with Jeff Goldberg, 1976, quoted in *Conversing with Cage*, edited by Richard Kostelanetz (New York: Limelight Editions, 1988), p. 11.

[85] John Cage, in an interview with Irving Sandler, 1966, quoted in *Conversing with Cage*, edited by Richard Kostelanetz (New York: Limelight Editions, 1988), p. 13.

[86] *Black Mountain College Bulletin* 6, no. 4 (May 1948):5.

THE RUSE OF MEDUSA, 1948: BUCKMINSTER FULLER WITH MERCE CUNNINGHAM. PHOTOGRAPH BY
CLEMENS KALISCHER. Courtesy of the artist.

THE RUSE OF MEDUSA, 1948: BUCKMINSTER FULLER, ELAINE DE KOONING
AND MERCE CUNNINGHAM. PHOTOGRAPH BY CLEMENS KALISCHER.
Courtesy of the artist.

POSTER FOR THE RUSE OF MEDUSA: A LYRIC COMEDY IN ONE
ACT BY ERIK SATIE, PERFORMED AT BLACK MOUNTAIN COLLEGE,
AUGUST 14, 1948. State Archives at North Carolina, Raleigh.

He gave piano recitals, as many as three times a week, of Satie's music. Albers suggested that Cage give a short talk introducing each recital, and one of these talks occasioned Cage's "Defense of Erik Satie," which was just as much an attack on Beethoven and the German Romantic tradition.

The culmination of the summer, for Cage, and for many who were there, was the performance of Satie's short play *Le Piège de Méduse (The Ruse of Medusa)*, which had only been performed once before. Poet M. C. Richards translated the text, and Cage performed the music. Buckminster Fuller, whom Cage and Cunningham had befriended, was enlisted to play the lead role of Baron Medusa, with Elaine de Kooning as his daughter, Frisette. Cunningham danced in the role of "a costly mechanical monkey," and student William Schrauger was Frisette's suitor. Willem de Kooning painted the sets. Fuller, although able to talk captivatingly for hours on end, froze when faced with the prospect of acting in conjunction with this extravagant gathering of geniuses. Nothing could deliver him from his crippling panic, until Arthur Penn was called upon to direct the production. Penn, a student, already had experience with Stanislavky's theories before coming to Black Mountain and eventually taught a popular class at the college in 1947 using the Russian master's *An Actor Prepares* as the textbook. Realizing Fuller was afraid of making a fool of himself, Penn himself proceeded to do the most ridiculous things he could imagine. Suddenly, when Fuller saw this, and everyone laughing at Penn, it unlocked him, and from then on he was the star of the show. On another occasion, Cunningham put on "A Program of Dances," with Sara Hamill and Louise Lippold, including the "Monkey Dances" with music by Satie and six other dances with music composed and performed by Cage.

PROGRAM OF DANCES BY MERCE CUNNINGHAM WITH SARA HAMILL AND LOUISE LIPPOLD, BLACK MOUNTAIN COLLEGE PRINT SHOP. State Archives at North Carolina, Raleigh.

As Penn felt his way into his Stanislavsky class, he got the idea of directing some one-act plays. These were among his earliest experiences directing, though he had worked before as a stage manager. His description of the "theater" is telling: "There was the vestige of a light board at one end of the dining hall, so I rebuilt that from my days of stage-managing and touring and bringing our own lights. . . . I knew enough to get that working. . . . We made wings. It was all flat. There was no stage. It was the dining room. Eventually, we made stuff and put it up. It was muslin, not real stage drapes. We made a makeshift stage for that period."[87] Penn continued his friendship with Fuller after Black Mountain. At one point, Fuller, who had left Harvard as an undergraduate, was to be awarded on honorary doctorate by the university. Again, he was petrified, and again he called on Penn, who told him, "Go with your impulse. Follow your unorthodox nature. Let what occurs to you come out. That's what they want. They don't know that they want it. They want to know what the secret of not being conventional is." For Penn himself, the legacy of Black Mountain was the ability to act, regardless of the consequences. "For so many of us there," he says, "we were just touching on something that a little later expanded."

Josef Albers must certainly have realized that the magic of summer 1948 was largely due to the inventive composer and choreographer, as he wrote them each uncharacteristically ecstatic, if brief, letters. His note to Cunningham read:

[87] This and other observations by Penn in this section are from an interview with Vincent Katz, 31 May 2001.

Dear Merce,
We all are terribly proud and grateful for your having been with us
and having worked here this summer.
God bless you.
Yours,

Josef Albers[88]

In January 1949, Cage's *Sonatas and Interludes* were performed at Carnegie
Recital Hall by Maro Ajemian and favorably reviewed by Virgil Thomson. By the
early 1950s, when Cage moved beyond the use of percussion and the prepared
piano into music that was composed using chance operations and indeterminacy,
he had moved into a different area, and a different era, of which he became the
leading exponent and theorist. "Chance operations" quite quickly became codified
for Cage as tossing three coins six times and using the results to select hexagrams
in the *I Ching*, or *Book of Changes*. These hexagrams would then be used to make
all decisions necessary in composing a piece of music, rendering the piece, as
Cage wrote in 1952, "free of individual taste and memory (psychology) and also
of the literature and 'traditions' of the art. The sounds enter the time-space centered
within themselves, unimpeded by service to any abstraction . . ."[89]

Imaginary Landscape No. 5, a piece Cage composed in 1952, uses chance operations to make a collage of fragments from 43 records of jazz music. With a gift
from former Black Mountain student Paul Williams, Cage was able to set up a studio to continue the expensive and time-consuming work of tape splicing. In 1952,
Cage and Cunningham were invited once again to spend the summer at Black
Mountain. This time, the invitation came from composer Lou Harrison. Cage continued work on a new tape piece, which became *Williams Mix*, whose score is more
than 400 pages for a piece of four minutes' duration. Cage also became very interested in the work of student Robert Rauschenberg, who was painting a now-classic
series of all-white paintings, along with another series that was almost entirely black.
In addition, Cage composed that summer what may be one of the most famous
pieces of contemporary music —*4'33"*, in which the pianist sits at the piano and
plays nothing. Cage credits the example of Rauschenberg's white paintings as having given him the push to compose his "silent" piece. He had been afraid that such
a piece would be taken as a joke, just as Satie's *Vexations* had been.

Cage also orchestrated what he later called *Theater Piece No. 1*, and which is
usually referred to as the first "Happening," a type of art event developed in the
late 1950s. *Theater Piece No. 1* was unusual as theater whose elements—music,
dance, light, design, text—were conceived independently, yet intended to exist
simultaneously, without anyone knowing what the combination would yield at any
given moment. As described earlier, Xanti Schawinsky, building on his Bauhaus
theater experiements, had already introduced at Black Mountain a theater whose

[88] Josef Albers, letter to Merce Cunningham, 7 September 1948, North Carolina Museum of Art, Black
Mountain College Research Project, North Carolina State Archives, Raleigh.

[89] John Cage, "Composition: To Describe the Process of Composition Used in *Music of Changes* and
Imaginary Landscape no. 4," originally published in *trans/formation* 1, no. 3 (1952), reprinted in John
Cage, *Silence* (Middletown: Wesleyan University Press, 1961), p. 57 ff.

elements were treated separately, and somewhat abstractly, but reading Schawinsky's script for *Spectodrama: Play, Life, Illusion*, one feels one is reading a traditional dramatic script, with the usual scene-setting, build-ups, climaxes, and denouments. A key catalyst to the 1952 performance, acknowledged by Cage, was M. C. Richards's translation of Antonin Artuad's *The Theater and Its Double*. As Cage describes it:

> . . . we got the idea from Artaud that theater could take place free of a text, that if a text were in it, that it needn't determine the other actions, that sounds, that activities, and so forth, could all be free rather than tied together. . . . So that the audience was not focused in one particular direction.[90]

Cage credits the atmosphere and people collected at Black Mountain with creating a climate conducive to such a piece, just as Schawinsky had felt emboldened by the intellectual openness at Black Mountain to conduct his theatrical experiments there. Cage says, ". . . the Happening business came about through circumstances of being at Black Mountain where there were a number of people present—Merce was there, David Tudor was there, there was an audience . . . there were many people and many possibilities and we could do it quickly. In fact, I thought of it in the morning, and it was performed that afternoon—I was able to sketch it all out."

Theater Piece no. 1 was not a free-form session. On the contrary, interested as he was in durations of activities, Cage assigned a duration, or "time bracket," to each of the actitivies. He also wrote an actual score, and indicated when each person was to be engaging in a particular action. The fact that there are different accounts of what actually took place that day is in part a function of this new type of simultaneous-action theater with which Cage was working. In such an experience, it is impossible to concentrate on everything that is occurring. Not only does each observer inevitably miss certain things, but their actual perception of what is occurring can be subtly altered, due to the simultaneity of events. In terms of what participants actually did, as Cunningham states, little was determined: "John Cage asked the four or five concerned to participate and gave them a vague idea and then told them to do whatever they wanted to do."[91] In terms of the physical set-up for *Theater Piece No. 1*, little was left to chance, as Cage màkes plain:

> The seating arrangement I had at Black Mountain in 1952 was a square composed of four triangles merging toward the center, but not meeting. The center was larger space that would take movement, and the aisles between those four triangles also admitted of movement. The audience could see itself, which is, of course, the advantage of any theater in the round. The larger part of the action took place *outside* of that square. In each one of the seats was a cup, and it wasn't explained to the audience what to do with this cup—

[90] John Cage, in an interview with Mary Emma Harris, 1974, quoted in *Conversing with Cage*, edited by Richard Kostelanetz (New York: Limelight Editions, 1988), p. 104.

[91] Merce Cunningham, in an interview with Vincent Katz, 28 March 2002.

some used it as an ashtray—but the performance was concluded by a kind of ritual, pouring coffee into each cup.[92]

Cage also made clear that the time frames within which a participant was to act were fixed. His description of what resulted follows:

> At one end of a rectangular hall, the long end, was a movie and at the other end were slides. I was up on a ladder delivering a lecture which included silences and there was another ladder which M. C. Richards and Charles Olson went up at different times. During periods that I called time brackets, the performers were free within limitations—I think you would call them compartments—compartments they didn't have to fill, like a green light in traffic. Until this compartment began, they were not free to act, but once it had begun they could act as long as they wanted to during it. Robert Rauschenberg was playing an old-fashioned phonograph that had a horn and a dog on the side listening, and David Tudor was playing a piano, and Merce Cunningham and other dancers were moving through the audience and around the audience. Rauschenberg's pictures were suspended about the audience. . . . He was also painting black ones at the time, but I think we used only the white ones. They were suspended at various angles, a canopy of painting above the audience.[93]

In a memoir of her time at Black Mountain, Francine du Plessix Gray includes the following journal entry, dated "August, 1952," and certainly the account written closest to the time of the event:

> At eight-thirty tonight John Cage mounted a stepladder until 10:30 he talked about the relation of music to Zen Buddhism while a movie was shown, dogs ran across the stage barking, 12 persons danced without any previous rehearsal, a prepared piano was played, whistles blew, babies screamed, Edith Piaf records were played double-speed on a turn-of-the-century machine. . . .[94]

As a direct result of *Theater Piece No. 1*, Cage wrote a piece entitled *Water Music*, 1952, in which the visual aspect of a musical performance begins to come to the fore, as certain actions, such as pouring water into a cup, are scored as much for the visual, as their aural, impact. He also composed a series of pieces he called Haiku, in which the visual aspect of the score is an important part of its existence. In each Haiku, there is one line of music at the bottom of a page. One of these was printed at Black Mountain in 1952, under the auspices of a music printing project, organized by Lou Harrison.

[92] John Cage, in an interview with Michael Kirby and Richard Schechner, 1966, quoted in *Conversing with Cage*, edited by Kostelanetz (New York: Limelight Editions, 1988), p. 103.

[93] Ibid., p. 104.

[94] Francine du Plessix Gray, "Black Mountain: The Breaking (Making) of a Writer," in *Black Mountain College: Sprouted Seeds*, edited by Mervin Lane (Knoxville: University of Tennessee Press, 1990), p. 300.

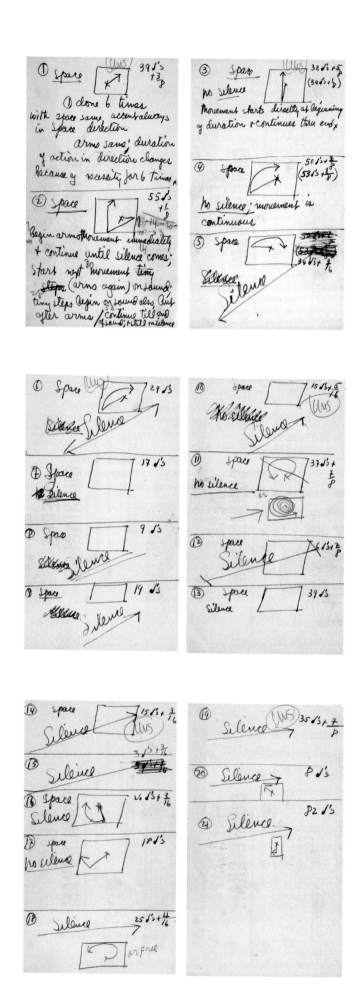

MERCE CUNNINGHAM
UNTITLED SOLO, 1953.
Six notes, each card: 3 9/16 x 5 13/16 inches.
Cunningham Dance Foundation Inc.

MERCE CUNNINGHAM AND VIOLA FARBER IN *BANJO*,
1953. PHOTOGRAPH BY ARNOLD EAGLE. Cunningham
Dance Foundation Inc.

MERCE CUNNINGHAM AND COMPANY: *BANJO*, 1953. PHOTOGRAPH
BY ARNOLD EAGLE. Cunningham Dance Foundation Inc.

MERCE CUNNINGHAM AND COMPANY: *SEPTET*, 1953. PHOTOGRAPH
BY ARA IGNATIUS. Cunningham Dance Foundation Inc.

ELLEN CORNFIELD IN *MINUTIAE*. SET BY ROBERT
RAUSCHENBERG. PHOTOGRAPH BY HERB MIGDOLL.

MERCE CUNNINGHAM DANCE COMPANY IN
NOCTURNES (1956). MUSIC: ERIK SATIE. DESIGN:
ROBERT RAUSCHENBERG. PHOTOGRAPH BY OSCAR
BAILEY. Cunningham Dance Foundation Inc.

Cunningham's interest in translating elements from daily life into art was shared by Cage and also Rauschenberg, who designed sets and costumes for most of Cunningham's dances between 1954 and 1964. In *Summerspace*, 1958, Rauschenberg designed matching set and costumes with many small points of color on a light ground, so that the dancers become evanescent, while in *Minutiae*, 1954, he turned various found objects into a sculpture, much in the vein of his "combine" paintings.

Buckminster Fuller was one of those figures oddly appropriate for Black Mountain. The illustrious, Harvard-educated generations of his family were spiced by radical non-conformists. Fuller, likewise, resists definiton: inventor, scientist, designer, architect, artist, poet, philosopher. One significant predecessor was his great-aunt, Margaret Fuller, a fighter for women's rights and cofounder, with Emerson, of the *Dial*, which she edited and which was the first journal to publish Emerson and Thoreau. Fuller himself did not graduate from Harvard; he found the teaching too strait-laced. After a stint in the Navy, he went into business, and there he began to analyze buildings.

What he discovered was that most structures were overbuilt in relation to the load they must bear. Thus began Fuller's search for the fomulas that would yield maxi-

VIOLA FARBER (*ABOVE*), AND CAROLYN BROWN (*RIGHT*) IN *SUMMERSPACE*
(1958). CHOREOGRAPHY: MERCE CUNNINGHAM. MUSIC: MORTON
FELDMAN. DESIGN: ROBERT RAUSCHENBERG. PHOTOGRAPHS BY RICHARD
RUTLEDGE. Cunningham Dance Foundation Inc.

BUCKMINSTER FULLER WITH MODEL. BLACK MOUNTAIN
COLLEGE, SUMMER, 1949. PHOTOGRAPH BY
MASATO NAKAGAWA.

mum strength with minimum expense and minimum material. He soon began thinking of ways of using technology to provide the maximum benefits to the maximum
number of people on the planet. He envisioned assembled dwellings air-lifted
around the world. That it was, and is, possible is now beyond doubt. The fact
that it has not happened yet does not make the vision a false one.

The term "Dymaxion," with which many identify Fuller's inventions, was not devised
by Fuller but by an advertising man, who combined parts of the words
"dynamism," "maximum" and "ions." Fuller designed a Dymaxion house, a Dymaxion car, and a Dymaxion bathroom. In 1936, working with the Phelps-Dodge Cor-
poration, Fuller produced prefabricated bathrooms at minimal cost and requiring
minimal installation. The Dymaxion Bathroom was divided into a bathtub/shower
space and a lavatory/toilet space. Air-conditioning was provided, and the tub
was wider than average. Twelve models were made and installed, but the Dymaxion
Bathroom was never mass-produced.

The Dymaxion Deployment Unit, patented in 1941, was a pre-fabricated dwelling
designed for emergency shelter, which could be easily transported by plane and
quickly assembled. It was used by the U.S. military in the Pacific and Persian Gulf
during World War II. One was also set up in the Museum of Modern Art's sculpture
garden. As the war continued, Fuller was consulted on how the Dymaxion Deployment Unit could help the aircraft industry shift to a post-war economy. Production of
inexpensive housing was considered of integral cog in this transition. With the support of Beech Aircraft in Wichita, Fuller designed the Dymaxion Dwelling Machine,

DYMAXION DWELLING MACHINE-WICHITA HOUSE, 1946.

BUCKMINSTER FULLER
THREE PIECES FROM THE PORTFOLIO OF
SCREENPRINTS ENTITLED *INVENTIONS:
TWELVE AROUND ONE*, edition 60, printed in
1981 by Colophon, Cincinnati. Each piece
contains two 30 x 40 inches screenprinted
sheets that may be presented separately or
together in overlay. One screenprint is in white
ink on clear polyester film; the second
screenprint is on Lennox paper; with each
piece, there is also a Curtis plan blue backing
sheet, which can be used under the print on
clear film to produce a blueprint.
Carl Solway Gallery, Cincinnati.

BUILDING CONSTRUCTION-DYMAXION DEPLOYMENT UNIT, 1941.

PREFABRICATED DYMAXION BATHROOM, 1938.

BUCKMINSTER FULLER
CLOSEST PACKING OF SPHERES, 1980.
Chrome-plated steel rods, molded thermoplastic connectors, smoked grey
acrylic spheres, 48 x 48 x 48 inches, edition of 10.
Carl Solway Gallery, Cincinnati.

BUCKMINSTER FULLER ARCHITECTURE CLASS, 1948
SUMMER SESSION IN THE ARTS. THE VENETIAN BLIND
DOME. *TOP*: BUCKMISTER FULLER WITH DIAGRAM;
MIDDLE: WILLIAM JOSEPH, ALBERT LANIER,
BUCKMINSTER FULLER, THEODORE DREIER AND ELAINE
DE KOONING; *BOTTOM*: BUCKMINSTER FULLER,
ELAINE DE KOONING AND JOSEF ALBERS.
PHOTOGRAPHS BY BEAUMONT NEWHALL.
Copyright 1948, Beaumont Newhall., © 2002, The
Estate of beaumont Newhall and Nancy Newhall.
Courtesy of Scheinbaum and Russek Ltd., Santa Fe,
NM.

patented in 1946. It featured a domed ceiling sixteen feet high at center, with a Plex-iglass window that circled the circumference of the structure. The total cost of the house to the consumer—including freight and installation—would be $6,500. At the end of the war, however, a different economic picture emerged than had been pre-dicted, and the Dymaxion Dwelling Machine never reached production.

Fuller was remarkable in synthesizing the latest thinking in many different spheres, including theoretical physics, architectural materials, and practical engineering. As recounted by Fuller and co-author Robert Marks, "Fuller saw clearly that men do not make structures out of 'materials'; they make large structures out of small structures—visible module associations out of non-visible module associations."[99] He wished to discover a mathematical system with rules that explained the way all physical structures behave:

> One phase of Fuller's exploration for a geometry of energy resulted in the discovery of what he named *closest-packing of spheres*, each sphere being conceived as an idealized model of a field of energy in which all forces are in equilibrium, and whose vectors, conse-quently, are identical in length and in angular relationships.[100]

There are certain regular principles that derive from the initial thought, or act, of taking a sphere and putting around it, in the closest possible manner, spheres the same size as the central one. The first layer completely surrounding the sphere would be composed of twelve spheres. A second layer, to surround the first in the same manner, would be composed of forty-two; a third, of ninety-two spheres. The structure formed by twelve spheres around a central sphere was a polyhedron with fourteen faces, six of which were squares, eight triangles. Fuller called this fourteen-faced figure the Vector Equililbrium.

From this discovery, Fuller was able eventually to discover the principles of the Octet Truss—a complex of Vector Equilibriums joined together to form alternating tetrahedrons and octohedrons. This led to the framed structures Fuller devised with "omnidirectional and equal dispersion of load pressures, with no member of the truss duplicating the function of any other. For this reason the truss has enormous load-carrying ability; and its strength to weight ration increases as the truss grows in size."[101] Namely, these were the Geodesic Domes, which Fuller worked on at Black Mountain in 1948 and 1949, and for which gained worldwide renown in the 1950s and 1960s. Although he never achieved his goal of providing high-quality housing to everyone on the planet, his engineering principles are still inte-gral to the most advanced thinking in dealing with global housing problems.

There are differing accounts as to what happened in Fuller's first attempt at raising a forty-eight foot diameter hemispheric Geodesic dome at Black Mountain Col-

[99] R. Buckminster Fuller and Robert Marks, *The Dymaxion World of Buckminster Fuller* (New York: Anchor Books, 1973), p. 40.

[100] Ibid.

[101] Ibid., p. 57.

lege in the summer of 1948. According to Elaine de Kooning, Fuller and his students calculated the tensile strength of the venetian-blind stripping they would use, and determined they had to double the strips everywhere. Though the College would only provide half the needed funding, Fuller decided to attempt raising the dome anyway, knowing it could not stand up. According to Fuller and Marks's account, "He intentionally designed this structure so that its delicate system gently collapsed as it neared completion."[102] His goal was to demonstrate that by gradually building a structure up to the precise structural level it needs to stand, one can create lighter, less expensive structures, which also, if they do collapse, will not be so hazardous as those made of extra-heavy materials: "The result was that the safe structure of the forty-eight foot dome was accomplished with one-hundredth of the weight of material customarily employed." The following summer, using a more formidable technique, a "necklace structure of tubular beads and continuous internal cable net," that he had perfected during a year at the Chica-

BUCKMINSTER FULLER ARCHITECTURE CLASS. 1949 SUMMER INSTITUTE. 31 GREAT CIRCLE NECKLACE STRUCTURE OF TUBULAR BEADS AND CONTINUOUS INTERNAL CABLE NET. THIS WAS CONSTRUCTED IN CHICAGO 1948–1949 AND WAS RECONSTRUCTED AT BLACK MOUNTAIN COLLEGE, IN SUMMER, 1949, WITH THE HELP OF SOME OF FULLER'S STUDENTS FROM THE INSTITUTE OF DESIGN. PHOTOGRAPHS BY MASATO NAKAGAWA.

[102] Ibid., p. 182.

go Institute of Design, and bringing with him from Chicago a crew of students, Fuller successfully erected a more modestly-scaled geodesic dome, its strength demonstrated by the entire crew hanging from its slender bars.

A concept that Fuller had worked on for years, Tensegrity—a "special discontinuous-compression, continuous-tension system"—also came into play at Black Mountain. As Fuller and Marks put it, "This Tensegrity network principle could also be demonstrated in a linear manner—as Fuller, enlightened by a linear Tensegrity discovery of his student colleague, Kenneth Snelson, showed by developing a series of Tensegrity masts."[103] Snelson had come to study at Black Mountain with Fuller in the summer of 1948 and returned the following summer with his discovery. Despite Fuller's respectful term "student colleague," Snelson still feels today that he was not given appropriate credit for his putting into practice of Fuller's theory. Tensegrity, or "floating compression," as he prefers to call it, has formed the basis of much of Snelson's prolific output of geometrically-based sculpture.[104]

In 1959, Fuller had an exhibition at the Museum of Modern Art, and a wall-mounted text for his "Tensegrity Mast," read, in part, "The principle involved in the tension integrity mast was first discovered by Kenneth Snelson in 1949, following his studies at Black Mountain College with Buckminster Fuller. The mast in the exhibition is based on the same principle but employs a different configuration of parts. . . . One of the most dramatic developments to grow out of Fuller's theories is the discovery made by Kenneth Snelson and analyzed by Fuller as tension integrity." The conclusion to this text, while disputed by Snelson, provides a key to the appropriateness of Fuller's presence at Black Mountain:

KENNETH SNELSON: *WOODEN FLOATING COMPRESSION COLUMN, WINTER 1948.* Wood, 11 x 5 inches. Photograph by Kenneth Snelson.

> In theory, structures organized on [the Tensegrity] principle have the astonishing characteristic of becoming stronger as their size increases. Domes or other shapes built with tensegrity elements could theoretically be of unlimited dimensions. The mastery of universal forces tensegrity implies is meaningful, however, not simply because it will enable us to make larger structures. More important, and perhaps central to Fuller's genius, is the insight his ideas give us into universal order. That is an acheivement which ranks him with other great poets, scientists, and artists.[105]

Snelson had been studying painting for two years at the University of Oregon when he decided to go to Black Mountain for the summer 1948 session. Although he enjoyed Albers's design class, what really hooked him was meeting Buckminster Fuller. He did a number of works at Black Mountain that make use of tension principles with which Fuller had been working. After leaving Black Mountain, Snelson enjoyed a successful career as a sculptor, with many public commissions. Much of his sculpture to this day employed the discontinuous pressure/continuous tension

KENNETH SNELSON AND JOY BALLON ON PIER BELOW DINING HALL. LAKE EDEN, SUMMER, 1949. PHOTOGRAPH BY MASATO NAKAGAWA.

[103] Ibid., p. 59.

[104] Kenneth Snelson, letter to R. Motro, published in *International Journal of Space Structures*, November 1990.

[105] Wall text to *Tensegrity Mast* in the exhibition by Buckminster Fuller, curated by Arthur Drexler, Museum of Modern Art, New York, 1959.

KENNETH SNELSON: *CONSTRUCTION, WINTER 1948.*
Marbles crazed by fire in chemistry building. "Location: If it is extant,
Buckminster Fuller would have it." Photograph and captions by Kenneth
Snelson.

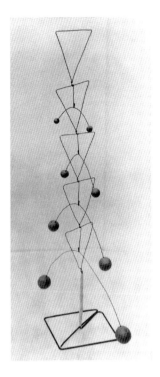

KENNETH SNELSON: *TENSION
STRUCTURE STAGE I, WINTER 1948.*
Iron wire and plasticine, 21 ⅔ inches
high, not extant. Photograph by Kenneth
Snelson.

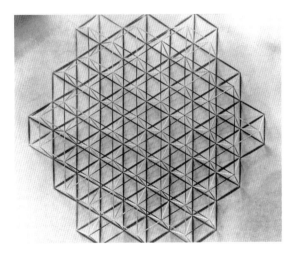

KENNETH SNELSON: *PLANAR SECTION THROUGH OCTA-TETRA-
HEDRON SPACE MATRIX,* BLACK MOUNTAIN COLLEGE, 1949.
Colored plastic toothpicks, not extant. Photograph by Kenneth Snelson.

ARCHITECTURE CLASSROOM. SECOND KENNETH
SNELSON TENSEGRITY STRUCTURE TO THE RIGHT, BLACK
MOUNTAIN COLLEGE, SUMMER, 1949. PHOTOGRAPH
BY KENNETH SNELSON.

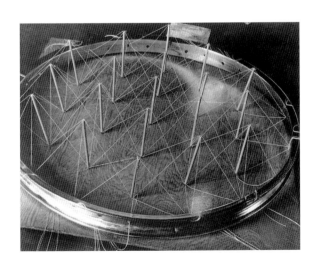

KENNETH SNELSON: *UNTITLED CONSTRUCTION,* JULY 1949.
Bicycle rim, aluminium tubes, fishing lines, ca. 24 inches in diameter, not extant.
Photograph by Kenneth Snelson.

BUCKMINSTER FULLER ARCHITECTURE CLASS (WITH
KENNETH SNELSON, JANO WALLEY, FULLER, CHARLES
PEARMAN, JOHN WALLEY). 1949 SUMMER INSTITUTE.
PHOTOGRAPH BY KENNETH SNELSON.

principle. He has often worked in photography as well, and is known for his 360 degree montage views.

After graduating from the Dalton School in New York in 1947, Susan Weil went to Paris for the summer, where she studied painting at the Académie Julian and drawing at the Académie de la Grande Chaumière. While there, she met Robert Rauschenberg, who was attending the same classes. Rauschenberg was twenty-four at the time. In the fall of 1948, both signed up to go to Black Mountain. Weil found Albers demanding, and, she says, "As a teenager, I wasn't to be told how to do everything. Albers had many rules and limitations, but I got a great deal out of his drawing classes. He was a dramatic speaker and could get very fierce about drawing. Everybody ended up in tears at least once a semester, including the most talented and favored students."[106] Rauschenberg also had mixed feelings. "Albers' rule is to make order," Rauschenberg later said. "[He] was a beautiful teacher and an impossible person. He wasn't easy to talk to, and I found his criticism so excruciating and so devastating that I never asked for it. Years later, though, I'm still learning what he taught me, because what he taught had to do wth the entire visual world. . . . The focus was always on your personal sense of looking."[107]

[106] Susan Weil, in an interview with Vincent Katz, 31 October 2001.

[107] Robert Rauschenberg, quoted in Tomkins, *The Bride and the Bachelors*, p. 199.

SUSAN WEIL AND ROBERT RAUSCHENBERG. BLACK MOUNTAIN COLLEGE, 1948. PHOTOGRAPH BY TRUDE GUERMONPREZ.

While at Black Mountain that first year, Weil created *Secrets*, 1949, a work emblematic of aspects of Weil's mature work until today. To make *Secrets*, Weil took a page from her journal, ripped into judiciously-selected shreds, and assembled the bits in such a way that the edges float off the surface, giving the impression of scraps in a pile on a desk or floor. The tantalizing character of this work, in which communication is intentionally obfuscated, derived from Weil's interest in fragmentation. Whereas in *Secrets* it was a text that fragmented, in later work it was the human body. In early 1949, Albers left Black Mountain, and Rauschenberg and Weil offered to transport some of Albers paintings to the Charles Egan Gallery in New York for an upcoming exhibition. As Weil recalls, "Egan put the lights on in the gallery and revealed a show of Franz Kline. I felt like I had been socked in the stomach. . . . It was as if the things we had learned in art school were suddenly invalid."[108]

In the spring of 1950, Rauschenberg and Weil married, and that summer, Weil introduced Rauschenberg to the blueprint technique of exposing sheets of light-sensitive paper with various objects on the paper. Beginning in 1950, they made a dozen large-scale blueprints using full human figures (often Weil herself) to block

[108] Susan Weil in an interview with Donna Stein, 1997, quoted in *Black Mountain College Dossiers*, no. 5 (Susan Weil), Black Mountain College Museum and Arts Center, Asheville, 1998.

156 >

SUSAN WEIL
SECRETS, 1949.
Pencil, collaged paper, 10 ⅔ x 10 ⅔ inches.
Collection of the artist.

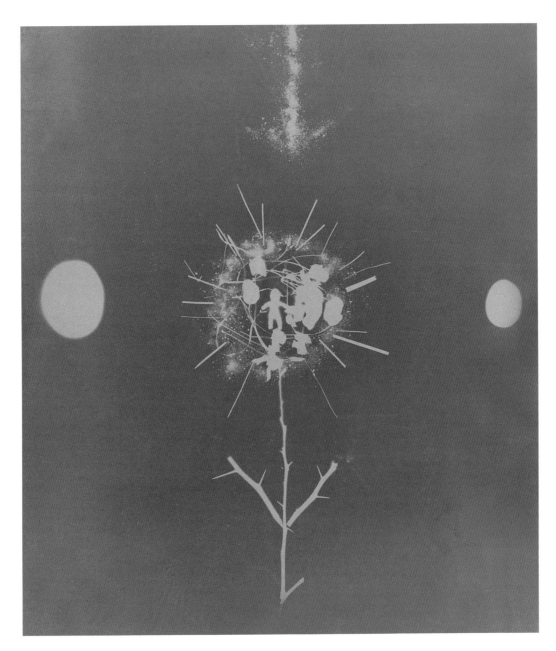

ROBERT RAUSCHENBERG
UNTITLED, 1952 (LARGE DETAIL).
Exposed blueprint paper, 18 x 16 inches.
Private Collection.

ROBERT RAUSCHENBERG PREPARING A MARDI GRAS
COSTUME. BLACK MOUNTAIN COLLEGE.
PHOTOGRAPH BY TRUDE GUERMONPREZ.

the light and thus create an image. Rauschenberg continued to work with this, as well as other photographic techniques. One such blueprint he gave as a 13th birthday present to Hermine Ford at Black Mountain College in the summer of 1952.

In the spring of 1951, Rauschenberg showed paintings at Betty Parsons Gallery and was included in the "Ninth St. Show" organized by Leo Castelli. After those shows, Rauschenberg began to do his Night Blooming series, in which he combined dirt and pigment to give the the impression of forms emerging organically from the surfaces. In *Untitled (Night Blooming)*, ca. 1951, a large, central image of a rising figure, like a tree or a stylized mountain peak is traced with blunt white strokes into the dark asphaltum. Just above the peak, the thinnest sliver of what could be a moon in the dense Blue Ridge night peeks through the gloom. In the summer of 1951, Rauschenberg returned to Black Mountain to study with Robert Motherwell, as did his new friend, Cy Twombly. Weil, Rauschenberg, and Twombly were all making mature work then. Rauschenberg's white paintings, many in multiple panels of different formats, represent an ultimate step in the idea of the progression of modern art to further and further states of elimination, or purity. His black paintings, which make use of collage and material embedded in the texture of the surface, are less conceptual and more tactile, though they do concern the use of non-art materials. As Fielding Dawson writes,

> Rauschenberg and Twombly on the gravel patio beneath the Studies Building, gazing down at a large canvas, covered in most part by tar. They tossed handfuls of pebbles on it. Motherwell, between them, gestured. Said to throw more, and they did.

ROBERT RAUSCHENBERG
UNTITLED (NIGHT BLOOMING), CA. 1951.
Oil, asphaltum and gravel on canvas, 82 ½ x 38 ⅜ inches.
Collection of the artist. Photograph by David Heald.

ROBERT RAUSCHENBERG
WHITE PAINTING (SEVEN PANELS), 1951.
Oil on canvas, 72 x 125 inches.
Collection of the artist. Photograph by David Heald.

"More."
They did.
"More."
They did.[109]

John Cage described the "principle of simplicity" in Satie's compositions, and he compared Robert Rauschenberg's white paintings to that principle:

> The most subtle things become evident [in Satie's *Vexations*] that would not be evident in a more complex rhythmic situation. We have, I believe, many examples in contemporary visual art of things brought to an extraordinary simplicity. I recall, for instance, the white paintings of Robert Rauschenberg, which don't have any images. It's in that highly simplified situation that we are able to see such things as dust or shadows carefully painted, [whereas] in Rembrandt, any other shadow entering the situation would be a disturbance and would not be noticeable, or if noticeable, a disturbance.[110]

Dorothea Rockburne remembers seeing Rauschenberg's white paintings when they were new: "When he met John and Merce, it was an instant understanding, and that's when he did the all-white paintings. It seemed natural and beautiful. I remember when he did the white paintings, he called me up to look at them. He lived in a loft-like structure that was there. He lived on one side of it and I lived on the other side of it. I thought they were so beautiful and full of light."[111]

Twombly became interested in Dada and Surrealism during the years 1947–1949. In September 1950 he moved to New York to study at the Art Students League, and he saw many museum and gallery exhibitions by Gorky, Kline, Motherwell, Pollock, and others. He met Rauschenberg at the art school and decided to attend Black Mountain in the summer of 1951. Apparently, Motherwell did not comment much on Twombly's work during the summer, saying only that he had nothing to teach him. He did recommend Twombly to his own dealer, Sam Kootz, who showed Twombly at the end of the year. Twombly also had a solo show at the Seven Stairs Gallery in Chicago in November of 1951, organized by Noah Goldowsky and Aaron Siskind. Motherwell wrote a short text for the exhibition:

> I believe that Cy Twombly is the most accomplished young painter whose work I happen to have encountered: he is a "natural" in regard to what is going on in painting now. . . . His painting process, of which the pictures are the tracks that are left, as when [one] walks on a beach, is org[i]astic: the sexual character of the fetishes half-buried in his violent surface is sufficiently evident (and so is not allowed to

FIELDING DAWSON: *CY TWOMBLY AT BLACK MOUNTAIN,* 1951.
Casein on butcher paper, 50 x 24 inches.

[109] Fielding Dawson, "Summer of '51" in *The Black Mountain Book: A New Edition* (Rocky Mount: North Carolina Wesleyan College Press, 1991), p. 113.

[110] John Cage, in an interview with Alan Gillmor and Roger Shattuck, 1973, quoted in *Conversing with Cage,* edited by Kostelanetz (New York: Limelight Editions, 1988), p. 47.

[111] Dorothea Rockburne, in an interview with Vincent Katz, 10 July 2001.

162 >

CY TWOMBLY
UNTITLED, 1951.
Bitumen and oil-based house paint on canvas,
49 ½ x 54 ¼ inches.
Staatliche Museum zu Berlin, Nationalgalerie.
Collection Marx.

CY TWOMBLY
MIN-OE, 1951.
Bitumen, oil-based house paint on canvas,
34 x 40 inches.
Robert Rauschenberg Foundation Collection.

CY TWOMBLY
UNTITLED, 1951.
Oil-based house paint on canvas,
24 x 30 inches.
Private Collection.

CY TWOMBLY
UNTITLED, 1951.
Oil-based house paint on canvas,
40 x 48 inches.
Private Collection.

PETER VOULKOS AT THE HOME OF MRS. IRA JULIAN
ON TRIP FROM BLACK MOUNTAIN COLLEGE TO NEW
YORK, 1953. PHOTOGRAPH BY MRS. IRA JULIAN.
Courtesy of North Carolina Museum of Art.

DAVID WEINRIB AND KAREN KARNES AT POT SHOP,
ROBERT TURNER ARCHITECT. LAKE EDEN CAMPUS,
BLACK MOUNTAIN COLLEGE (BUILT 1949–50).
PHOTOGRAPH BY EDWARD DUPUY.

POTEAT HOUSE INTERIOR, JOSEPH J. ROBERTS
ARCHITECT. DESIGNED AND CONSTRUCTED 1954.
CERAMIC PANEL BY DAVID WEINRIB. BLACK
MOUNTAIN COLLEGE. PHOTOGRAPH BY EDWARD
DUPUY.

LIDDED JARS (1952–54) BY KAREN KARNES.
PHOTOGRAPH BY EDWARD DUPUY.

emerge any more). Yet the art in his painting is rational, often surprisingly simply symmetrical and invariably harmonious.[112]

Charles Olson also wrote something on Twombly's work at the time, after being impressed by a visit to his studio at Black Mountain. Twombly and Olson share vital common interests, particularly the study of "pre-Western" cultures, although Twombly later became increasingly enamored of classical Greece.

By his summer at Black Mountain, Twombly was painting pictures that broke free of obvious indebtedness to such abstract expressionist models such as Franz Kline. The effect of Twombly's paint, though applied in a seemingly casual manner, is slow, and in fact his insouciance is careful and precise. Working with a severely reduced palette, and interested in a palpable physicality of surface created by mixing dirt and other materials into the house paint he was using, Twombly painted the first in a lifelong series of totemic images—figures with bulbous bodies and spindly legs or else simple circles, furiously traced, with spiky, dragging appendages dangling from them. In these early works, Twombly reveals his mastery of paint handling and his individual vision. Some of these images were inspired by African fetish objects, and certainly a wide-ranging interest in Mexico, Native American, and later, North African cultures would inform the facture as well as the symbolism of Twombly's early paintings.

Peter Voulkos taught a ceramics workshop at Black Mountain in the summer of 1953. He had received his Master of Fine Arts degree the previous year from the California College of Arts and Crafts in Oakland when he was invited. Ceramics had begun to be an important part of Black Mountain's activities with the pottery workshop renovated and amplified by David Weinrib and Karen Karnes. Then there was the pottery workshop of 1952 with Bernard Leach, Shoji Hamada, Marguerite Wildenhain, and Soetsu Yanagi. At the time he was at Black Mountain, Voulkos was making exquisite vases with a Japanese style and finish. A few years later, partly due to to his contact with painters, poets, and musicians at Black Mountain and New York, Voulkos transformed his idea of a pot. He made "dropped" vases, and ceramic pieces from separate, modular units. *Vase*, 1956, was an example of the latter, its cylindrical forms on top of one another giving the impression of two figures very close, possibly embracing.

It is difficult to think of Ray Johnson as an obedient follower, but at Black Mountain, he was a serious student in Josef Albers's class. Later he became known for his independence, as someone who eschewed normal artistic career channels, such as gallery exhibitions, and who encouraged people who were not artists to participate in his collaborative mail-art project, The New York Correspondance School. But in photographs from Albers class, he appears as an attentive student. In fact, he was in the same class with Rauschenberg and Weil their first year. Later, Johnson would move to New York with Richard Lippold, sharing space in the same Monroe Street building where John Cage had his studio. Thus Johnson came under Cage's influence, which ultimately effected him more than Albers'. Or perhaps Johnson learned how to design from Albers, but learned how to rebel from Cage. Besides his fine art, Johnson is known for his graphic designs, such as the book covers he did for New Directions Press. There was fruitful cross-fertilization between his art and graphic work: in becoming intimate

[112] Robert Motherwell, published in *Cy Twombly: Paintings and Sculptures 1951 and 1953* (New York: Sperone Westwater, 1989).

PETER VOULKOS
VASE, 1956.
Stoneware, brushed slip and glaze,
wheel thrown and slab construction,
39 ½ x 17 x 13 inches.
Collection American Craft Museum, New York. Gift of
Mr. and Mrs. Adam Gostomski, 1962. Donated to the
American Craft Museum by the American Craft
Council, 1990. Photograph by Eva Heyd.

PETER VOULKOS
ROUND BOTTLE, CA. 1953.
Stoneware, sgraffito through wax resist, inlaid cobalt and copper
line drawing, 14 3/4 inches high x 12 inches diameter.
Private Collection. Photograph by Schopplein Studio.

RAY JOHNSON
UNTITLED, 1953.
Inks, paint, paper board mounted on board, 14 ¾ x 13 ⅜ inches.
Collection of Richard Lippold. © The Estate of Ray Johnson.
Photograph by Max Yawney, New York.

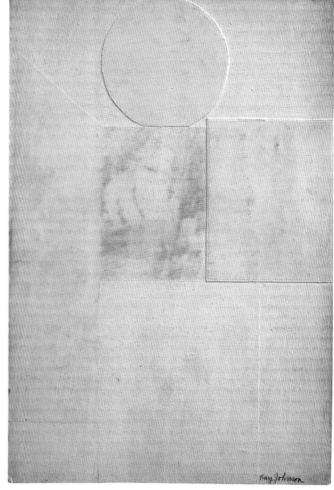

RAY JOHNSON
WHITE CIRCLE, 1960.
Paper circle, paint, on corrugated cardboard, 17 x13 inches.
© The Estate of Ray Johnson. Courtesy Richard L. Feigen & Co.

ELAINE SCHMITT AND RAY JOHNSON.
BLACK MOUNTAIN COLLEGE.

JOSEF ALBERS DRAWING CLASS (RAY JOHNSON IN
PROFILE AT RIGHT). BLACK MOUNTAIN COLLEGE,
SUMMER, 1944. PHOTOGRAPH BY JOSEF
BREITENBACH.

JOSEF ALBERS DRAWING CLASS (RAY JOHNSON IN
SWEATER, HAZEL-FRIEDA LARSEN IN GLASSES AND LEG
BRACE). BLACK MOUNTAIN COLLEGE, SUMMER,
1944. PHOTOGRAPH BY JOSEPH BREITENBACH.

with the power of commercial graphic, particularly photographic, imagery, he brought that to bear on his own work, while bringing his uniquely refined sensibility to commercial design.

In Johnson's early cut cardboard pieces, which he called "moticos" (the word, made up by Johnson, is an anagram for "osmotic"), there is a delicate balance of cut-out painted and attached forms. Johnson was also capable of minimalist purity—inspired by Rauschenberg, though not as extreme—as in his *White Circle*, 1960. Many works were outright homages to mentors and personages, whether Albers, Cage, Black Mountain College, or simply a friend or celebrity. Johnson, like many collagists, liked the idea of recycling, or re-using "outside" images, as well as re-copying his own favorites. In *Untitled (f.x. profumo)*, ca. 1948–1980, Johnson used an air-mail envelope mailed to "f. x. profumo" at Black Mountain College. In *Untitled (Black Mountain College)*, ca. 1953–1959–1980, the words "Black Mountain College, Black Mountain, N. C." are visible. With his fondness for puns, Johnson perhaps thought of college/collage, and Black Mountain as a collage of disparate spirits. Johnson was certainly one of the funniest Black Mountain artists, and *A Shoe (John Cage Shoes)*, 1977, was witty for a number of reasons—partly because it makes us think of "john" and "cage" as words instead of names, partly because the shoes seemed to be dancing shoes, and the kind of dancing they suggest was not usually associated with the composer.

Johnson took copious notes in Albers's classes, which he burned in the 1950s in a classic act of self-liberation. In a later piece, *Untitled (Dear Josef Albers with Slant Step)*, 1991–1992, Johnson appeared to be addressing his early master, who died in 1976: an ambiguous silhouette of a man (from the feet, he seems facing away, but from the head he seems to be facing the viewer), with a stark graphic shape superimposed on his chest. Despite the shape's geometric intimations, it is biomorphic, not rectilinear, expressing a poignant inability to communicate. Johnson took his own life in 1995.

RAY JOHNSON: COVER FOR NEW DIRECTIONS 1957
EDITION OF RIMBAUD'S *ILLUMINATIONS* TRANSLATED BY
LOUISE VARÈSE. Collection of Vincent Katz. Photograph
by Joaquín Cortés.

168 >

RAY JOHNSON
UNTITLED (F.X. PROFUMO), CA. 1948–1980.
Collage, 20 ½ x 15 ½ x 1 ½ inches.
Collection of Frances Beatty Adler and Allen Adler.
© The Estate of Ray Johnson.

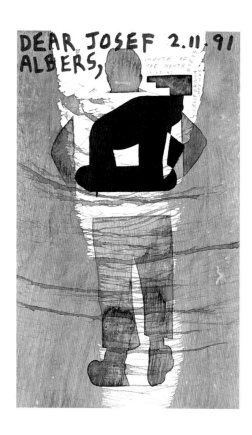

RAY JOHNSON
UNTITLED (BLACK MOUNTAIN COLLEGE), CA. 1953–1959–1980.
Collage, ink on cardboard panel, 20 x 13 x 1 ½ inches.
© The Estate of Ray Johnson. Courtesy Richard L. Feigen & Co.

RAY JOHNSON
UNTITLED (DEAR JOSEF ALBERS), 1991–1992.
Collage, 10 x 6 ¼ x ⅛ inches.
© The Estate of Ray Johnson. Courtesy Richard L. Feigen & Co.

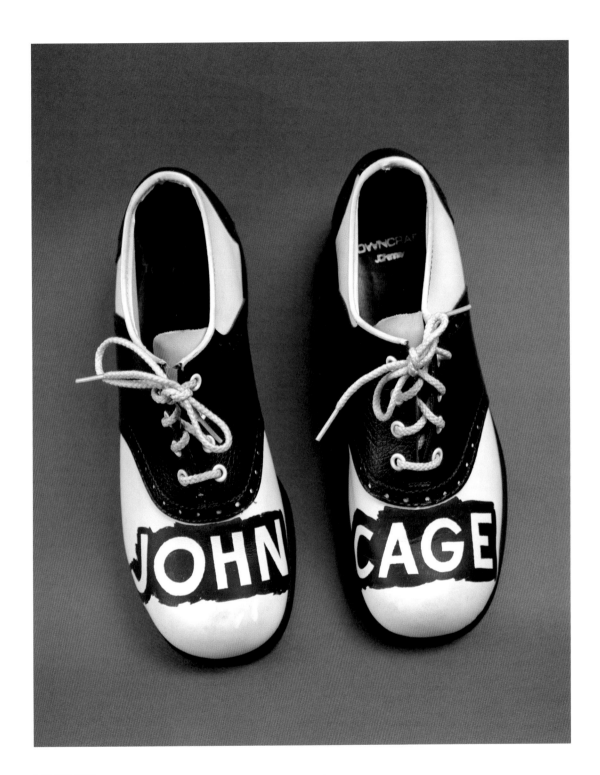

RAY JOHNSON
A SHOE (JOHN CAGE SHOES), 1977.
Shoes with painted addition, 12 x 8 ¾ x 5 ¼ inches.
© The Estate of Ray Johnson. Courtesy Richard L. Feigen & Co.

VI. Photography

Photography played a key role in the art pedagogy at Black Mountain, as it had at the Bauhaus, and photographic artists were invited to teach at Black Mountain. Barbara Morgan visited during the summer of 1944 to lecture and give several days of workshops. Beaumont Newhall taught at Black Mountain several times in the 1940s. Born in 1908, he received a Master of Fine Arts degree from Harvard in 1931, and after further studies at the Institute d'Art et d'Archeologie in Paris and London's Courtauld Institute, began a career as a museum curator and photography critic. He was curator of photography at the Museum of Modern Art, New York, in 1940–1942 and 1944–1946. He was the author of *Photography: A Short Critical History*, Musuem of Modern Art, 1937, and a later book, *The History of Photography*, Museum of Modern Art, 1964, a carefully researched and argued introduction to the photographic issues of the day, including Callahan, Frank, and Siskind. Albers wrote to Newhall in April of 1946, inviting him to lecture at that year's Summer Art Institute. Newhall spent two weeks at Black Mountain, accompanied by his wife, Nancy Newhall, also a curator and photography critic. Both Newhalls were photographers and took striking photographs during their stays, including portraits of Leo Amino, Ilya Bolotowsky, Gwendolyn Knight, Jacob Lawrence, and Fuller's venetian-blind experiment. In 1947, the Newhalls returned, and Beaumont taught introductory and advanced photographic technique, and also lectured. For the 1948 summer session, Newhall, writing to Albers, stressed an approach that located photography in the context of the history of other media:

> A new lantern slide technique which I have mastered has enabled me to start making a collection of 2 x 2 inch slides of photographs of all periods. The year of research and work which I have put into the new completely revised edition of my Short History has given me a grasp on the subject which I believe will enable me to make these talks more vivid and more related to the development of other art forms and to the history of America, than I have been able to previously.[113]

Newhall felt he was more valuable as a lecturer on photography's history and esthetics than as an instructor on technique. He had the clarity to write, "Although I photograph, I am not a photographer."[114] He organized an exhibition of photographs by Helen Levitt at Black Mountain that summer of 1948, her first show in five years.

Clemens Kalischer was at Black Mountain twice, in 1948 and 1954, both times in an unofficial capacity, but it is fortunate he decided to show up, as he took, among other splendid images, a series of photographs that document the historic 1948 production of Satie's *Le Piège de Méduse*. Kalischer had first heard of the college from Joseph Breitenbach, a photographer who had taught in the summer of 1944. Kalischer came to Black Mountain in 1948 at the suggestion of Beau-

JOSEF ALBERS. BLACK MOUNTAIN COLLEGE, SUMMER, 1944. PHOTOGRAPH BY ROBERTA BLAIR.

[113] Beaumont Newhall, letter to Josef Albers, 11 March 1948, North Carolina Museum of Art, Black Mountain College Research Project, North Carolina State Archives, Raleigh.

[114] Ibid.

mont Newhall, who had informed Kalischer he would be there. Kalischer's landscape photography manifests a stillness that borders on abstraction, an impression abetted by its rich tonal contrasts. His photographs of the Satie play captured the production's serious frivolity—Fuller's gregariousness and Cunningham's technical control—preserving the interaction of these disparate talents. Kalischer also made remarkable portraits—Cage sitting erect while playing the piano, and from his 1954 visit, a pensive Stefan Wolpe.

Hazel-Frieda Larsen was a photograhy student and later became an instructor. Her esthetic was formed at Black Mountain, and she produced work that one might call archetypal Black Mountain photography—based on a classical, yet modernst sense of balance, tempered by a humanistic reverence for life expressed in her photographs' gentleness of detail. In 1949, she exhibited at the Photo League in New York, and received a substantial review in the *New York Times*. The photograph reproduced with the review was part of a series she did of the entrance to the Quiet House at Black Mountain, a place for meditation built to commemorate the death of Ted and Bobbie Dreier's son Mark. Larsen's photographs blend proportional balance with the warmth of someone who appreciates the labor and achievement of another.

After Albers's departure, and Larsen's transition from student to teacher, she took an active role in the life of photography at Black Mountain. She conceived the idea for the most significant summer for photography in the college's history. In 1951, as had been the case in the other visual arts for years, Larsen decided to invite prominent photographers to teach, securing the presence of Harry Callahan, Alfred Siegel, and Aaron Siskind. Callahan and Siegel were teaching at

Chicago's Institute of Design, while Siskind lived in New York as the only photographer among a cricle of Abstract Expressionists.

Aaron Siskind began photographing seriously at twenty-nine and for the next nine years did social documentary photography, much of it under the auspices of the Photo League. Around 1940, he made a shift toward abstraction, leaving behind the social commentary of his earlier work and suddenly entering an art world populated mainly by painters and sculptors. In the mid-1940s, during summers on Martha's Vineyard and near Gloucester, Massachusetts, Siskind began to explore a vision that depended on a shallow plane, and utilized delicate, minimal designs.

In 1947, Barnett Newman suggested to Siskind that he show his photographs to the dealer Charles Egan. Egan was impressed and gave Siskind a solo exhibition that spring. Painters such as de Kooning, Kline, and Tworkov became admirers of Siskind's work, and Josef Albers arranged an exhibition of forty Siskind abstractions at Black Mountain in March of 1948. In May of 1948, de Kooning showed his black and white abstract paintings at Egan, and in June, Siskind had his second show at the gallery. In May of 1951, Siskind was the only photographer invited to participate in the Ninth Street Show of abstract expressionist painters, which included de Kooning, Kline, Motherwell, Tworkov, and the sculptor Grippe.

While at Black Mountain in 1951, Siskind had his second exhibition at the college, again showing forty photographs. He made a remarkable series of photographs that summer in North Carolina, Kentucky, and Tennessee, which further developed his stress on the two-dimensionality of the photographic image, and explored in depth what was to a signature motif—the close-up of a wall with tattered posters and fragmentary language. Many times, as in *North Carolina 30, 1951*, Siskind's perspective is tightly cropped, perception of scale alters, and isolated letters of words from advertisements acquire vivid monumentality. At the same time, as Siskind was often drawn to hand-painted or hand-drawn signs, usually in a state of decay, this monumentality of scale is counter-balanced by porousness of texture. In *North Carolina 9, 1951*, the viewer is tantalized by distant mountains and sky, while mysterious shapes (probably chipping paint on a window) assume the foreground. Likewise in the beguiling *North Carolina 33, 1951*, a quasi-geometric form looms palpably close, its textural details clearly displayed, while cropping prevents a decisive conclusion as to its whereabouts—probably a window again, with mysterious reflections doubling as dark forms. Three other pieces show Siskind's ability to transform the everyday—the geometry of the side of a clapboard structure (*North Carolina 21, 1951*), a brick wall with electric boxes (*North Carolina 29, 1951*), and an image of particular resonance for Black Mountain's association with Charles Olson and his ambitions for the school's literary life: *North Carolina 10, 1951*, an open book lying on a dusty, stark floor under the legs of a table, light streaming on it, as if to say, literature's light will survive in the starkest environments.

Harry Callahan picked up photography as a hobby in his late twenties. In 1945, he stayed in New York for half a year and met Beaumont and Nancy Newhall, and Paul Strand. In 1946, he began to teach at the Institute of Design in Chicago. In 1948, he met Steichen and Siskind and was included in the group exhibi-

TABLE-STOOL BY MARY GREGORY (BLACK MOUNTAIN COLLEGE, 1941–1947). PHOTOGRAPH BY HAZEL LARSEN ARCHER.

PLATES BY MARY GREGORY. PHOTOGRAPH BY HAZEL LARSEN ARCHER.

CLEMENS KALISCHER
LANDSCAPE WITH REEDS, 1948.
Gelatin silver print, 11 x 14 inches.
Courtesy of the artist.

CLEMENS KALISCHER
LAKE WITH DOCK, 1948.
Gelatin silver print, 11 x 14 inches.
Courtesy of the artist.

HAZEL LARSEN ARCHER
QUIET HOUSE DOORS, 1948.
Gelatin silver print, 9 ½ x 6 ⅝ inches.
Black Mountain College Museum and Arts Center, Asheville.

tion, "In and Out of Focus" at the Museum of Modern Art, as was Siskind. Callahan was also in the Modern's 1951 exhibition, "Abstraction in Photography," curated by Edward Steichen; Siskind was also included.

Callahan had worked with abstraction since the early 1940s, sometimes in a geometric vein, as in phone lines against the sky in *Detroit*, 1945. He could be enamored of the regularity of clapboard, as in *Wisconsin*, 1949, an extreme, more intensely proximate version of Paul Strand's formal vision. By 1950, Callahan's work assumed an expansive, less theoretical, tone, in such photographs as *Lake Michigan*, c. 1950, in which the plane of the lake's surface occupies nearly the entire picture plane, save for a tiny strip of beach with waves quietly breaking on it. One of the few photographs taken at Black Mountain that Callahan allowed to be printed, *Asheville*, 1951, is unusual for Callahan as it shows street action taking place in an actual "scene." A woman walks past a darkened portal in downtown Asheville, her stylish white purse the only irregular biometric form, the whole scene witnessed, with a wink of irony, by the staring eye of an optometrist's placard. After leaving Black Mountain, Callahan continued an extended series of photographs of his wife, Eleanor, as well as working with the abstract properties of nature.

The third invited photographer, Arthur Siegel, came for only two weeks. Siegel grew up in Detroit and made his living as a photographer during the Depression, photographing portraits, window displays, and working for newspapers and wire services. He majored in Sociology at Wayne State University, where he became enamored of social documentary and at the same time studied the manipulation of understanding which photography makes possible. Siegel's turning point was a lecture given in Detroit in 1937 by Moholy-Nagy, who invited Siegel to study at the New Bauhaus in Chicago on a scholarship, where he went on to become head of the photography department at the Institute of Design, as the New Bauhaus was later called. When Callahan arrived there in 1946, the two photographers became close, using similar techniques of multiple exposures and printings. While Callahan's images were coolly spare, Siegel tended to overload repeated forms, creating dense abstract fields. Siegel pursued color photography as early as 1946 and joined Beaumont Newhall on a visit to Kodak in 1948 to determine the quality with which dye-transfer prints could be made from transparencies. Apparently satisfied, Siegel continued to make color work as his resources permitted. Fourteen of his color pieces were published in *Life* magazine on November 20, 1950, as "Modern Art by a Photographer."

Callahan and Siskind spent most of July and August at Black Mountain, teaching photography to students, while Siegel came to lecture on Contemporary Photography for two weeks in July. Joseph Fiore, Robert Motherwell and Ben Shahn were teaching painting that summer, and Katherine Litz taught dance. Photography was one of the main attractions in the bulletin sent to attract students. The anonymous bulletin text, possibly written by Hazel Larsen, echoes the philosophy of Larsen's master, Josef Albers:

> At Black Mountain College . . . We take on the responsibility of a
> human mind controlling a beautiful piece of mechanism so that it may
> be used to record a particular kind of vision. We try to become alert

177 >

AARON SISKIND
NORTH CAROLINA 9, 1951.
Gelatin silver print, 10 1/16 x 12 9/16 inches.
San Francisco Museum of Modern Art. Gift of Robert Menschel.
© Aaron Siskind. Photograph by Ben Blackwell.

AARON SISKIND
NORTH CAROLINA 16, 1951.
Gelatin silver print, 10 1/2 x 13 7/16 inches.
Gift of Emanuel and Edithann M. Gerard, 1991.1041. © Aaron Siskind.
Image © The Art Institute of Chicago.

AARON SISKIND
NC 33, 1951.
Silver print, 10 1/4 x 13 1/4 inches.
Robert Mann Gallery.
© Aaron Siskind.

AARON SISKIND
NC 10, 1951.
Vintage silver print, 10 x 8 inches.
Robert Mann Gallery.
© Aaron Siskind.

AARON SISKIND
NC 21, 1951.
Vintage silver print, 10 ¼ x 13 ½ inches.
Robert Mann Gallery.
© Aaron Siskind.

and watchful of the world around us, and we begin to see. The world is open wide to the photographer who can see. And one can never be bored if one can see.[115]

The summer of 1951 was significant in Rauschenberg's development, as photography became central to his later work. Sheryl Conkelton noted an array of vital activity: "Over the summer Weil and Rauschenberg worked on a series of life-size figurative blueprints, Twombly made pinhole camera photographs, and Siegel made a large multiprocess mural. Siskind made his first sustained group of photographs incorporating fragments of language."[116]

While some photography students that summer were beginners, others had already studied the art. Jonathan Williams, after dropping out of Princeton, had been briefly at the Institute of Design and went to Black Mountain in 1951 to study with Callahan and Siskind. "I can't remember any elaborate instructions in learning to use my Rolleiflex," Williams has written. "Still, within a month under the scrutiny of Callahan and his compadre Aaron Siskind, I was taking some of the best photographs of Olson ever made."[117] This might seem immodest were it not patently true. Siskind and Callahan taught basic camera technique to individual students, occasionally gathering them for a class critique. There was also much informal discussion. As Williams described it, "Much of what I learned from Harry and Aaron was over a beer or three at Ma Peek's Tavern, a desolate redneck joint a couple of miles in towards town. Closing time was 11:00 P.M. Armed with a case or two in hand, the palaverer/scholars would go back to the College and talk late into the night."[118] Williams wrote a note on Siskind to accompany eight photographs in the *Black Mountain Review* no. 5, and Creeley provided the text for eight photographs by Callahan in the *Black Mountain Review* no. 7.

Williams, one of the most distinguished photographers to have been a student at Black Mountain, typifies a late Black Mountain multi-disciplinary approach to the arts, having been prolific as poet, photographer, critic and publisher. His writing is partly collage, where found thoughts and sounds collide with giddy erudition. As a photographer, Williams began with a classic group of portraits of the Black Mountain circle, including Creeley, Duncan, du Plessix Gray, Harrison, Litz, Olson, Oppenheimer, Rice, and Wolpe. Williams did not so much "capture" his subjects as collaborate with them. As a colleague, or one of the gang, there is no defensiveness on the part of his subjects, but rather an opening and relaxed acceptance of time and occasion in which the photographer can pause, think, and achieve an ultimate exposure—whether it be Duncan's languor leaning against a building, Creeley's evil grin as a "Spanish Assassin," or Olson's piercing stare as he drapes a Mexican serape over his business suit.

[115] Black Mountain College Bulletin, Summer Session 1951.

[116] Sheryl Conkelton, "Aaron Siskind: the fragmentation of language" (New York: Robert Mann Gallery, 1997), p. 4.

[117] Jonathan Williams, "A Callahan Chrestomathy," in *Harry Callahan*, Masters of Photography Series, Aperture, New York, 1999, p. 5.

[118] Ibid.

182 >

HARRY CALLAHAN
DETROIT, 1941.
Gelatin silver print. Image size 3 ⅝ x 4 ⅘ inches,
paper size 5 x 8 inches.
Courtesy of the Estate of Harry Callahan and Pace MacGill
Gallery, New York. © The Estate of Harry Callahan.

HARRY CALLAHAN
PORT HURON, MICHIGAN, 1952.
Gelatin silver print. Image size 8 x 10 ¼
inches, paper size 11 x 14 inches.
Courtesy of the Estate of Harry Callahan and Pace
MacGill Gallery, New York.
© The Estate of Harry Callahan.

HARRY CALLAHAN
WISCONSIN, 1947.
Vintage gelatin silver print. Image size 7 ¾ x 7 ⅝ inches,
paper size 8 3⁄8 x 7 7⁄8 inches.
Courtesy of the Estate of Harry Callahan and Pace MacGill Gallery,
New York. © The Estate of Harry Callahan.

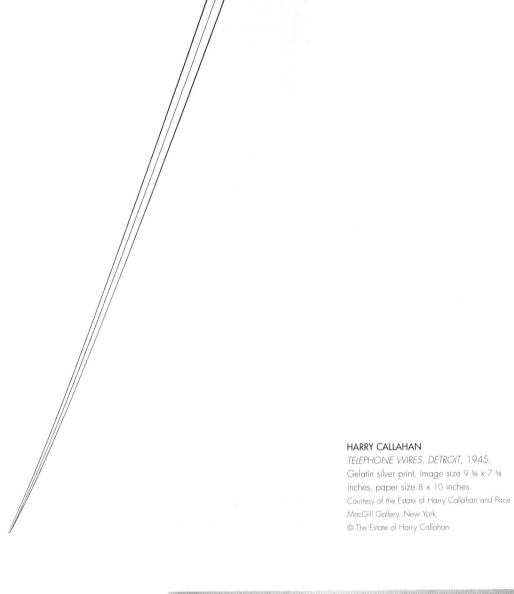

HARRY CALLAHAN
TELEPHONE WIRES, DETROIT, 1945.
Gelatin silver print. Image size 9 ⅝ x 7 ⅝
inches, paper size 8 x 10 inches.
Courtesy of the Estate of Harry Callahan and Pace
MacGill Gallery, New York.
© The Estate of Harry Callahan.

HARRY CALLAHAN
LAKE MICHIGAN, CA. 1950.
Gelatin silver print, 4 ¹⁵⁄₁₆ x 6 ⁵⁄₁₆ inches.
National Gallery of Art, Washington,
anonymous gift 1997. © The Estate of Harry
Callahan. Photograph by Lorene Emerson.

ARTHUR SIEGEL
SKATING, LINCOLN PARK, 1951.
Dye imbibition print, 6 ½ x 9 ⅔ inches.
Peabody Fund, 1954.1227. Image © The Art Institute of Chicago.
Photograph by Greg Williams.

ARTHUR SIEGEL
BACK OF TRUCK, 1952.
Dye imbibition print, 6 ⅖ x 9 ⅘ inches.
Peabody Fund, 1954.1228. Image © The Art Institute of Chicago.
Photograph by Greg Williams.

ARTHUR SIEGEL
CEMENT MIXER, 1953.
Dye imbibition print, 6 ⁹⁄₁₆ x 10 inches.
Gift of Arthur Siegel, 1956.1070. Image © The Art Institute of Chicago.
Photograph by Greg Williams.

VII. Landscape & Space

*I take SPACE to be the central fact to man born
in America, from Folsom cave to now. I spell
it large because it comes large here. Large,
and without mercy.*

—CHARLES OLSON
Call Me Ishmael[119]

*You know, a poet, when he's alive, whether
he talks or reads you his poems is the same
thing. Dig that!*

—CHARLES OLSON
"Reading at Berkeley"[120]

The last years of Black Mountain College, the 1950s, had a character distinct from the college's earlier history. With the departures of the Albers and Ted Dreier in 1949, the last links to those earlier times were severed, and with them went the feeling, inherited from the Bauhaus and Rice's vision, of the school as a good-natured camp, where artists and students mingled, and worked hard, striving to better themselves and possibly the world. Black Mountain College, always financially insecure, was now intellectually up for grabs as well. Through a fortuitous set of events, a poet, Charles Olson, now moved in to the power vacuum at the college, ultimately becoming its final rector and exerting a dominating, if not exactly controlling presence over its final years. Depending on a person's point of view, these years were either a pitiful decline, the ignominious squashing of grand ideals, or they were a fantastic incubation chamber for some of the most original literature to emerge out of the United States in the postwar period. Perhaps both versions are correct.

Literature was always taught at Black Mountain, and big names had been both regular teachers and visitors. At various times, Thornton Wilder, Aldous Huxley, Henry Miller, Irwin Panofsky, and Anais Nin paid visits. Eric Bentley, Paul Goodman, and Alfred Kazin taught at Black Mountain in the 1940s, and Galway Kinnell, James Leo Herlihy, and Ebbe Borregard were students. M. C. Richards taught creative writing, and Hilda Morley taught 17th to 19th century literature. Edward Dahlberg taught briefly at the College, and it was he who, in 1948, suggested that Charles Olson would be a good person to fill a gap and deliver lectures on a variety of topics.

Olson first arrived in the fall of 1948 to pick up the slack created by Dahlberg's abrupt departure. As Ann Charters has summarized: "[Olson] was also there in the summer and fall, 1949, and lectured during an evening in May, 1950. His

[119] Charles Olson, *Call Me Ishmael,* first published (New York: Reynal & Hitchcock, 1947), reprinted (Baltimore: The Johns Hopkins University Press, 1997), p. 11.

[120] Charles Olson, "Reading at Berkeley," 23 July 1965, published in *Muthologos: The Collected Lectures and Interviews,* vol. 1 (Bolinas: Four Seasons Foundation, 1978), p. 111.

most extended teaching began in the summer, 1951, continuing with short leaves of absence until Black Mountain closed in the fall, 1956. . . ."[121] The years 1948 to 1956 were critical to Olson's career as a writer. He had excelled in Latin and Oratory in school, studied at Wesleyan and Harvard, worked for the Office Of War Information during World War II, where he collaborated on a project with Ben Shahn, and worked on FDR's election campaign of 1944. Disenchanted by the Democratic Party's turn to the right, he left politics and concentrated on writing. His 1946 *Encounter at St. Elizabeth's* is a powerful literary document, in which he confronts the demons in his poetic master, Ezra Pound, thus staking out new ground for himself. Just what that ground was to be was still unclear. Olson made his name with his groundbreaking—in scholarship and style—study of Melville, *Call Me Ishmael*, published in 1947. Although thirty-seven, Olson had not yet published much poetry.

Olson's Black Mountain years found him attempting to encompass everything in a mind-boggling attempt at universality as inspiring as it is on occasion disappointing: he needed a grand cultural theory, incorporating anthropology, archeology, psychology, Heisenberg's indeterminacy principle, theater, performance, the act of the word in the moment of literary creation—a theory powerful enough to vanquish the staid academics he believed blocked his way to publication and power—and he wanted, to top it all off, to write an epic poem, so that the grandness of his creative and intellectual stature would be forever established in art as it was in theory. In some ways, he succeeded. Against the prevailing winds, Olson—rightly most critics would say today—elevated Herodotus's approach to history over Thucydides': that is, an approach based on philosophy more than chronology; history as ideas, not facts. Olson's study of Mayan glyphs in Lerma, in the Yucatan, led to a theory of a people in touch with primal forces, untainted by American or European alienating and exploitive commercial passions, and further, the glyph served powerfully as symbol of something that both acted in itself and carried additional significance—a keystone to Olson's esthetic.

Perhaps the most memorable event in Olson's literary career was the 1950 publication of his essay "Projective Verse." In this essay, he clearly staked out the territory he wished to occupy, along with such staunch allies such as his "running mate," Robert Creeley.[122] Projective Verse was composition by field; that is, it regarded the page as a canvas on which words could be dropped in a variety of positions, not simply one after another. The space between them indicated the pause appropriate to timing one's reading of the verse. This emphasis on the visual aspect of poetry made the typewriter an instrument for determining precise spatial delineations, and a key tool, relating Olson's preoccupations to those of the contemporaneous Concrete Poets of Brazil. The other key aspect to Projective Verse was the demand that it be written in the moment, that one word, one thought, spur the next, that it, in other words, not be a "meditation" on a "theme" but capable of such "abstraction" as painters and musicians were exploring.

ERIC BENTLEY TEACHING. LAKE EDEN CAMPUS, BLACK MOUNTAIN COLLEGE, CA. 1942–1944.

[121] Ann Charters, introduction to Charles Olson, *The Special View of History*, edited and with an introduction by Charters (Berkeley: Oyez, 1970), p. 1.

[122] Tom Clark, in his biography *Charles Olson: The Allegory of a Poet's Life* (Berkeley: North Atlantic Books, 2000), quotes on page 180 a letter from Charles Olson to Robert Duncan, summer 1951, in which Olson calls Creeley "my running mate, my tandem."

186 >

CHARLES OLSON
"COSMOS," CA. 1951–1956.
Paper, manuscript in pencil and black ink, 11 x 8 ½ inches.
Archives and Special Collections at the Thomas J. Dodd Research Center,
University of Connecticut Libraries.

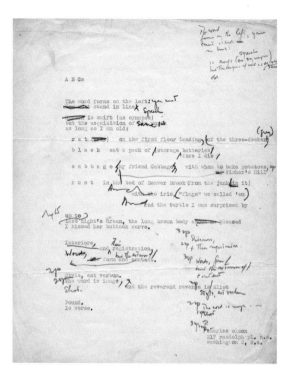

CHARLES OLSON
ABCS, CA. 1950.
Paper, typescript with pencil notations, 11 x 8 ½ inches.
Archives and Special Collections at the Thomas J. Dodd Research Center,
University of Connecticut Libraries.

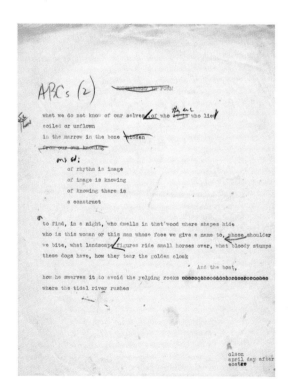

CHARLES OLSON
ABCS (2), APRIL 10, 1950.
Paper, typescript with pencil notations, 11 x 8 ½ inches.
Archives and Special Collections at the Thomas J. Dodd Research Center,
University of Connecticut Libraries.

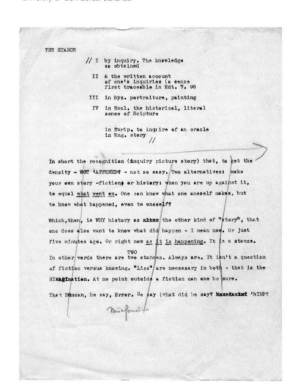

CHARLES OLSON
"THE STANCE," CA. 1951–1956.
Paper, typescript with pencil and red ink notations, 11 x 8 ½ inches.
Archives and Special Collections at the Thomas J. Dodd Research Center,
University of Connecticut Libraries.

```
        words are wonders and their laws
        aee what a man brings


        words are wonders and their laws
        are what a man brings to them, those
        xxxinxiixxx possibilities


        words are wonders and their laws
        are what a man brings to them, those
        possibilities, the xxxxxixxxxx right side of the moon new,
        in an afternoon sky,as slight as a cloud, then, west, with night
        white inxihx and clear, shining, and seeming twice
        what it was as we picked apples off the ground not being able
        the tree was too high to knock them down, the black top road
        as we drove to see how it was, new as it is, covered with hens
        curiously eating off it, maybe seeds stick to it, stopping us
        who had no place to go really, so ihx we dawdled, and turned
        before that gray stretch where my soul is always dampened, and I won't
        go there any more, mabking time, rushing always towards the next
        event, some new crisis


        to find out how to write poems
        which sound as though I belonged
        on this earth. I have this personal problem:
find    that I don't/that so easyX, however much other men,
        I take it, do seem to.
```

```
        god is value. he is prior, and useful, simply that how to find out
        that one's life is a value, and is to be spent as such, and not a
        commodity, mere goods, is not so easy. but when, like Echart had
        itx the god in,is the otherhalf of the truth, then the transcendent
        (which is only in timexxxixxxxxxxxinxihx god out) gives way to you,
        the mortal. That, then, is the primary. And much of the ixxx falsity
        of doubles as universals comes from the failure to distinguish God
        as prior to the coming into existence of god in the self. For example,
        life & death are phoney compliments. Death, in the eye of God, is
        as asx "free" as life is when it is lived. The kicker, of course,
        is that life is only such when it is value. And for it be takes
        all that any human can muster, shall we say, without loading anything.
        Just, goofed off, too much, real cool.
```

Goofed off

Constance & Kate & Charles Ol̄ live at Black Mt Coll̄

CHARLES OLSON

"WORDS ARE WONDERS," CA. 1951–1954.

Paper, typescript with black ink notations, 11 x 8 1/2 inches.

Archives and Special Collections at the Thomas J. Dodd Research Center,
University of Connecticut Libraries.

In 1951, Olson spent several months in Lerma, the Yucatan, and his letters from there to Creeley were edited by Creeley and published as *Mayan Letters* (Divers Press, 1954). As usual, Olson tackled his material with a fresh eye, aware but skeptical of previous approaches. He wrote from Lerma:

> Christ, these hieroglyphs. Here is the most abstract and formal deal of all the things this people dealt out—and yet, to my taste, it is precisely as intimate as verse is. Is, in fact, verse. Is their verse. And comes into existence, obeys the same laws that, the coming into existence, the persisting of verse, does.[123]

Back at Black Mountain for the summer of 1951, Olson transmitted his excitement regarding glyphs to the community there. As Katherine Litz describes it, "The Glyph dance grew out of an exchange of 'glyph-gifts' among the faculty. Charles Olson presented Ben Shahn with a glyph poem and in turn Shahn presented Olson with a glyph painting. I then presented the community with a glyph dance with music by Harrison and decor utilizing the Shahn painting enlarged. The common idea of a Glyph expressed by the different art forms was simply a compound image contained in a single work."[124] There is no poem entitled "A Glyph" in *The Collected Poems of Charles Olson*, although there is one called "A Round & A Canon." The latter poem, written in July of 1951 and published in *Origin*, no. 3, fall 1951, as printed in the *Collected Poems* has no dedication, but a typescript of the beginning of the poem in the Olson papers at the University of Connecticut adds the dedication "(for Katy Litz, and for Lou Harrison)." Also at Connecticut is an undated typescript of another poem:

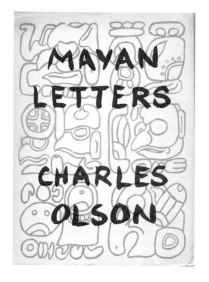

Mayan Letters by Charles Olson, 1954, Divers Press, edited by Robert Creeley.
Archives and Special Collections at the Thomas J. Dodd Research Center, University of Connecticut Libraries.

A GLYPH

Romans, my contrymen [sic]
your daemons
are neglected, abundance
is what you have, all
that you produce

so you should be surprised
what is left to us, except
to shut us up in our houses
like fattening birds and gorge
our bellies in the dark until
we burst with fat

This could be the "glyph" poem given in the summer of 1951 to Ben Shahn, an attack on the Western way of life that confronted Olson on his return from the Yucatan. The disgust, and despair, in this short piece echo familiar Olsonian polit-

[123] Charles Olson, *Mayan Letters* (Divers Press, 1954), republished (London: Cape Editions, 1968), p. 43.

[124] Katherine Litz, "Statement on the Summer Dance Program at BMC," previously unpublished, North Carolina Museum of Art, Black Mountain College Research Project, North Carolina State Archives, Raleigh.

ical sentiments, such as the oft-quoted condemnation from the beginning of *Call Me Ishmael*: "We are the last 'first' people. We forget that. We act big, misuse our land, ourselves. We lose our own primary."[125]

In "Human Universe," an essay published in 1951, Olson wrote, as part of an attempt to get away from the blind acceptance of form, "There is only one thing you can do about kinetic, re-enact it. Which is why the man said, he who possesses rhythm possesses the universe. And why art is the only twin life has—its only valid metaphysic. Art does not seek to describe but to enact."[126] Olson had been seeking poetry's roots in performance for several years, first in his 1948–1949 class in "Verse and the Theatre," which called for woodwinds and percussion, flute, slides and color projections, masks, "various combinations of the human voice, without music, without dance, but with gesture, posture, the skill of speech." There had also been the LIGHT SOUND MOVEMENT WORKSHOP, in which Elizabeth and W. P. (Pete) Jennerjahn had participated, she as dancer, he as percussionist. In Elizabeth's words:

> I remember especially rehearsing "The Kingfishers" with Charles Olson. We were near the kitchen; Olson was reading; I was dancing; Pete was playing; and a sharp light was on me, and the whole rest of the dining hall was dark. And there were a lot of LIGHT SOUND MOVEMENT rehearsals with Nick Cernovich and Tim LaFarge, and moving in our green- and red-striped tights through red and green saturated light created by the red- and green-striped slides.[127]

The LIGHT SOUND MOVEMENT workshop the Jennerjahns lead in 1949 and 1950 is an important link at Black Mountain between the early multi-media experiments of Schawinsky and Evarts and the historic Happening of 1952. As Pete recalls:

> We had dancers, composers, musicians, and idea people who were interested in getting together to DO something. We were limited only by the meager facilities available at the dining hall and the studies building. No light control panel: no curtain to open and close, etc. Events were limited to a minute, or so. All costumes and props were hand-done for the bit. What I liked was that all the components in the final version of the piece were thrown into the mix early on. No adding in of the music late in the game and costume and lighting in the last minute. Sometimes a

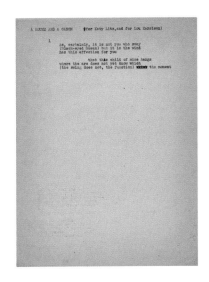

CHARLES OLSON: "A ROUND AND A CANON," JULY 31, 1951.
Newsprint, typescript, 10 ¹³/₁₆ x 8 ⁷/₁₆ inches.
Archives and Special Collections at the Thomas J. Dodd Research Center, University of Connecticut Libraries.
THIS WOULD SEEM TO BE AN EARLY VERSION OF THE BEGINNING TO "A ROUND & A CANON."

---

[125] Charles Olson, *Call Me Ishmael* (Baltimore: The Johns Hopkins University Press, 1997), p. 14. Pound had said of Olson's book, "I read with joy—made it unnecessary to read Melville," though he later added, "I thought you might be a serious character when I read that labor-saving device of yrs on H. Melville. But that was 2 yrs ago, bro." See Charles Olson, *Charles Olson And Ezra Pound: An Encounter At St. Elizabeths*, edited by Catherine Seelye (New York: Paragon House, 1991), p. 103.

[126] Charles Olson, "Human Universe," published in *Origin*, no. 1, winter 1951–1952, reprinted in Charles Olson, *Collected Prose*, edited by Donald Allen and Benjamin Friedlander (Berkeley: University of California Press, 1997), p. 155 ff.

[127] Elizabeth Jennerjahn, "Betty Schmitt, How Ever Did You Get Here?" in *Black Mountain College: Sprouted Seeds*, edited by Mervin Lane (Knoxville: University of Tennessee Press, 1990), p. 132.

DOROTHEA ROCKBURNE WITH JORGE FICK.
BLACK MOUNTAIN COLLEGE,
CA. 1950–1953. PHOTOGRAPH BY MARIE TAVROGES.

DOROTHEA ROCKBURNE. BLACK MOUNTAIN COLLEGE,
CA. 1950–53.

whole piece would snowball from a costume idea as the spark, or a dance movement, and all the other components would weave in. These pieces were like sparks which glowed, briefly, and were done.[128]

Betty and Pete Jennerjahn arrived at Black Mountain in the summer of 1948 (Betty had also studied there in 1943). Betty learned dance with Merce Cunningham and weaving with Anni Albers, producing such textiles as *Cross*, 1949. Pete studied with Josef Albers, and became a prized assistant. When Albers departed the following year, Pete took over some of the art instruction, dividing it with Joseph Fiore, who also made the transition from student to instructor.

MERCE CUNNINGHAM TEACHING, 1948 .
PHOTOGRAPH BY CLEMENS KALISCHER.
Courtesy of the artist.

Dorothea Rockburne, who arrived at Black Mountain in 1951 and stayed for the next four years, took the LIGHT SOUND MOVEMENT workshop, in lieu of Color Studies or classes, though she also took a drawing class from Joe Fiore. She remembers the workshop as "very feisty," and says, "We learned a lot about lighting, the way gels work in terms of negative colors."[129] She was seventeen when she arrived from Montreal, having already studied at the Ecole des Beaux Arts there and having gained a firm knowledge of drafting, grinding pigments, and other traditional skills. She married and had a daughter at Black Mountain, but found the environment less than ideal: "It was strange and wonderful place, but it was very sexist. Olson was extremely sexist, and I'd never experienced that before. You would talk, and it was like you were invisible. Except as a sexual object." Rockburne studied dance with Cunningham and photography with Larsen, where her fellow students were Rauschenberg and Twombly. The three formed a friendship that continues until today. Edward Steichen would come to the college occasionally to perform critiques. Lou Harrison wrote a piece for her to sing.

Her most significant experience, in relation to her future work, were her studies with mathematician Max Dehn, a renowned thinker and teacher, who enjoyed teaching non-specialists. While Rockburne insists she is neither a mathematician

---

[128] W. P. Jennerjahn, e-mail to Vincent Katz, 15 July 2002.

[129] The quotes of Dorothea Rockburne in this section are from an interview with Vincent Katz, 10 July 2001.

ELIZABETH JENNERJAHN
CROSS, 1949.
Woven wool tapestry, 12 ½ x 10 ½ inches.
Collection of the artist.

PETE JENNERJAHN
ADVENTURES OF RED, 1951.
Oil on hardboard, 25 ½ x 13 inches.
Collection of the artist.

nor a physicist, her devoted studies in these areas have informed the range of her mature work. Partially, it was the actual math she learned, probability theory and topology, that impacted her; partially it was the experience of confronting the unknown: "I realized that I liked to read things I couldn't understand. I found that it opened doors . . . when I started to take Max's classes, at first I was at sea. . . . We'd go on walks that were tutorials. . . . It was as though I had blinders on and somebody raised the shade. It was quite an experience." She did study painting with Kline and Tworkov and remembers Kline saying to her, "You were meant to work in color. You're not black and white. I've had a tragic life, and I am black and white." Later, she would use black and white, as well as vibrant color.

If Hazel Larsen was the archetypal Black Mountain photographer, Joseph Fiore was its archetypal painter. Both artists were trained at Black Mountain by Josef Albers, and both went on to become instructors, thus embarking on their professional careers while still at Black Mountain College. Though Fiore is an artist known to many in the New York art world, his 1950s work may come as a surprise. Fiore heard about Black Mountain while in high school in Cleveland and later read Adamic's article, first published in *Harper's* and then collected in his book *My America*, published in 1938. Fiore attended the summer session of 1946 and was impressed by the use of color in Jacob Lawrence's paintings. "It was more interesting to me than Albers's color class, which I didn't take," Fiore remembers.[130] Fiore gravitated toward Bolotowsky, when he filled in for Albers. What he learned from Bolotowsky has helped Fiore throughout his career: "We did a lot of work from still lifes that was Cubist-derived. That has stayed with me all through, because I keep going back to it, in certain ways." After a year in San Francisco, Fiore returned to Black Mountain for the 1949 summer session. That fall, four former students were appointed faculty members. Fiore would teach painting and drawing, Pete Jennerjahn would teach design and color, Betty Jennerjahn would teach dance, and Hazel Larsen would teach photography. From then until Black Mountain's closing Fiore would be the painting instructor.

One change in the school, gradually apparent during this period, was how the learning experience became less structured. While students had been free to create their own course of study, often on a tutorial basis, there had been, certainly in Josef Albers's classes, strictly organized activities. After Albers's departure, art instruction came to be more individually based. There were indeed classes, particularly a drawing class, but painting was often done in private, followed by critiques. As Fiore puts it: "Some people still say they felt free for the first time in lives. They could do something on their own, not forced by anybody. It was a way of finding yourself. Albers had such a focus in a certain way that some students were overly influenced by him, and he even advised them they should do something else, or go somewhere else, as they were just sopping up what he had to offer."

Through the late 1940s and early 1950s, Fiore had been aware of artistic developments in New York and he was able to witness them first hand through visits by de Kooning, Kline, Tworkov and others. The experience with de Kooning was the

[130] The quotes of Joseph Fiore are from an interview with Vincent Katz, 26 July 2001.

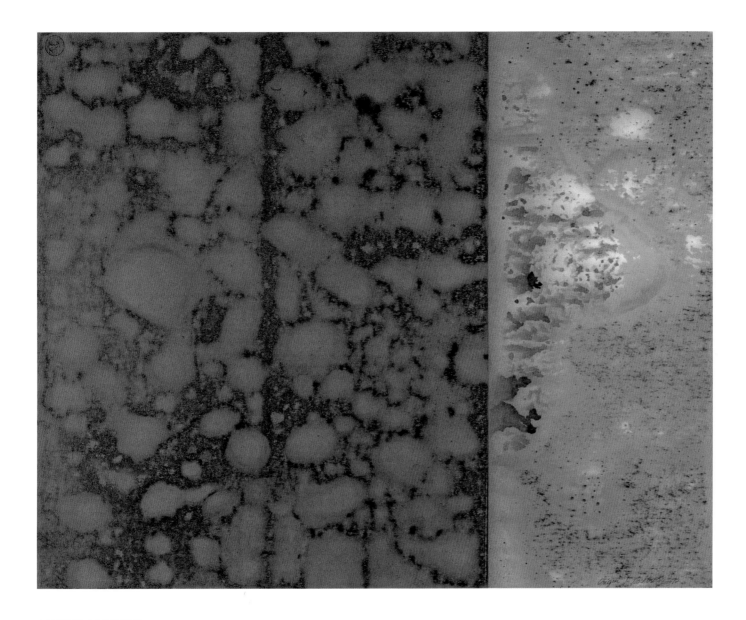

DOROTHEA ROCKBURNE
ORIGIN, 1972.
Oil on paper, 23 x 29 inches.
Walker Art Center, Minneapolis. Gift of Sharon and Jerry Zweigbaum, 1996.

JOSEPH FIORE
2-52, 1952.
Oil on canvas, 40 x 34 inches.
Collection of the artist.

JOSEPH FIORE
8-54: YELLOW FIELD, 1954.
Oil on canvas, 34 x 50 inches.
Collection of the artist.

JOSEPH FIORE
LARGE COLLAGE, 1953.
Paper on cardboard, 18 ¼ x 23 ⅞ inches.
Black Mountain College Museum and Arts Center, Asheville.

JOSEPH FIORE
PAINTING, 1954.
Oil paint on crescent board, 8 1/16 x 10 7/16 inches.
Archives and Special Collections at the Thomas J. Dodd Research Center,
University of Connecticut Libraries.

of poetry he intended, Creeley started fully-formed, writing in his twenties exquisitely carved lyrics, which maintain a live-wire edge through their reluctance to settle into conventional habits of thought. From his earliest poems, and always with an intense awareness of the contemporary—in music, speech, and art—Creeley developed by adding over the years compassion and wisdom's solace, and by collaborating with innumerable artists on books and art works.

Creeley visited Black Mountain in 1954 and returned in 1955. As he recalls, the college was rapidly becoming a place with meager provisions for its dwindling population: "There was no longer a dining room. People cooked on their own. Cadged or ate with friends or managed modest cooking with hotplates. I was living on five dollars a week. That was my salary. Dan Rice and I would pool our resources." Even so, Creeley sensed an impressive devotion to, even a hunger, for knowledge: "Black Mountain felt like a graduate school, despite the ages of the students. The students were various and there was a marked emotional shifting."[133] In an early previously unpublished poem, "An Ode (For Black Mt. College)," Creeley wrote:

> Why go to college. Or, as a man said, it
> is too far away.
>
> Why go.
> If I don't get there,—I did
> once
>
> If I don't get there, this year
> anyhow I know some of the names, I know
> what it might have been like, say, or
>
> you say.

Cy Twombly asked Olson to write a preface for an exhibition in 1952. Olson responded with a brilliant piece, one that matched the raw sophistication he had saw Twombly display in a room in the Studies Building. Olson's words about Melville are also about Twombly, and perhaps Rauschenberg: "There came a man who dealt with whiteness. And with space. He was an American. And perhaps his genius lay most in innocence rather than in the candor now necessary. In any case, he was not understood." Olson took the reader into his own thought processes confronting the newness of Twombly's paintings, revealing with intelligence his own inability to see them:

> It was just then, just when in this particular canvas I didn't see it—or
> saw more than I needed to see, saw what is death to see, the innocence of it is such a dissolve—when Twombly himself had, by going too far not gone far enough (that is, as a painter, so confined, had not gone far enough) had, in fact, gone outside himself, had, as so many most able men have gone outside the canvas gone to tech-

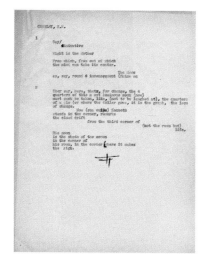

CHARLES OLSON: "CREELEY, N.H.," CA. 1951-1952. Paper, typescript with black ink notation, 11 x 8 1/2 inches. Archives and Special Collections at the Thomas J. Dodd Research Center, University of Connecticut Libraries.
THIS POEM IS A RE-WORKING OF ROBERT CREELEY'S POEM "LITTLETON, N.H.".

---

[133] The quotes of Robert Creeley in this section are from an interview with Vincent Katz, 30 July 2001.

nique—when, in this one case, Twombly had tried to solve it outside the place where he almost every time does battle it out (he is that pure), look at his canvases. . . .

Ultimately Olson did find vindication in Twombly's surfaces, his use of the real *in* his painting: "the dug up stone figures, the thrown down glyphs, the old sorells in sheep dirt in caves, the flaking iron—there are his *paintings.*"[134]

In "The Present Is Prologue," Olson declared his belief in the need to work "from Homer back," to avoid the strait jacket imposed by Platonic/Aristotelian theory, and from Melville forward, forming that ancient/modern pinion sought by Albers and many modern artists. At the end of this essay, Olson struggled to define himself without reference to standard terminology: ". . . how to use oneself, and on what. That is my profession. I am an archeologist of morning." He pointed to Melville, Dostoevsky, Rimbaud, and Lawrence, who "put men forward into the post-modern, the post-humanist, the post historic, the going live present. . . ."[135]

Teacher, talker, unescapable reference point for Black Mountain, Olson was an active principle. Not only his ideas, but his methods were challenging, provoked people out of their customary skins, and stimulated some to become artists. Jonathan Williams described the extremes to which his methods could go:

> . . . and there was Olson, who *was* the biggest man in the world. In those days he was maybe as light as 240. He was certainly a vast spectacle. So I signed up for his writing course, which met one night a week, after dinner. I do remember that one of those classes that summer started at 7 o'clock and it went to 11, at which point everybody rushed to Ma Peek's place . . . the local beer joint, and so everybody loaded up on beer, went back to the college, the class went on all night, it went on all the next day, we went back to Peek's place the following night, and I think there were three people still sort of stumbling about next day and mumbling at each other. That class lasted almost two days. That was the kind of experience that Black Mountain could offer.[136]

The range of Olson's teaching is evident from his course titles at Black Mountain: "Verse & The Theatre," which combined poetry with music and dance, "Mayan Hieroglyphic Writing and Ovid's *Metamorphoses*" (to which, he added, in the prospectus, "For use, now."), "The Act of Writing in the Context of Post-Modern Man" ("The effort is definitely non-literary."), "The Present," for which students

[134] Charles Olson, "Cy Twombly," published in *Olson: The Journal of the Charles Olson Archive*, no. 8, edited by George F. Butterick, University of Connecticut, Storrs, Fall 1977, reprinted in *Charles Olson, Collected Prose*, edited by Donald Allen and Benjamin Friedlander (Berkley: University of California Press, 1997), pp. 175–78.

[135] Charles Olson, "The Present Is Prologue," first published in *Twentieth Century Authors, First Supplement*, 1955, reprinted in Charles Olson, *Collected Prose*, Allen and Friedlander, pp. 205–207.

[136] Jonathan Williams, interview with Martin Duberman, 3 November 1968, North Carolina Museum of Art, Black Mountain College Research Project, North Carolina State Archives, Raleigh.

were required to read that day's entire *New York Times* and *Asheville Citizen* before class, "Projective Verse," as well as courses in Sumerian and Hittite "lamentations, hymns, and epics," Theocritus, Melville, William Carlos Williams, and Ezra Pound.

Olson instilled in his students the importance of independence for the writer, which inevitably entailed self-publishing: "Olson said, don't ever be intimidated by the disdain or the disinterest of the world. Get yourself some type, get yourself some paper, and print it."[137] Williams and Olson's other students took this advice, and sometimes assignments for his classes were turned in already in handprinted editions. At a poetry conference in Berkeley in 1965, with Allen Ginsberg, Ed Sanders and other politically active poets in the audience, Olson reiterated the importance of self-publishing as an avenue to power. In a rambling talk, he kept returning to the idea that poetry—any art, any activity—had its own politics, and that poetry also had a role to play in the wider political scheme:

> You need to know that experience and society is a complex occasion, which requires as much wit and power as only poets have. . . . Writing is publishing. . . . I am now publishing, tonight, because I'm talking writing. . . . I mean, I think this is a political occasion. . . . What's that guy's name that really is one of the examples of why we're here, and why we're as political as we are, and why, in fact, we're better than Madison Avenue—those of us who are. And there's some men in this hall that surely are. . . . If you don't know, brother, that poetics is politics, poets are political leaders today, and the only ones, you shouldn't have come. . . .[138]

In the early 1950s, Olson and Creeley, with some other cohorts, decided to mount an attack on academic poetry. They did not mean to infiltrate, however. They would forge entirely other paths and ways of living alien to those for whom comfort was primary, and establish other avenues of publication. Critical pieces and poems were published in periodicals, but in particular in their own venue, the *Black Mountain Review*, and in the slight, startlingly beautiful books they insisted come into existence.

The printing press at Black Mountain was busy producing poetry broadsides and other small-run editions, usually with artwork. In 1951, Olson put out the broadside *Letter to Melville*, printed by Larry Hatt at Black Mountain, as well as *Apollonius of Tyana*, "A Dance, with some Words, for two Actors," a book designed by Larry Hatt with a map by Stanley Vanderbeek. Both Hatt and Vanderbeek were students. Those were followed in 1952 by *This*, a broadside poem by Olson with graphic work by Nicholas Cernovich, printed on four different stocks by Cernovich at the Black Mountain College Graphics Workshop as Black Mountain Broadside No. 1. Cernovich also printed in 1952 *The Song of the Border-Guard*, a poem by Robert Duncan, with cover by Cy Twombly.

---

[137] Ibid.

[138] Charles Olson, "Reading at Berkeley," 23 July 1965, published in *Muthologos: The Collected Lectures and Interviews*, p. 97 ff.

By the mid-1950s, Robert Creeley in Mallorca and Jonathan Williams in North Carolina were publishing books of such high quality and frequency as to become key elements in the literary movement that would be known as the Black Mountain School of writers. Creeley's Divers Press put out books by Paul Blackburn, Duncan, Larry Eigner, as well as Creeley's own short stories and poems. When Williams began publishing his series Jargon, which continues until today, it was Joel Oppenheimer, a student who became adept at working the moveable type, who printed on the college press the second number, *The Dancer*, a collaboration between Oppenheimer and Rauschenberg dedicated to Katherine Litz. Other Jargon publications included *The Maximus poems 1–10* by Charles Olson, 1953, the first publication of what would become Olson's epic; *The Immoral Proposition* by Robert Creeley, 1953, with drawings by René Laubiès; *All that Is Lovely in Men* by Robert Creeley, 1955, with drawings by Dan Rice and cover photo by Jonathan Williams; *Anecdotes of the Late War* by Charles Olson, 1955; *The Maximus Poems 11–22* by Charles Olson, 1956; *The Dutiful Son* by Joel Oppenheimer, 1956; and *The Empire Finals at Verona: Poems 1956–57* by Jonathan Williams, 1959, with illustrations by Fielding Dawson.

Fiore's 1956 report on the art department observed that "[Tom] Field was the first to collaborate with Jonathan Williams's Jargon Press, in the publication of Charles Olson's poem 'Anecdotes of the Late War,' for which Mr. Field designed, executed, and printed the cover for the author's edition of 30, in the fall of 1955. I myself have been commissioned by Mr. Williams to do a color litho cover for the author's edition of Joel Oppenheimber's collected poems, to be published late this spring." With evident pride, Fiore added, "I do not know offhand of any other school in the country offering a lithography course, which has these possibilities of publication, and a close and fruitful collaboration between artist, writer, and publisher."[139]

Fielding Dawson, a student at Black Mountain who became a writer and artist, took Olson's message to heart and published his own work, including *2 & 4 Poems*, by Jack Boyd and Dawson, 1950, printed by Dawson at Black Mountain; *6 Stories of the Love of Life*, ca. 1950, Black Mountain College print shop; *Elizabeth Constantine*, 1955, Biltmore Press, Asheville (the same press at which Albers had done some prints); *Krazy Kat and One More*, Jargon, 1955; and *Ajax*, a Jargon broadside, 1956. Regarding the first two, Dawson states, "At Black Mountain in 1950–51, I published two little booklets of poems. It's like kid stuff and baseball, but they're also attacks on racism."[140] Dawson painted and drew as much as he wrote in those days, contributing in 1956 a series of woodcuts to Creeley's book of poems *If You*.

Dawson had two mentors, or father figures, at Black Mountain—Charles Olson and Franz Kline—and he wrote extensively about both. Olson was "the master," someone who put students through trial by fire, after which some came out writers. He could also be careless in his treatment of his students. Dawson recalls that

LETTER FOR MELVILLE BY CHARLES OLSON, 1951, PRINTED AT BLACK MOUNTAIN COLLEGE. Archives and Special Collections at the Thomas J. Dodd Research Center, University of Connecticut Libraries.

DAN RICE, FRANZ KLINE, FIELDING DAWSON. "THE DOG'S NAME WAS ANXIOUS." PROVINCETOWN, SPRING, 1959. COMMENT BY FIELDING DAWSON.

[139] Joseph Fiore, "Some Notes on the Nature of Painting Instruction at Black Mountain College," mimeograph printout, dated 5 May 1956, North Carolina Museum of Art, Black Mountain College Research Project, North Carolina State Archives, Raleigh.

[140] Fielding Dawson, in an interview with Vincent Katz, 22 August 2001.

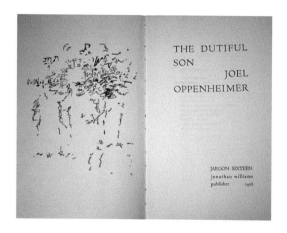

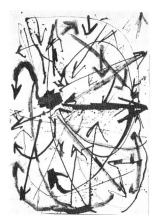

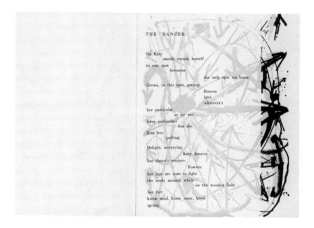

The Dutiful Son by Joel Oppenheimer, Jargon 16, Jonathan Williams. Frontispiece by Joseph Fiore, 1956. Collection of Ann van de Wiele.

The Kind of Act of by Robert Creeley, 1953, Divers Press. Printed by Mossén Alcover in Palma de Mallorca. Cover by René Laubiés. The Poetry/Rare Books Collection, State University of New York, Buffalo.

2 & 4 Poems, by Jack Boyd and Fielding Dawson, August 1950. Archives and Special Collections at the Thomas J. Dodd Research Center, University of Connecticut Libraries.

Robert Rauschenberg: Cover drawing for Joel Oppenheimer's *The Dancer*, 1951 (Jargon 2, Black Mountain College). Ink on paper, 7 x 5 inches. Collection of James S. Jaffe.

The Dancer, 1951, poem by Joel Oppenheimer, drawing by Robert Rauschenberg. Printed at Black Mountain College by Oppenheimer and Jonathan Williams, Jargon 2. Archives and Special Collections at the Thomas J. Dodd Research Center, University of Connecticut Libraries.

once, "I sent copy of 'Krazy Kat' to Olson, asking what he thought of it. He kept it a year, it was almost lost, and he finally sent it back without comment."[141] Kline, conversely, was utterly charismatic, and had much to impart to young artists. In *An Emotional Memoir of Franz Kline*, Dawson recalls studying with Kline at Black Mountain:

> He talked of the face, and difference in depth from the ridge of the nose to the hollow of the eye, following the nose planes down and then back up to the eye cavities giving strength to the cheekbones— he spoke enthusiastically of the upslanting hollow below the cheekbones, and when he put his hands flat against his own cheekbones his eyes were intent, and brilliant: "From there on it cuts in," and he pressed in on his eye cavities—really the structure of his face, talking of light on the planes, he ended, depth and surface, as in Rembrandt.
>
> "If you can get that right," he gestured about his face, "you've got the whole works."[142]

[141] Ibid.

[142] Fielding Dawson, *An Emotional Memoir of Franz Kline* (New York: Pantheon Books, 1967), p. 7.

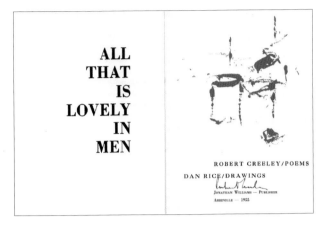

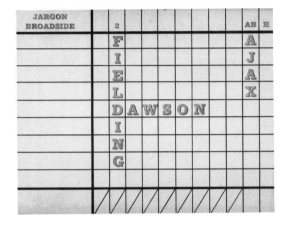

THE MAXIMUS POEMS 11–22 BY CHARLES OLSON, 1956, JARGON 9, JONATHAN WILLIAMS PUBLISHER, STUTTGART, EDITION OF 350. Archives and Special Collections at the Thomas J. Dodd Research Center, University of Connecticut Libraries.

ALL THAT IS LOVELY IN MEN BY ROBERT CREELEY, 1955. JARGON 10, JONATHAN WILLIAMS PUBLISHER. The Poetry/Rare Books Collection, State University of New York, Buffalo.

APOLLONIUS OF TYANA BY CHARLES OLSON, SUMMER 1951, BLACK MOUNTAIN COLLEGE, BOOK DESIGNED BY LARRY HATT, MAP BY STANLEY VANDERBEEK, EDITION OF 50, 20 BOUND AND SIGNED, 30 PAPER. Archives and Special Collections at the Thomas J. Dodd Research Center, University of Connecticut Libraries.

AJAX BY FIELDING DAWSON, 1956. JARGON BROADISE 1. Archives and Special Collections at the Thomas J. Dodd Research Center, University of Connecticut Libraries.

IF YOU BY ROBERT CREELEY, 1956, POEMS & PICTURES NO. 8, WOODCUTS BY FIELDING DAWSON. PORPOISE BOOKSHOP, SAN FRANCISCO. The Poetry/Rare Books Collection, State University of New York, Buffalo.

While staying at Kline's loft in New York, Dawson painted a remarkable Kline-influenced portrait of Olson, whose thick black lines have a vital attenuation, with occasional sharp definition. All in all, a masterful one-shot, adding up to an exagerration perfectly appropriate to Black Mountain's dynamic and larger-than-life central figure. At Black Mountain, Kline also did a fast-paced ink drawing of Dawson's seated figure.

Other writing students in the 1950s at Black Mountain who went on to become acclaimed figures in postwar American literature include Ed Dorn, Joel Oppenheimer, Michael Rumaker, and John Wieners. Dorn developed a relationship with Olson, whose "Bibliography for Ed Dorn," a key document in Olson studies, was literally a note, following a conversation, dropped on the windowsill of Dorn's kitchen. Creeley affirms that, "Olson's repsect for Ed's writing is substantial. He spoke of Ed's having 'an Elizabethan ear.' He had an extraordinary ear for cadence and precisions of rhythms. . . . The feeling about Ed was that he was Malvoglio. He's not sinister, but he has a kind of ironic depression, ironizing vibes and senses of a black world—an exquisite writer, particularly his poetry."[143]

[143] Robert Creeley, in an interview with Vincent Katz, 30 July 2001.

205 >

BMC prospectus for Spring Semester, Feb, 11–June 7, 1952*

BLACK MOUNTAIN COLLEGE is heretical because it has practiced from its founding (1933) two of the simplest & oldest principles on which higher learning—when it has been higher—has rested.

I. that **the student**, rather than the curriculum, is **the proper** center of a general education, because it is he and she that a college exist for

II. that a faculty fit to face up the student as the center have to be measured by **what they do with what they know**, that it is their dimension as teachers as much as their mastery of their disciplines that makes then instuments capable of dealing with what excuses their profession in the first place, their ability to instruct the student under hand.

Several things follow these two base principles, so far as the instruction at Black Mountain College goes. One characteristic, from the beginning, has been the recognition that ideas are only such as they exist in things and in actions. Another worth emphasizing (it is still generally overlooked in those colleges where classification into fields, because of curriculum emphasis, remains the law) is that Black Mountain College carefully recognizes that, at this point in man's necessities, it is not things in themselves but **what happens between things** where the life of them is to be sought.

THE PRESENT FACULTY, herein presented, is a measure, both in their number (1 to every 2 students) and in the range of their accomplishments as well as the disciplines offered, of what the standard of teaching and of life Black Mountain has tried to give students for 19 years.

These are the present faces and facts. In offering them, the College takes pride in carrying before them some of the philosophy of teaching they represent as that philosophy got variously stated by the leader in the founding of the College, John A. Rice:

Our central consistent effort is to teach method, not content; to emphasize process, to invite the student to the realization that the way of handling facts and himself amid the facts is more important than facts themselves. For facts change, while the method of handling facts —provided it is life's own free, dynamic method— remains the same. The law of a teacher at Black Mountain is to function as a working "artist" in the teaching world, to be no passive recipient or hander-out of mere information, but to be and increasingly to become, productive, creative, **using** everything that comes within his orbit, including especially people.

There is a technic to be learned, a grammar of the art of living and working in the world. Logic, as severe as can be, must be learned; if for no other reason, to know its limitations. Dialectic must be learned: and no feelings spared, for you can't be nice when truth is at stake. The hard, inscrutable facts of science must be learned, for truth has a habit of hiding in queer places. Man's responses to ideas and things in the past must be learned. But they are not all. There are subtle means of communication that have been lost by mankind, as our nerve ends have been cauterized by schooling. The arts, especially the performing arts, are more and more valuable in such restorations. For these nerves must be renewed, in both ourselves as faculty and in the students who come to us to communicate and to learn to communicate. To learn to move, at least without fear, to hear, see, touch, also without fear or at least without denials of first hungers, to be aware of everything around us (again, including especially people)—this is to start to penetrate the past and to **feel** as well as mentally see our way into the future.

A good teacher is always more a learner than teacher, making the demand of everyone to be taught something. A man who never asks himself any questions had better not try asking others. In the center of his being a teacher should be calm, quiet, **tough**. He must have in him the principle of growth; like the student, a sense of justice and a great capacity for dejection.

Teachers in a place like this, where education is taken seriously, should always bear in mind that they are the central problem; **that we would provide the students with a liberal education if we merely gave them the privilege of looking on while we educated ourselves.**

---

* Although this text is unsigned, the writing style, layout, and typography of the original strongly indicate that its author was Charles Olson. (*Ed.*)

FIELDING DAWSON
CHARLES OLSON, 1956.
Ink on paper collaged on board, 12 x 12 inches.
Collection of Jonathan Williams. Photograph by Reuben Cox.

FRANZ KLINE
DRAWING OF FIELDING DAWSON, BLACK MOUNTAIN COLLEGE, AUGUST 1952.
Ink on vellum, 23 x 18 inches.
Estate of Fielding Dawson.

Rumaker studied prose writing with Creeley and poetry with Olson. Creeley was stunned by Rumaker's stories, and Rumaker went on to become a fiction writer, although "fiction" seems idadequate for stories so hard-hitting and palpably every-day.

Gerald van de Wiele grew up in Detroit and attended the School of the Art Institute of Chicago for a few months, but found it too rigid. A letter from student George Fick enticed van de Wiele down to Black Mountain. Van de Wiele visited and became enamored of the place and of Olson. He enrolled as a student for the school's final two years, looking more for a place to paint than to pile up credits. Classes were suspended during the winter of 1955, and van de Wiele returned to Chicago. While there, he convinced two friends to follow him back in the spring—Richard Bogart and John Chamberlain. All three had been students at the Art Institute of Chicago.

When van de Wiele went to Black Mountain to study in September of 1954, there were only seven students, but he was not disappointed. On the contrary, he found the setting conducive to the self-exploration he wished to undertake. He was interested in the poetry of Olson and Williams before arriving, and the relationship with the master poet was an important one for the young painter: "He was very approachable. There wasn't anything about him that put you off, yet he inspired enormous awe in the writing students."[144] What van de Wiele most took away was an interaction among the arts: "There was no science at the time. . . . There were sometimes drawing classes, but never a painting class. You painted in your studio and people would come by. Everyone got involved in what everyone else was doing and would come by. Stefan Wolpe taught a class for writers and painters, people who knew nothing about music, but he could talk about the creative process for a composer. That was enormously interesting. Everybody seemed to be interested in the other arts—that was probably the thing that was the most exciting."

The actual painting instruction was delivered by Fiore: "Joe Fiore was the painting teacher. Joe was very low key in the way he taught. He'd let you bring out what you needed to bring out in yourself. He didn't push ideas. He allowed you to develop what you wanted to develop." Van de Wiele's large painting *The Quarry*, 1956, is the perfect counterpart to Fiore's *The Harbor*. Both are large-scale verticals that deal with the plunging, expanding use of paint, in a way not so remote from what Clement Greenberg had called for, a loosening of line into paint, a spreading from beyond adherence to the Cartesian into a more open approach. The way van de Wiele and Fiore used color might not have appealed to Greenberg, as they were perversely muddying it, not letting it shine with either purity or a diluted mystique. They obfuscated with paint, building up motions or intimations that did not preach, but sat back and waited for the next utterance. Richard Bogart made a large-scale collage almost photographic in effect, combining fragments of various of his own abstract paintings.

FIELDING DAWSON: *ABSTRACT DRAWING*, UNDATED. Pencil on paper, 6 x 4 inches. Archives and Special Collections at the Thomas J. Dodd Research Center, University of Connecticut Libraries.

[144] The quotes of Gerald van de Wiele are from an interview with Vincent Katz, 5 July 2001.

GERALD VAN DE WIELE
THE QUARRY, 1956.
Oil on canvas, 84 x 51 inches.
Collection of the artist.

RICHARD BOGART
BLACK MOUNTAIN, 1956.
Oil and collage, 32 x 22 inches.
Collection of the artist.

JOHN CHAMBERLAIN
UNTITLED, 1955.
Steel, 21 x 8 x 9 inches on an iron base.
Collection of Ann van de Wiele.

JOHN CHAMBERLAIN
UNTITLED, 1955.
Steel, 18 x 15 x 8 inches on a wooden base.
Collection of Ann van de Wiele.

JOHN CHAMBERLAIN
G. G., 1956.
Steel, 77 x 24 x 23 inches.
Collection of Robert Natkin and Judith Dolnick Natkin.

JOHN CHAMBERLAIN
THAT'S MY HEART, 1955.
Ink on paper, 8 ½ x 11 inches (detail).
PaceWildenstein. Photograph by Eleanor P. Labrozzi.

Van de Wiele believes that Black Mountain was important for John Chamberlain in providing him with a positive environment that allowed him to flourish as an artist. In 1954, Chamberlain had been in a group exhibition juried by Robert Motherwell and Betty Parsons. At Black Mountain, Chamberlain worked on welded sculptures that partook of the sculptural language of David Smith, although even then Chamberlain's pieces possessed a distinct raw energy and formal invention. Working on his own at Black Mountain, as opposed to doing much studying of art, what influence he took from the school came more from its writers than from its visual artists. "I was going to Charles's class," Chamberlain recalls, "but I didn't write poems. The rest of the people brought their poems and read them, and I brought four drawings. . . . When I made those drawings, I couldn't figure out how to deal with the edge of the page. I'd make a drawing and it would get tight, staking the borders. So I made sure I went off the edge, and then I could do it. I had to teach myself."[145] According to van de Wiele, Chamberlain was respected at Black Mountain in a way he had not been in Chicago, and this gave him the self-confidence to mature into the artist who would work with automobile bodies and ultimately say of himself, "I'm an Abstract Expressionist using Pop Art materials." Creeley, from whom Chamberlain learned the clarity that comes from juxtaposing simple ideas in descriptive sentences, noted the sculptor's independence: "John was very much an unknown quantity. He was not a student by any simple definition, insofar as he went about his own work and stayed marginal determinedly. . . . He was one of the most intelligent people I'd ever met."[146]

Dan Rice, another artist at Black Mountain for a number of years, and a charismatic figure, was coaxed into painting partly by Fiore's calm example. He had played trumpet with the bands of Tommy Dorsey, Benny Goodman, Woody Herman, and Stan Kenton. After going to Black Mountain intent on studying musical composition, and while subsequently in San Francisco studying architecture, Rice connected with Joe Fiore: "Joe bought me some brushes and paint and said, 'Stop fooling around, paint if you're going to.' In a way, Fiore sent me on my way."[147] They both returned to Black Mountain, and Rice, like Fiore and van de Wiele, worked with an idea of landscape in the illustrations he did for books and in a series of spare ink drawings preserved in the Robert Creeley papers at Stanford University. Rice sometimes enclosed forms, building modules of rectilinear force, while other times the force was from brushed ink, always sufficiently withheld so that they were not simple brushstrokes, but mysteriously appeared as defined shapes. Many suggest forms of animals, especially cattle, while others possess more energy of movement and imply dance. Rice also collaborated in performances at Black Mountain, making sets on various occasions for Cage, Cunningham, Olson, and Wolpe. He was "Olson's favorite," and "approved" by Kline, in Creeley's words. As Creeley remembers his friend, "Dan was very attractive, not just as a physical presence, but classically manly. He was actually quite small, but he had a quick, deft capability—humor and savvy. He was looked to among the males as the canny, resourceful person. I liked his art a lot."[148]

[145] Quotes of John Chamberlain are from an interview with Vincent Katz, 27 September 2001.

[146] Quotes of Robert Creeley are from an interview with Vincent Katz, 30 July 2001.

[147] Dan Rice, in an interview with Vincent Katz, 17 October 2001.

[148] The quotes of Robert Creeley are from an interview with Vincent Katz, 30 July 2001.

Another figure from that era, though arriving later, was Tom Field, at Black Moun tain during Creeley's time, and like Dawson both a writer, who was published in the *Black Mountain Review*, and a painter. His *Bird in Flight*, 1954, is from his Black Mountain period, and it shows an ability to deal with a large central image in a composition—a little domestic, but weird. Field moved to San Francisco after Black Mountain folded and appears in a memoir by Michael Rumaker about Robert Duncan and the life out west. Field became legendary, especially among poets, and many collected his work. Field's *The Kerouac Painting*, 1960, was a much more open piece than *Bird In Flight*, reminiscent of Twombly's ability to exit a painting without overworking it with thick and heavy conspicuous insistence. Here a whitish ground prevails, with hints of bright orange, while activity is dom- inated by a profusion of delicately balanced lines, whose calligraphic quality lends itself to thoughts of writing. Thus it is no surprise to learn that Jack Kerouac contributed a collaborative element to this painting, a small pencil drawing of a stick figure.

Basil King, born in London in 1935, emigrated with his parents to Detroit and entered Black Mountain in 1951 at age 16. With some absences, he remained until the school's closing in 1956. King studied painting with Fiore and Vicente, and he took classes with Creeley, Duncan, Olson, and Wolpe. In his student days, King was painting in the mode of abstract expressionism that was trying to continue in looking for roots in nature, in landscape, as in *Riverbed*, 1956.

In the final year of the College, Robert Duncan arrived to teach and found the situ- ation one of decay. The school had dwindled to a handful of students and faculty:

> My first impression of Black Mountain was that it was very run down.
> It was winter, between semesters. We stayed in the so-called Gropius
> building, which by that time was a derelict piece of modernism—noth-
> ing looks more run down than an art moderne building ten years later.
> Nothing was gracious about it. It was meant to be shipshape and if it
> isn't it's a very wrecked old left-over of the ship. By spring, 1955,
> Black Mountain had lost its lands. It no longer was the Black Mountain
> one had heard about in the late 1930s, when there was a coordina-
> tion between the land and its farms and the college. By spring, 1956,
> when I actually thought there, the large dormitory building was not too
> bad to live in, but the school was very noticably derelict. One had
> only to walk about to find deserted laboratories with broken glasses,
> and splendid kiln equipment which had just gone to ruin.[149]

Michael Rumaker, a student of Olson's and later acclaimed fiction writer, wrote a memoir of Duncan, in which he also recalled the "hanging-on" days of Black Mountain:

> This was near the final closing of the school and in the year since I'd
> left there was drastic change. There was a psychotic, unpredicatable

---

[149] Robert Duncan in an interview by Anne Charters, 5 June 1969, quoted in the introduction to Charles Olson, *The Special View of History*, Charters, p. 7.

215 >

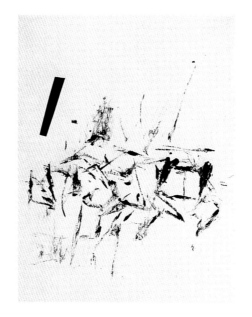

DAN RICE
DRAWINGS.
Ink on paper, 6 ⁵⁄₁₆ x 4 ¾ inches.
Special Collections, Stanford University Libraries.

TOM FIELD
BIRD IN FLIGHT, 1954.
Oil on canvas, 35 x 60 inches.
Collection of Denise N. Di Salvo.

TOM FIELD
THE KEROUAC PAINTING, 1960.
Oil and graphite on canvas, 71 x 67 ¹⁵⁄₁₆ inches.
Collection of the Morris and Helen Belkin Art Gallery,
Vancouver. Gift of Ernie Edwards, 1997.
Photograph by Howard Ursuliak.

KING, 1958

BASIL KING
RIVERBED, 1956.
Oil on paper, 22 x 26 inches.
Collection of the artist.

energy in the air. Jerry van de Wiele, the painter, told me that when certain students came to visit, when he was living at Last Chance on the road to the farm, he was careful to put the axe he used for cutting firewood in a safe place, out of sight and reach.

During my stay, Olson and Betty Kaiser, with whom he was now living after first wife Connie's departure, invited me up to supper one night and Charles gleefully told me (but with a touch of bewilderment and exasperation in his voice since the quality of the work of what writing students there were had dropped considerably) that the remaining faculty should vote to take down the Black Mountain College sign over the Gatehouse entrance and "run up a bright red flag that says 'SECONAL' on it in big letters!"[150]

Those were grim days, alleviated partly by Duncan's theater productions, which got everyone collaborating again, in a new way, yet with some of the old Black Mountain spirit. What remained, as legacy, was partly that sense of community, which persisted not only as active efforts to publish or write criticism of one another, but also in poems, works of art, dedicated to other artists with shared affinities. Olson wrote poems to or addresing some aspect of Blackburn, Cage, Cernovich, Creeley, Cunningham, Dawson, Duncan, Goodman, Larsen, van de Wiele, Wieners, Williams.

John Wieners developed close friendships with a number of people at Black Mountain, including his two teachers whose spontaneity impressed him: "[Olson] would come down the Studies Building and talk off the top of his head. I never figured out just who he spoke of. . . . I took classes and conversation with Robert Duncan the following summer. It was excellent, early in the morning. He'd come up and wake us up in the lodge. I don't think he knew exactly what he was going to say. No notes were prepared."[151] He noted, interestingly, "tolerance" as being the main thing he learned from Olson, citing, "political overtones to the work, even though it's set in the 17th century." In a previously unpublished poem, "Black Mountain Blues," John Wieners wrote, as the refrain of a blues ballad, of longing to return to that time of simple pleasures: "I want to go back to old black mountain this morning,/I want to sing old songs with Dorn and charlie O . . ."

In a 1958 letter to Creeley, Wieners wrote of *Measure*, the magazine he had begun to edit in Boston, which picked up threads of *Origin* and the *Black Mountain Review*, adding other patterns to a still developing tapestry: "The REASON for Measure is you & Charles, & Jonathan, whoever else I respect. That it is not my generosity, but yours that will allow Measure to mark the end of the decade. . . ."[152] In a letter to *Measure*, Robert Duncan wrote, addressing Wieners, "I shall continue to send you (as I do to *The Black Mountain Review*) the central work. With the joy, for me, that you demand it. Let's ride the outer edge of

[150] Michael Rumaker, *Robert Duncan in San Francisco* (San Francisco: Grey Fox Press, 1996), pp. 2–3.

[151] John Wieners, in an interview with Vincent Katz, 1 August 2001.

[152] John Wieners, letter to Robert Creeley, 24 July 1958, Robert Creeley Papers, Department of Special Collections, Stanford University Libraries.

the risk; the central work does. It's the peripheral rests in the sure thing of the accomplished."[153]

It should be noted that Olson did not seek to revolutionize Black Mountain College—he admired his predecessors and the history and philosophy of the college, and he was proud to be the successor to their mantle. A college propspectus for the Spring semester of 1952, almost certainly written by Olson, stated, "These are the present faces and facts. In offering them, the College takes pride in carrying before them some of the philosophy got variously stated by the leader in the founding of the College, John A. Rice." It went on to paraphrase Rice: "Our central and consistent effort is to teach method, not content; to emphasize process. . . . The law of a teacher at Black Mountain is to function as a working 'artist' in the teaching world. . . . Teachers in a place like this, where education is taken seriously, should always bear in mind that they are the central problem; that we would provide the students with a liberal education if we merely gave them the privilege of looking on while we educated ourselves."[154]

This pride in self-education and a concomitant fearlessness in the face of facts was Olson's pedagogical banner for the final years. By the time Creeley arrived, in 1954, there was no science class being offered, and although he had little actual knowledge of the sciences, Olson convinced him to teach a course in biology. Olson's lecture topics were notoriously wide-ranging, and Duncan, according to Gerald van de Wiele, "seemed to know everything about everything." Creeley supported the view that method was more important than subject:

> Teaching is not determined by subject in any real sense at all. At one point, we had no science courses, and part the requirement for our qulification as a legitimate educational institution was that we had to have something offered in the sciences, no matter how little. So Olson said, "Well, Bob, why don't you teach biology?" I said, "That's the one thing I never took. I never had it in high school. I never took anything remotely involved with biology in college." He said, "Terrific, you can learn something." And I learned later that that was a very practical comment. I thought it was at the time, but I just didn't want to learn biology, for whatever reason. Subsequently, I realized that teaching is teaching. It has, paradoxically, nothing to do with the subject. It's a way of being with someone in an unpresumptive manner, as he or she learns to find ways to get to or to use or to recognize whatever it is that's being addressed.

> Black Mountain was an extraordinarily useful preparation for confidence. I'd never been in a situation where I didn't feel defensive, where I didn't feel isolated by the rest of the company, where I didn't feel tacitly alone or contesting. At Black Mountain, I was suddenly with peers and people who were like-minded, who both respected

153 Robert Duncan, "Letter—1st of a series," in *Measure*, no. 2, winter 1958, p. 63.

154 Black Mountain College prospectus for the Spring Semester, 1952, North Carolina Museum of Art, Black Mountain College Research Project, North Carolina State Archives, Raleigh [see p. 202 of this book].

me for what I did and paid attention. And paid attention to the people I much revered, as Williams, for example. That changed my life, when I found a company that was forever sustaining. I'd never had a sense of fitting in anywhere, and Black Mountain was it. Chamberlain put it most aptly. Someone asked him what was it about Black Mountain that he particularly respected, or what had been the attraction he felt toward the place, and he said, "Black Mountain was the only place he'd gone to where people were more interested in what they didn't know than in what they did."[155]

VIII. Recent Work

The period after Black Mountain closed was one of esthetic uncertainty. Abstract artists had defined an approach that already had imitators. The theory of abstraction, Greenberg's move away from a Cubist-derived base in the horizontal and vertical, and away from the easel, was followed by some artists, but others doubled back. The 1960s were a time of crisis in the arts, and artists had to decide whether to pursue Greenberg's ideas to their logical conclusions—the abandonment of traditional modes of fracture, and ultimately, the traditional activity of art itself—or to "go back" and try whatever it was they felt like. Once the rules fell away, there was little guidance.

Some artists, like Fiore and van de Wiele, began to paint what they could see. Van de Wiele painted abstractly until 1963, the time of his solo exhibition at the Leo Castelli gallery. As Fiore describes the show, "It was like an abstract expressionist view of a 15th-century portrait."[156] Having come through abstraction, through that dense passage, there could be a use in painting realistically, although that term is as problematic as abstraction. In recent years, both Fiore and van de Wiele have returned to a more abstracted base, influenced by the symbolism of indigenous peoples, and their renewed desire for dynamics comparable to Olson's glyph. Richard Bogart, dissatisfied with abstraction, has been painting landscape-derived works, drenched in a personally opaque reverence for veils of enveloping glow. Gwendolyn Knight still uses recognizable imagery. Her recent work relies less on color effects, coaxing emotion from carefully drawn forms.

Others responded to the seductive allure of photography, the gratification of working with the image machine. Being the artists they are, they have taken photographic processes in diverse directions. For Rauschenberg, photography, and what he learned about it in 1950–1951, from Weil and from Callahan and Siskind, became the grist for his artistic mill to the present day. In the Black Mountain spirit, he has treated both found photographs and his own as *objets trouvés*. Most recently, he devoted two portfolios to photographs from his Black Mountain days—one of diverse images, the other photos of his friend, Cy Twombly, whom he continued to photograph on their subsequent travels to Italy and Africa. Twombly too seems to have entered the *temenos*, or sacred ground of memory

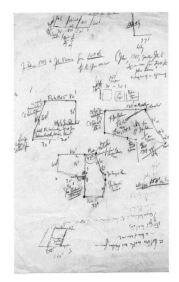

CHARLES OLSON: *SALE OF LAND DIAGRAM,* CA. 1959–1961.
Paper, manuscript in pencil and blue ink, 12 x 8 inches.
Archives and Special Collections at the Thomas J. Dodd Research Center, University of Connecticut Libraries.
THIS STUDY OF LAND PLOTS, PART OF OLSON'S RESEARCH FOR THE MAXIMUS POEMS, BEARS A SIMILARITY TO SOME OF JOSEF ALBERS' STUDIES FOR ABSTRACT PAINTINGS IN ITS CONCERN FOR MEASURED EDGES.

[155] Robert Creeley, in an interview with Vincent Katz, 30 July 2001.

[156] Joseph Fiore, in an interview with Vincent Katz, 26 July 2001.

226 >

GERALD VAN DE WIELE
ZOE, 1975.
Oil on board, 14 ¼ x 12 ¾ inches.
Collection of the artist.

JOSEPH FIORE
HOMAGE TO PICASSO II, 2001.
Oil on paper, 16 x 24 inches.
Collection of the artist.

RICHARD BOGART
LAST LIGHT, 2000.
Oil on canvas, 35 x 60 inches.
Collection of Denise N. Di Salvo.

GWENDOLYN KNIGHT
STANDING HORSE, 1999.
Etching, 18 ½ x 18 inches.
Courtesy of the artist and Francine Seders Gallery, Seattle. Artwork copyright Gwendolyn Knight Lawrence,
courtesy of Jacob and Gwendolyn Lawrence Foundation. Photograph by Spike Mafford.

ROBERT RAUSCHENBERG
QUIET HOUSE, BLACK MOUNTAIN, C. 1949.
Gelatin silver print, 20 x 16 inches.
San Francisco Museum of Modern Art. Purchased through a gift
of Phyllis Wattis. Photograph by Ben Blackwell.

ROBERT RAUSCHENBERG
MERCE, 1952.
Gelatin silver print, 19 15/16 x 16 inches.
San Francisco Museum of Modern Art. Sale of Paintings
Fund purchase. Photograph by Ben Blackwell.

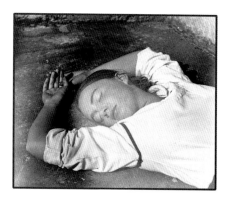

ROBERT RAUSCHENBERG
PORTFOLIO I, 1952.
Portfolio of 7 gelatin silver contact prints mounted to rag board.
Conceived and published in 1998.
Each image: 5 ⅝ x 3 ¼ inches, each board: 14 ½ x 12 inches.
Courtesy of the artist and Pace MacGill Gallery, New York.

ROBERT RAUSCHENBERG
PORTFOLIO II, 1952.
Portfolio of 6 gelatin silver contact prints mounted to rag board.
Conceived and published in 1998.
Each image: 5 ⅝ x 3 1/4 inches, each board: 14 ½ x 12 inches.
Courtesy of the artist and Pace MacGill Gallery, New York.

CY TWOMBLY

ROBERT RAUSCHENBERG, TETUÁN,
1952–1999.
Dry print, 16 15/16 x 11 inches.
Collection of Nicola del Roscio, Rome.

FRANZ KLINE, BLACK MOUNTAIN COLLEGE,
1952–1999.
Dry print, 16 15/16 x 11 inches.
Collection of Nicola del Roscio, Rome.

JOHN CAGE, BLACK MOUNTAIN COLLEGE,
1952–1999.
Dry print, 16 15/16 x 11 inches.
Collection of Nicola del Roscio, Rome.

BAY OF NAPLES, 1994–1999.
Dry print, 16 15/16 x 11 inches.
Collection of Nicola del Roscio, Rome.

PEONIES, BASSANO IN TEVERINO,
1980–1990.
Dry print, 16 15/16 x 11 inches.
Collection of Nicola del Roscio, Rome.

JOHN CHAMBERLAIN
UNTITLED NUMBER 34109.03, 1991.
Ektacolor print, edition 3 of 9, 24 x 20 inches.
Courtesy of PaceWildenstein, New York.
Photograph by Kerry Ryan McFate.

JOHN CHAMBERLAIN
UNTITLED NUMBER 34105.05, 1997.
Ektacolor print, edition 5 of 9, 20 x 24 inches.
Courtesy of PaceWildenstein, New York.
Photograph by Kerry Ryan McFate.

IRWIN LUBROTH
THE LANDSCAPE CORRECTED I, OCTOBER 1999.
Color Photograph, 39 ⅖ x 26 ⅖ inches.
Collection of the artist.

FANNIE HILLSMITH
OVER THE CITY, 1991.
Acrylic on canvas, 36 x 36 inches (nine panels, 12 x 12 inches each).
Courtesy of Susan Teller Gallery, New York.

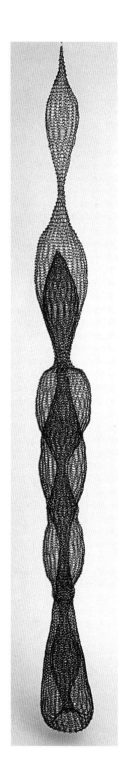

RUTH ASAWA
UNTITLED, CA. 1954.
Black and brown iron wire,
81 x 8 inches.
Black Mountain College Museum and Arts
Center, Asheville.

JAMES BISHOP
UNTITLED NUMBER 1, CA. 1990.
Oil on paper, 11 13/16 x 11 13/16 inches.
Courtesy of Galerie Jean Fournier, Paris. Photograph by Julien Fileyssant.

JAMES BISHOP
UNTITLED NUMBER 2, CA. 1990.
Oil on paper, 7 7/8 x 8 1/4 inches.
Courtesy of Galerie Jean Fournier, Paris. Photograph by Julien Fileyssant.

JAMES BISHOP
FOR VIOLA FARBER, 1964.
Oil on canvas, 59 x 59 inches.
Collection Jean-François et Marie-Aline Prat, Paris.

 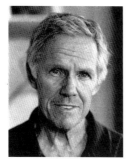  

JOSEPH FIORE. JEFFERSON, MAINE, 2001.
PHOTOGRAPH BY VINCENT KATZ.

GERALD VAN DE WIELE IN HIS STUDIO. NEW YORK,
2001. PHOTOGRAPH BY VIVIEN BITTENCOURT.

JOHN CHAMBERLAIN. SHELTER ISLAND, 2001.
PHOTOGRAPH BY VIVIEN BITTENCOURT.

KENNETH NOLAND IN HIS STUDIO. PORT CLYDE,
MAINE, 2001. PHOTOGRAPH BY VINCENT KATZ.

that the camera allows, his latest series of dry prints of photographs taken in various periods, some from his Black Mountain days. John Chamberlain uses the photographic image as a sculptural element, bending it to his will as easily as he does the body of an automobile. Irwin Lubroth, who studied with Callahan at Chicago's Institute of Design and then at Black Mountain with Albers and Fuller, moved to Madrid as an architect and photographer who pushes the styles he learned early on into new phases. Lubroth is a devotee of abstraction in nature, using filters and shifts of focus to turn a fields into a glowing areas of color. The classicism of his technique seduces the viewer, while the intensity of his hues blinds him. Williams continues to publish exquisite books and to make stunningly affecting portraits.

Some artists have stuck to the guns of their modernist education. James Bishop has continued to make paintings and works on paper that are dazzling examples of reduction. Despite their simplicity, a roiling emotion exists in a brushstroke or the depth of a tone, perhaps a testimony to Bishop's studying with Esteban Vicente at Black Mountain. Certainly, Bishop moved in his own direction in the 1960s, as in the powerful *For Viola Farber*, 1964. In this period, Bishop worked with simple shapes neither rectilinear nor hard-edge, although they sometimes gave those impressions. Their blockiness recalls the 1960s' need to strip to essentials. The title puts one in mind of Farber's work with the Cunningham company. There too, one senses shared concerns of simplicity, for removing the deeper significations from a work, leaving simply movement. Bishop is a cunning colorist too, as this piece makes clear, and the effect of his choices is not simply in interaction, but in the plain quality of each color, alone. Focus on a single tone was something he pursued in the 1970s. Today he works on paper on an intimate scale to pursue expression with the unpredictable sweep of a brush or line. Perhaps, sometimes, he thinks back on Vicente's strokes.

Fannie Hillsmith is another artist who continues to work within a modernist vision in such paintings as *Over the City*, 1991, where she accesses a formalist version of a particular view—in this case houses in a community—and treats it with pla-

nar division and subdivision, nevertheless allowing the whole to breathe with a democratic grace. Ruth Asawa has always been one of the most admired members of the Black Mountain community. Having lived through the Japanese-American internment camps during World War II, Asawa successfully maintained an inner decorum, creating works such as *Untitled*, ca. 1954 that suggest that history is simply how things happen, yet one must be personally accountable for every link in the continuing folly.

Betty and Pete Jennerjahn still work and think spontaneously. Betty makes an analogy between her attitudes toward dance and painting in *Fiesta*, 1997, while Pete's series of paintings poured onto canvas, entitled "Wounds," reference the wounds of Christ. *Threadbare Rose*, 2001, is a painting that grew out the "Wounds" series.

Basil King's art has taken a different path since his student days. At a certain point in the 1960s, King, who had worked as an assistant to Gottlieb, Motherwell, Newman and Rothko, turned to the figure as a major source of inspiration. "My first love was abstract expressionism," writes King. "When I stopped being an abstract expressionist, I had the courage to look for something new, and I believe I got that at Black Mountain. The people there were brave. They persisted at a time when nobody wanted them."[157] In *Mirage CN*, 1993, King makes use of a free reference to human physiognomy, rendering the figure more fantastical than realistic, allowing its emotional and formal valences to take precedence.

Gregory Masurovsky, born in New York in 1929, studied with Bolotowsky at Black Mountain and later with Will Barnet at the Art Students League in New York. He moved to Paris in 1954 with his wife, painter Shirley Goldfarb, and has lived there ever since. He works almost exclusively in ink on paper, making large drawings that utilize a pointillist technique to highlight the breakdown point in

PAT PASSLOF IN HER STUDIO. NEW YORK, 2001. PHOTOGRAPH BY VINCENT KATZ.

DOROTHEA ROCKBURNE IN HER STUDIO. NEW YORK, 2001. PHOTOGRAPH BY VIVIEN BITTENCOURT.

ROBERT CREELEY. WALDOBORO, MAINE, 1998. PHOTOGRAPH BY VIVIEN BITTENCOURT

JOHN WIENERS. BOSTON, 2001. PHOTOGRAPH BY VINCENT KATZ.

[157] Basil King, e-mail to Vincent Katz, 11 July 2002.

234 >

ELIZABETH JENNERJAHN
FIESTA, 1997-2002.
Oil on canvas, 24 x 30 inches.
Collection of the artist.

PETE JENNERJAHN
THREADBARE ROSE, 2001.
Acrylic on canvas, 48 x 44 inches.
Collection of the artist.

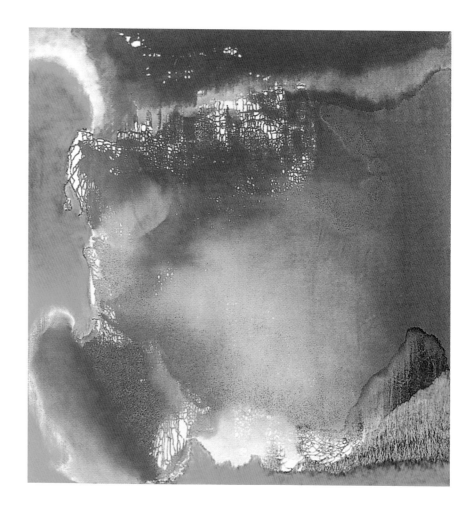

BASIL KING
MIRAGE CN, 1993.
Oil on canvas, 25 x 22 inches.
Collection of the artist.

GREGORY MASUROVSKY
PASSAGE I, 1999.
Pen and ink on Ingres MBM Arches paper, 24 ⅘ x 18 ¹⁵⁄₁₆ inches.
Collection of the artist. Photograph by J. Hyde.

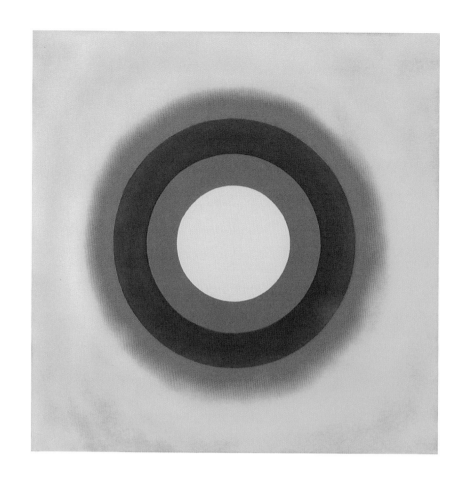

KENNETH NOLAND
MYSTERIES: RED IMAGE, 2001.
Acrylic on canvas, 36 x 36 inches.
Collection of the artist.

PAT PASSLOF
CHESTNUT, 2001.
Oil on linen, 36 x 36 inches.
Collection of the artist.

DAN RICE
BARBARA'S GARDEN SURROUNDS THE HOUSE THAT JACK BUILT, 1992.
Oil on canvas, 69 x 69 ½ inches.
Collection of the artist.

DAN RICE
DON WESTLAKE AS SEEN FROM ABOVE, 1978.
Oil on canvas, 26 x 24 inches.
Collection of the artist.

EMERSON WOELFFER
UNTITLED, 1995.
Acrylic on canvas, 24 x 20 inches.
Courtesy of Manny Silverman Gallery, Los Angeles.

#10

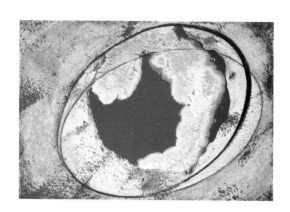

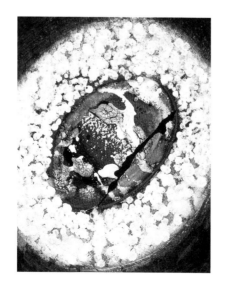

DOROTHEA ROCKBURNE
PARAMETERS, PERIMETERS AND SHADOW,
1991.
Lascaux Aquacryl, colored pencil and
watercolor stick on paper, 26 x 39 ⅞ inches.
Courtesy Artemis Greenberg van Doren, New York.

REINVENTING THE ELEMENTS: COPPER,
EGYPTIAN BLUE & ISAAC NEWTON (Nº 10),
2001.
Lascaux Aquacryl, pencil, copper, on Holbein
paper, 6 x 4 inches.
Courtesy Artemis Greenberg van Doren, New York.

REINVENTING THE ELEMENTS: COPPER,
EGYPTIAN BLUE & ISAAC NEWTON (Nº 31),
2001.
Lascaux Aquacryl, pencil, copper, on Holbein
paper, 6 x 4 inches.
Courtesy Artemis Greenberg van Doren, New York.

RED AND BLUE, 1999–2001.
Aquacryl, Caran D'Ache, silver One Shot
enamel, Deka-white enamel, on Moulin de
Larroque paper, 12 ½ x 17 ⅛.
Courtesy Artemis Greenberg van Doren, New York.

STAR FORMATION, 1999–2000.
Aquacryl, Caran D'Ache, silver One Shot
enamel, Deka-white enamel, on Moulin de
Larroque paper, 17 ⅛ x 12 ½.
Courtesy Artemis Greenberg van Doren, New York.

KENNETH SNELSON
FOREST DEVIL'S MOON NIGHT, 1990.
Digital image made on Silicon Graphics work station using
Wavefront Technologies software, dimensions variable.

SUSAN WEIL
BLUE CONFIGURATION, 2000.
Acrylic paint on fragmente paper, 60 x 66 inches.
Collection of the artist.

CLAIRE ZEISLER: *BUDDY BALLS*, 1972.
Styrofoam covered in wool pile, dimensions variable.
The Minneapolis Institute of Arts.
The Ethel Morrison Van Derlip Fund.

image perception. Masurovsky's drawings are closer to Michaux's than to Seurat's, though Masurovsky's centralized forms are more unified than the French painter and writer's squirming masses.

Noland has maintained the geometric provision with which he began at Black Mountain. His most recent work glows with a tonal richness merely schematic when he was a student. Passlof continues with painterly abstraction, but in an area where the shapes she devises take precedence over the field, as in *Chestnut, 2001*, and often these shapes have geometric derivations. Woelffer paints lyrical abstractions in which the stroke maintains much of its former glory, though in a cadence that can seem geometrically regulated. Rice's recent paintings effectively bring abstraction and landscape into an enduring embrace, and he is now producing some of the most exciting work in this area.

Rockburne has said that, "Black Mountain was a terrific experience educationally. I use some aspect of it every day of my life, and that's what education should be." She goes on to stress the accumulated power of her math lessons in creating the energy-laden drawings she makes today, in which pigment applied in a manner so labor-intensive ends up being so light in effect. Work is a daily practice, and that too comes from Black Mountain: "I couldn't be doing this work if I hadn't done those classes with Max Dehn. I use some translations. But this is all Black Mountain-based."[158]

Kenneth Snelson still works with floating compression—sometimes in large sculptures, sometimes in computer-generated images that demonstrate his readiness to carry his principles of new thinking into the future. Susan Weil still imagines the body fragmented in sections and paints them, arriving at imposing large-scale friezes that cover a wall with mysterious conclusions about the body's allure and defenselessness.

Claire Zeisler took the "female" art of weaving into realms unpredicted even by the prescient Anni Albers. Zeisler created monumental free-hanging sculptures from hand-knotted fabrics. She has made offbeat sculptures with fabric surfaces, such as *Buddy Balls*, 1972, while a more traditional format, as in *Chamois*, allowed Zeisler to exhibit her masterful invention in design and technique.

Just before Black Mountain shut down in 1956, Charles Olson typed up a diagram projecting a life for the college after its closing: a rebirth in various temporary satellite projects linked to specific geographical settings: a theater institute under Duncan in San Fransciso, a "weekend academy," perhaps with Kline's involvement, in New York, etc. In a strange way, looking back now, these communities, cognizant or not of Olson's diagram and directive, did in fact come into existence. In particular, Black Mountain people and ideas continued to thrive in New York, San Francisco and elsewhere. The Cedar Bar in New York was a nexus for Chamberlain, Creeley, Dawson, de Kooning, Kline, et al., while San Francisco was home to Alexander, Borregard, Duncan, Field, and Rumaker, with

[158] Dorothea Rockburne, in an interview with Vincent Katz, 10 July 2001.

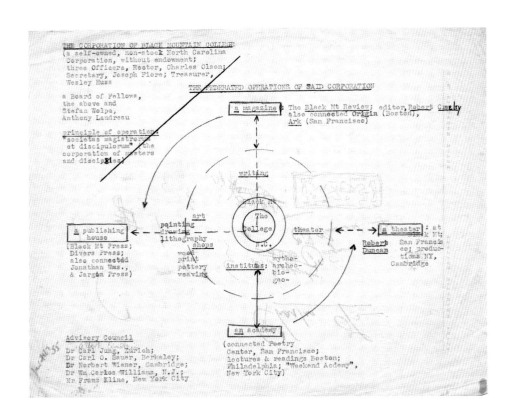

PLAN FOR THE OPERATION OF BLACK MOUNTAIN
COLLEGE AFTER 1956 BY CHARLES OLSON, 1956.
Archives and Special Collections at the Thomas J. Dodd
Research Center, University of Connecticut Libraries.

memorable visits by Creeley, Olson, and Wieners. Even today, these and other satellites continue to spin in uncanny orbit, as a new generation of poets arises devoted to Black Mountain writers, and Black Mountain aesthetic issues in the other arts are revived.

This may be the final thought (for now): the need to set foot there, wherever there now is, the need to be absolutely in the place, thereby knowing not only that place, but all other places.

V. K.

Martin Brody

THE SCHEME OF THE WHOLE:
BLACK MOUNTAIN AND THE COURSE OF
AMERICAN MODERN MUSIC

"Soon? Why not now? Here goes!"
—LOU HARRISON
Letter to Frank Wigglesworth,
written at Black Mountain in 1951.

WHAT OCCURRED there still seems implausible:

1944: A Schoenberg Festival, the most significant gathering of émigré and American Schoenbergians to occur in the U.S.

1946: the German musicologist, Edward Lowinsky, completes a groundbreaking study of chromatic practice in the Renaissance.

1948: Cage presents a series of "Amateur" Satie performances; Arthur Penn stages Satie's *Le Piège de Méduse*, with Merce Cunningham, Buckminster Fuller, and Elaine de Kooning; Cage orates a "Defense of Satie," exposing the fault lines of avant-garde debate for the coming decade.

The epochal works composed in the 1950s: Stefan Wolpe's *Enactments*, John Cage's *Williams Mix*, Lou Harrison's *Praise for the Beauty of Hummingbirds*, the '52 "Happening" . . .

MUSIC CUBICLE, PAUL BEIDLER ARCHITECT. CONSTRUCTED BY STUDENTS. LAKE EDEN CAMPUS, SUMMER 1945.

David Tudor's comprehensive exploration of experimental and avant garde piano music: The Boulez Sonatas, Cage's *Music of Changes*, Wolpe's *Passacaglia*, works of Morton Feldman, Christian Wolff, Earle Brown; and the prior generation—Schoenberg, Webern, Messiaen . . .

The mythic collaborations and dialogues: Cage/Cunningham, Cage/Rauschenberg, Tudor/Wolpe, Harrison/Litz, Tudor/Cage, Cage/Fuller, Wolpe/Kline, Wolpe/Olson . . . .

How did a provincial experimental college become a vortex of musical modernism, a haven for middle European composers and musicologists and a breeding ground for the American musical avant-garde?

DINNER GONG. BLACK MOUNTAIN COLLEGE. PHOTOGRAPH BY BEAUMONT NEWHALL. Copyright Beaumont Newhall, © 2002, The Estate of Beaumont Newhall and Nancy Newhall. Courtesy of Scheinbaum and Russek Ltd., Santa Fe, NM.

I. The Scheme of the Whole

The explosion of musical activity that would occur at Black Mountain and the unique role it would play in the American music scene could not have been antici-

[1] I am grateful to Vincent Katz for providing material from the Black Mountain archives and excerpts from his interviews with Black Mountain alumni—and for stimulating conversation about Black Mountain and music. Thanks, also, to Caroline Jones for discussions of John Cage and for her article, "Finishing School: John Cage and the Abstract Expressionist Ego," Critical Inquiry 19, Summer 1993, 643–674, which helped me enormously to think about Cage.

pated in September 1933, when an aspiring young composer named John Evarts offered his credentials to the college's Rector, John Andrew Rice. It was only a week before students began to gather at Robert E. Lee Hall; a faculty was quickly being assembled. To support his candidacy for a faculty post, Evarts submitted a self-effacing, even apologetic, artistic autobiography. The young musician confessed that he had learned to read the bass clef only a few years earlier, while a junior at Yale College:

> My musical elders impressed it upon me that if I wished to go farther in composition I should learn to read music—piano music. The dubious gift of being able to approximate the effect of a piece of music without reading it had made me lazy about trying to read. Having been trained along the one stave of violin music I was like a frightened rabbit when confronted with the double stave of a piano score and could do little with it.

Studying in Germany two years later, he was still resigned to improving his basic skills. "[M]y Herr Professor decided that my weakness in reading demanded full concentration on the piano," he admitted, before concluding his résumé with a short list of his professional credentials: a single year of preparatory school teaching and a brief stint as assistant music critic for the *Brooklyn Daily Eagle* ("the income from [which] was little more than enough for car fare"). He signed off with characteristic candor: "Though my musical abilities are still limited, I think I might fit in to the scheme of the whole."[2]

Despite his dubious credentials, Evarts had conspicuous advantages for employment at the new college. He was a protégé of Thomas Whitney Surette, Director of the Concord Summer Music Institute and mentor to Black Mountain's co-founder, Ted Dreier. In imagining a scheme of the whole for their educational experiment in the Blue Ridge Mountains, the founders had been deeply influenced by Surette's resonant pronouncements about the centrality of musical and artistic experience in the development of the humane person. "There is in every one of us a region of sensibility in which mind and emotion are blended and from with the imagination acts," Surette intoned in an article in *The Atlantic Monthly* written in 1917, "and it is to this sensibility that music appeals.[3] In a retrospective account of the music program, Evarts summarized the practical proposals of his mentor that he had imported to Black Mountain: "Expose students to only the best in musical literature—the best in 'serious' music, the best in folk music. Learn as much as possible through doing: through singing and through playing and instrument . . . Music is not only important as a field of study, it should become a part of daily life," and so forth.[4] Such truisms had little relevance to the self-proclaimed "ultra-modern" composers of Surette's generation, who set the terms for an urban American avant-garde in the years just before Black Mountain opened. While Surette spoke about

[2] Letter from John Evarts to John Andrew Rice, September 7, 1933, Black Mountain College Papers, vol. III, North Carolina Museum of Art, North Carolina State Archives, Raleigh.

[3] "The Symphony," *Atlantic Monthly*, January 1917, 71. Surette wrote a series of influential articles in the *Atlantic Monthly* in 1916–1917.

[4] John Evarts, "Music at Black Mountain College, 1933–1942," ms.

the civic virtues of music to a broad intelligentsia, the advocates of the avant-garde pondered the technical implications and metaphysics of dissonance. Charles Seeger developed advanced theories of dissonant counterpoint, Dane Rudhyar meditated on dissonance and theosophy, Henry Cowell extended dissonance procedures to rhythm; and the American avant-garde perennially debated the rationale of Arnold Schoenberg's "emancipation of the dissonance" and his "twelve-tone method."

Surette's "moderns," however, were not Schoenberg, Seeger, or Rudhyar, but Walt Whitman, T.S. Eliot and Herbert Spenser—who he conjured in an erudite argument placing music at the heart of liberal education.[5] Surette's pedagogy filled a void for progressive-era music teachers, searching for a rapprochement of European musical high culture and modern, "American" values: democracy, group participation, learning through direct engagement and experience. Evarts, like Dreier, was a true believer. "I enjoyed those weeks [at Surette's Concord School]— the enthusiasm of the place, the participation in so much great music, more than I can say," he gushed to Rice in his letter of introduction. Just as importantly, Evarts would work for free: "Mr. Surette sent me a telegram, saying he had recommended me for the music post in a college on the point of being founded," he recalled years later, in a memoir of Black Mountain, "no salary, but an exciting job."[6] Evarts joined the faculty immediately and he remained at the college until enlisting in the army in 1942. Black Mountain provided him with a range of opportunities unimaginable in more conventional music departments. The young instructor eagerly threw himself into each disparate project, teaching a handful of music appreciation courses and private piano lessons, directing a madrigal group, leading community singing, and playing popular songs for social dances.

With a population that grew from only twenty-two to seventy-four students between 1933 and 1939 and included no music majors, few spaces for private practice, and a miscellaneous, ever-changing ensemble of performers, the music curriculum at Black Mountain seemed destined to remain modest. The registration records for the spring of 1939 list only nine participants in what was euphemistically called "orchestra," while twice as many students were enrolled in folk dancing.[7] For experienced musicians who joined the Black Mountain faculty, the college's blurry academic categories and haphazard music offerings might be more appealing in principle than in practice. Alan Sly, a British composer and pianist (himself an alumnus of the Surette School), joined the faculty in 1935. Like Evarts, Sly participated in all aspects of the music program, arranging music for Black Mountain's erratic ensembles, even building bamboo flutes for students who had no other instruments at hand. But Sly seemed less inclined than Evarts to submit to the college's inchoate scheme of the whole. "Please don't say 'Advanced Piano' any more," Sly wrote in a 1938 curriculum memo, "as there ain't no such animal at

SATURDAY NIGHT PARTY (JOHN EVARTS AT PIANO, JOSEF ALBERS IN SUSPENDERS WITH CIGARETTE). BLACK MOUNTAIN COLLEGE, 1930S.

[5] See, for example, "What is Music?," *Atlantic Monthly*, February 1916, pp.188–197 and "Music and Life," Atlantic Monthly, March 1917, pp. 372–380.

[6] Evarts, "Music at Black Mountain College."

[7] "Registration, Spring Semester, December 15, 1938," Black Mountain College Papers, vol. II Box 35, North Carolina Museum of Art, North Carolina State Archives, Raleigh.

SPECTODRAMA: PLAY, LIFE, ILLUSION (1924–1937) BY XANTI SCHAWINSKY, PRESENTATION AT BLACK MOUNTAIN COLLEGE 1936–1937, DIRECTED BY SCHAWINSKY, MUSIC BY JOHN EVARTS, PART IV, SCENE 1 (*LEFT AND ABOVE*), AND PART III, SCENE 2.

THE DANSE MACABRE: A SOCIOLOGICAL STUDY, DESIGNED AND DIRTECTED BY XANTI SCHAWINSKY, BLACK MOUNTAIN COLLEGE, SATURDAY, MAY 14 TH, 1938. Bauhaus-Archiv, Berlin.

BMC." He preferred the term "'Individual Msuic [sic] Lessons' [to] allow for private lessons in ukele, harp, or anything else that takes their little fancies."[8] Sly decamped shortly thereafter for a position at the College of William and Mary.

However, even in the inchoate, first phases of the music program, there were extraordinary opportunities for artistic experimentation. In 1936–1937, Evarts, with Alan Sly's assistance, participated in a series of collaborations with a genuine avant-garde firebrand, Alexander Schawinsky, a Bauhaus alumnus and former assistant to Oskar Schlemmer. Evarts, who already had copious experience improvising music for popular films, extemporized for Schawinsky's *Spectodrama: Play, Life, Illusion* and produced a fully scored composition (based on improvised variations on the *Dies Irae*) for *Danse Macabre, a Sociological Study*. Describing *Spectodrama* in one of his memoirs of Black Mountain, Evarts seems intrepid, but there is an unusually quizzical undertone: "the play of abstract forms and sounds, with original musical accompaniment. It was all quite strange to us Americans and its values were much debated, but it was a provocative eye-opener."[9]

"The Lady of Great Estate," section III of Evarts's score from *Danse Macabre* reveals no such ambition to provoke.[10] The composition appears to have been notated in haste; there are no dynamics, articulations, or phrase markings in the score. And Evarts's music is conventional in its texture, phrasing, and melodic structure, though inflected with hints of "exoticism": temperate modal inflections and gently jazzed-up harmonies. Evarts's description of his role in the ("mystifying") *Spectodrama*, suggests an unresolved relationship between his music and Schawinsky's more radical conception: "Perhaps the music added a certain humanizing sauce to the whole."[11]

Indeed, neither Evarts nor the college's leadership was prepared to forge a rapprochement between the advanced modernism of Albers and Schawinsky and the high-minded humanism of Surette. Nor were they equipped to steer a course through the shifting terrain of America's burgeoning modern music sub-culture. In the fall of 1935 Henry Moe (Secretary to the Guggenheim Foundation and advisor to the Black Mountain elders) in consultation with Surette, installed Dante Fiorillo as resident composer at the college. The prolific, if eccentric, Fiorillo produced lyricalworks with such pertinent titles as *The Black Mountain Suite*, *The John Andrew Rice Suite*, and *The Surette Suite*. However, as Mary Emma Harris recounts in The Arts at Black Mountain College, the resident composer was forced to leave the college ignominiously. At a time when few contemporary music scores were published and recordings of new music were virtually non-existent, Fiorillo had solicited numerous pieces from European colleagues, with the apparently altruistic goal of securing performances for them in the United States. Alan Sly suspected Fiorillo of less benevolent intentions when he detected a strong similarity between a work of Fiorillo

XANTI SCHAWINSKY, 1929. PHOTOGRAPH BY JOSEF ALBERS. Bauhaus-Archiv, Berlin.

[8] Ibid., "Registration, 1938–39"

[9] Evarts, "Music at Black Mountain College."

[10] Thanks to Vincent Katz for providing a photocopy of the ms. "The Lady of Great Estate."

[11] Evarts, "Music at Black Mountain College," p. 5.

and one of the solicited scores. Sly reported his suspicions of plagiarism to Moe and Surette, and Fiorillo was banished. (Henry Moe, however, continued to advocate his protégé, who received an unequalled four consecutive terms as a Guggenheim Fellow between 1934 and 1938. By 1950, Fiorillo had disappeared completely from the music scene, leaving behind a catalogue listing hundreds of compositions, but only a handful of extant manuscripts.)[12]

II. The Necessary Attributes of a "Real" Composer

The vagaries of the music curriculum and the uncertain role that "advanced" composition would play in the scheme of the whole may have been especially evident at a small, unaccredited experimental school where the arts had been placed front and center. But the ambiguous status of music at Black Mountain was hardly unique among institutions of higher education, experimental or otherwise, in the United States in the 1930s. Although an inchoate structure for the performance of modern music had emerged in New York and a few other American cities by the time Black Mountain was founded, the role of modern music in civic and academic life had hardly been defined.[13] For ambitious, urbane, American musicians, the decade of the 1930s was a critical time. Composers such as Henry Cowell, Aaron Copland, and Roger Sessions believed that they were founding a new culture that might emerge out of the ashes of Europe. But the questions of how to interpret and assimilate the European legacy and the innovations of European modernists—especially those of Arnold Schoenberg—seem as perplexing as they were urgent. "There can no longer be any question that music, like every other manifestation of Western culture, stands under the sign of crisis," Roger Sessions wrote in the essay, "Music and Crisis" in 1933.[14]

Sessions's student, Milton Babbitt, emphasized that this was equally a time of opportunity as well as peril, an "era during which, first mainly in New York but eventually throughout the country, thinking in and about the total musical environment was transformed." However, for Babbitt, the signal event of the season was not the inauguration of a new college in the Blue Ridge Mountains, but Schoenberg's arrival in the Harbor of New York, six weeks later. Schoenberg's landing marked "the sudden, unforeseen transplantation of all that were the diverse, often revolutionary modes of contemporary musical creation, re-creation and explication, from—mainly—Austria and Germany to, mainly, this country, and by—mainly—those very persons, even celebrities, who had invented, molded, and developed those modes."[15]

---

[12] See Mary Emma Harris, *The Arts at Black Mountain College* (Cambridge and London: MIT Press, 1988), p. 35; and C. Matthews "Berthold Goldschmidt: Orchestra Music," *Tempo*, 184 (1984), 12.

[13] Both the Pan American Association of Composers (led by Edgar Varèse, Henry Cowell, Carlos Chávez, and Carl Ruggles) and the Copland-Sessions Concerts began in 1928, following the inauguration of Cowell's publication *New Music: A Quarterly of Modern Compositions* a year prior. (See Carol Oja, *Making Music Modern*, New York: Oxford, 2000.)

[14] Roger Sessions, "Music in Crisis, Some Notes on Recent Musical History," *Modern Music*, X/2, p. 63.

[15] Milton Babbitt, "My Vienna Triangle at Washington Square, Revisited and Dilated," in *Driven into Paradise*, ed. Reinhold Brinkmann and Christoph Wolff (Berkeley and Los Angeles: University of California Press, 1999), p. 39.

Babbitt and Sessions labored unceasingly to analyze these "often revolutionary modes" and argue for their significance to American composition and for the role of modern music in American universities and culture as a whole. For Sessions, the redemption of Western music on American soil would require nothing less than a revitalization of the human spirit through the "emergence of really commanding personalities. [I]t is obviously only through the emergence of such personalities that collapse can be avoided, or [social and cultural] crisis, even in its purely temporary aspects, be resolved," he announced gravely in "Music and Crisis."[16] In turn, Sessions's "commanding personalities," models for young Americans to emulate, would be found among the European musicians who were beginning to emigrate to the United States, most notably his own teacher Ernst Bloch, and (as Sessions only later came to believe) Schoenberg and the surviving members of his Viennese circle.

By contrast, Babbitt prophesied that a new generation of sophisticated Americans would be uniquely positioned to clarify and thus redeem the accomplishments of their Viennese elders. Recalling his first encounters in New York City with the grand figures of the European modern music diaspora—the pianist, Edward Steuermann, the violinist, Rudolph Kolisch, and Schoenberg himself—Babbitt recounted a wistful fantasy: "[I] wish[ed] that [the Viennese music theorist] Schenker and his students, as well as Schoenberg and his students, had been aware that right around the Ringstrasse in Vienna was the "Vienna Circle" . . . with its concern for responsibility and [the] clarity of discourse and the techniques of rational reconstruction [which would have made Schenker's and Schoenberg's theories more logically consistent and accessible]."[17]

Babbitt's fantasy provided an agenda for American musicians, who could be trained both in compositional methods and music theories and in positivist philosophy: to clarify and extend the accomplishments of the Schoenberg and Schenker schools and thereby establish America's modern music credentials.

For these sophisticated and ambitious American composers, like the ultra-moderns of the prior decade, Black Mountain seemed a remote location. Sessions—who had traveled extensively in Europe, studied with a bona fide émigré master, and published careful evaluations of the sophisticated music theories emanating from Vienna—dismissed Surette as "quite superficial," his Concord Institute at best "a little dull [though causing] no harm."[18] Indeed, the musical life of Black Mountain during its first half decade would only have confirmed the anxieties of such cosmopolitan composers as Sessions and Babbitt—that American music had not yet matured and that American composers would not be taken seriously by their European forebears. "[W]hile I gladly admitted and exposed myself further to the foreign influences," Babbitt wrote in a memoir of the thirties, I remained, in the eyes (and probably the ears) of those older and surely educationally differently oriented

[16] Sessions, "Music in Crisis," p. 77.

[17] Babbitt, "My Vienna Triangle," p. 47.

[18] "Letter to John Duke," in *The Correspondence of Roger Sessions*, ed. Andrea Olmstead (Boston: Northeastern University Press, 1992), p. 116.

JALOWETZ COTTAGE, A. LAWRENCE KOCHER
ARCHITECT. PHOTOGRAPH BY A. L. KOCHER.

«INTERIOR OF JALOWETZ COTTAGE, WITH ALBERS
DRAWING ABOVE FIREPLACE [MADE OF TRANSITE —
ASBESTOS CEMENT — ALSO USED ON OUTSIDE OF
STUDIES BUILDING — INEXPENSIVE MATERIAL]».
PHOTOGRAPH AND CAPTION BY A. LAWRENCE
KOCHER.

European musicians, a young American, perhaps "clever" and "knowledgeable," but forever doomed by the absence of that *Geist und Seele* which was not acquirable but was the necessary attribute of a "real" composer.[19]

Babbitt's fear—that America would remain forever young, forever locked in the gaze of a superior European sensibility, and always deficient of the "necessary attributes" of a "real" composer—could hardly have been assuaged by Surette's genteel pieties, Evarts's hapless charm, or Fiorillo's eccentric mischief.

Ironically, however, Black Mountain's savvy innocence, its receptivity to foreign influence, and its embrace of the experimental came to play a crucial role in linking Viennese and American modernism. While the elite American academic establishment found little use for the émigré modernist composers in its midst during the years following the *anschluss*, Black Mountain's doors were open.[20] From the outset, of course, Black Mountain had Albers and, briefly, Alexander Schawinsky. When Heinrich Jalowetz, one of Schoenberg's most admired students, came to the U.S. in 1939, he and his family took the advice of Ernst Krenek and headed straight to Asheville. Jalowetz, who stayed at the college until his death in 1946, had impeccable Old World credentials. A key figure of the Schoenberg circle, he had also studied with the great Viennese musicologist, Guido Adler, knew Mahler, served as conductor of the Cologne Opera, and led premiere performances of works by Schoenberg, Berg, Webern, and Krenek, among others. Just as significantly for the fate of Black Mountain, he seems to have had the character of a saint. While the imperious Schoenberg became a revered but feared mentor to a handful of American students (and while the young Babbitt to feel the cool condescension of his Viennese elders in New York), Heinrich and his wife Johanna Jalowetz embraced the communal life of the college and its idiosyncratic curriculum. "Jalowetz . . . was probably the single most beloved figure in Black Mountain's history," according to Martin Duberman.[21] The middle European composer quickly substituted as father figure for John Evarts when Thomas Whitney Surette died in 1941. Evarts recalled that "Jalowetz [was] entirely in harmony with his [Surette's] ideas"—a tribute to the depth of feeling Evarts felt for both mentors and a sign of the Schoenberg student's magnanimous embrace of the Black Mountain ethos.[22]

Just as Albers had intuitively grasped the ideological compatibility between American progressivism and Bauhaus modernism, Jalowetz seemed to understand the potential synergy between the college's homespun music program, its impressive credentials in abstract art and avant-garde theater, and the culture of central European modern music. Two more émigré musicians, the composer Frederic Cohen (who arrived with significant experience in writing for avant-garde dance and theater) and the musicologist Edward Lowinsky (who had begun a controversial study of chromaticism in Renaissance music), joined him on the faculty in 1942. While prominent guest lecturers and performers had appeared intermittently on campus

[19] Babbitt, "My Vienna Triangle," p. 39.

[20] Exceptionally, Schoenberg taught at UCLA for several years and Krenek at Vassar.

[21] Martin Duberman, *Black Mountain: an Exploration in Community* (New York: Dutton 1972), p.172.

[22] Evarts, "Music at Black Mountain College," p. 4.

MUSIC FACULTY. 1944 SUMMER MUSIC INSTITUTE, BLACK MOUNTAIN COLLEGE, 1944. (FREDERIC COHEN, ELSA KAHL, MARCEL DICK [SEATED ON GRASS], JOHANNA GRAUDAN, HEINRICH JALOWETZ, LOTTE LEONARD [SEATED], NIKOLAI GRAUDAN, RUDOLF KOLISCH, LORNA FREEDMAN KOLISCH, EDWARD LOWINSKY, MARK BRUNSWICK, EDWARD STEUERMANN, ERNST KRENEK, TRUDI STRAUS, ROGER SESSIONS [STANDING]). PHOTOGRAPH BY BARBARA MORGAN. Barbara Morgan Archive.

since the opening of the college, there was now a distinguished staff of European composers and musicologists on the regular faculty. Jalowetz's lectures on the Mozart operas excited the entire community, and he conducted instrumental and vocal ensembles, transcribed the latest of Schoenberg's twelve-tone works (the *Ode to Napoleon*) for performance at the college, and planned a book on his Viennese master. Cohen continued his work in musical theater and assisted Jalowetz in the organization of the 1944 Summer Music Institute. Lowinsky taught innovative courses on early music and completed his study of *musica ficta*, his *Secret Chromatic Art in the Netherlands Motet*.

In the summer of 1945, Lowinsky directed an historic institute at the college, focused on the study of polyphonic music and featured a world-class, guest musicologist, Alfred Einstein. More momentously, it inaugurated a sequence of appointments of African-American musicians and scholars at Black Mountain. Lowinsky recruited the alto, Carol Brice, for a month-long residency. She was joined, at the end of her stay, by the tenor, Roland Hayes, who remained for two weeks after her departure. As a student at Juilliard and the first black winner of the prestigious Naumberg performance prize, Brice had already broken through formidable racial barriers. Hayes was also an imposing figure. The son of a slave, he had been effectively banished from performing in the United States during the early phases of his career. Both performers electrified the community. "It is not the voice alone; it is the whole man, the musician, the artist, the perfection of training as a matter of course . . . what he has to give, to present as a gift," wrote Julia Feininger, after Roland Hayes's recital. "It is very difficult to describe in words, as

ROLAND HAYES, HIS WIFE, AND DAUGHTER AFRICA. BLACK MOUNTAIN COLLEGE, SUMMER, 1945. PHOTOGRAPH BY MARGARET WILLIAMSON.

it is sound and picture in one and the forthpouring soul of the man."[23] Hayes's recital, which itself combined European song repertory (Monteverdi, Haydn, Mozart, Schubert, Saint-Saens, and Debussy) with African-American spirituals and Creole and Afro-Brazilian music, was attended by a uniquely large and integrated audience of several hundred people. In anticipation, Lowinsky had instructed the student ushers for the event to inform visitors that seating would not be segregated—this, in itself, a courageous move in rural North Carolina, in 1945. "[O]ne realizes sharply how much human substance this country is still wasting by its discriminating policies," he ruminated, shortly after meeting Hayes.[24] The college continued in its efforts to integrate and hired the black composer, Mark Fax, for the spring term of 1946.

A year before, Jalowetz had initiated the first of Black Mountain's Summer Music Institutes, a prodigious celebration of Arnold Schoenberg's seventieth birthday. Virtually all of the prominent émigrés of the Schoenberg circle and several of the most ardent American Schoenbergians made the pilgrimage to Black Mountain. Jalowetz launched the festival—which included performances by Steuermann and his students, the singer, Lotte Leonard, and a resident quartet assembled by Rudolf Kolisch—with a grand statement on the role of the arts in "reconstructing our shaken world." His forceful rhetoric must have resonated strongly with at least one of the American participants in the Institute: Roger Sessions. And the Schoenberg Festival offered a unique opportunity for Sessions to interact intimately on a daily basis with precisely the strong personalites (who Milton Babbitt later dubbed the "celebrities" of modern music) that he had summoned in his own writing. The experience at Black Mountain was especially telling for Sessions, who now at least briefly considered the college to be an essential destination. He reported on the Summer Institute to the *New York Times* with breathless enthusiasm:

> I have just returned from attending the first summer Music Institute held at Black Mountain College, N.C., which came to an end recently. The college, which is situated in the Blue Ridge Mountains, was founded in the early Thirties by a group of idealists who believed that education is a kind of collaboration between individuals differing in experience and knowledge but between whom barriers arising from positions of authority are minimized to the utmost extent. In practice this results, as I was able abundantly to observe, in an amazing freedom of discussion which to one coming quite unprepared from the outside world, is extremely impressive in its testimony to the maturity and seriousness of which young Americans are capable. [25]

For a few months, Black Mountain was Sessions's vision of utopia. "Maturity" and "seriousness," the words he summons to describe the "young Americans" who studied there, were strong words for Sessions—the key terms he repeatedly invoked to

[23] Harris, *The Arts at Black Mountain*, p.101.

[24] Duberman, *Black Mountain: An Exploration*, p. 211.

[25] Roger Sessions, "Report on Black Mountain," *New York Times*, September 24, 1944.

describe the great artistic personalities who would rehabilitate culture. While stating his admiration for the free exchange of ideas across "barriers" of "experience and knowledge" (what Babbitt would, more sarcastically, called *Geist und Seele*), Sessions must himself have been enormously grateful for the unprecedented access to the "outstanding personalities" that the Summer Institute afforded:

> Those who worked there in music this summer had the privilege of daily comradeship with the regular music staff, including such outstanding personalities as Heinrich Jalowetz, formerly conductor of the opera at Cologne; Frederic Cohen, who was a leading spirit in organizing the institute, and Edward Lowinsky, eminent musicologist. The summer staff included such distinguished musicians as Edward Steuermann, Ernst Krenek, Marcel Dick, Rudolf Kolisch, Nicolai and Joanna Graudan, Yella Pessi, Lotte Leonard and others.[26]

The Institute also yielded a direct link to Schoenberg. A month after it ended, Sessions sent a copy of his Schoenberg lecture to the master himself. Schoenberg replied effusively in early December, citing the "profound ideas in this article, [which are] of the greatest assistance for a future understanding of my music," and sending a "little '*cadeau*'" to Sessions, the first page of the score of *Die Jakobsleiter*.[27] As Sessions recalled in 1972, "partly as a result of this article, I acquired a very satisfying and quite unforgettable personal relationship with Schoenberg, never as a 'disciple' but rather a loyal friend." He cited this new relationship as a primary reason for his changing appraisal of Schoenberg's accomplishment.[28]

Sessions had, indeed, modified his assessment of the Viennese master. In "Music and Crisis," he had catalogued the Schoenberg school's "tortured and feverish moods, its overwhelming emphasis on detail, its lack of genuine movement, all signs of a decaying musical culture, without fresh human impulses to keep it alive."[29] However, by the time he came to Black Mountain, he had softened his critique and found fresh relevance in Schoenberg as an "American" composer. "As for Vienna, Schoenberg has outlived it as he has outlived Alban Berg. Had he not done so his position might be today less evident than it is," Sessions now argued, further suggesting that in the "works written since 1936 [while living in the U.S.] Schoenberg has achieved a freedom and resourcefulness which carries them . . . far beyond his earlier works." While insisting that he was "in no sense a spokesman" for the "12-tone technique," Sessions stressed that "one must distinguish carefully between technical principles in the abstract, and the works in which they become embodied."[30] Perhaps most importantly, Schoenberg now

---

[26] Ibid.

[27] "Letter from Arnold Schoenberg to Roger Sessions," December 3 [–8], 1944, in *Correspondence of Roger Sessions*, pp. 337-338.

[28] "Roger Sessions, "author's note to "Schoenberg in the United States," in *Roger Sessions on Music*, ed. Edward T. Cone (Princeton: Princeton University Press, 1979), p. 353.

[29] Sessions, "Music in Crisis," p. 73.

[30] Sessions, "Schoenberg in the United States," passim.

represented "uncompromising integrity and independence." He had survived the political and cultural crises of central Europe and might now teach young Americans how to survive as artists in a market-driven culture. "[I]n the face of the most bitter and persistent opposition, score and neglect, [he] has always gone his own way in uncompromising integrity and independence [and] has been and is still the most dangerous enemy of the musical status quo."[31]

Writing eight years after the Summer Institute and only months after his "loyal friend's" death, he went even further in rehabilitating Schoenberg, even assuming the role of a "spokesman" for the twelve-tone system. In 1952, Sessions pronounced Schoenberg's discovery of the twelve-tone meted to be a "historical necessity." What Sessions had previously understood to be a decisive "lack of genuine movement" in the Viennese composer's early music, he now reinterpreted as a phase in a heroic process: Schoenberg had shown the courage to internalize an historical crisis, "living it through to its furthest implications" and emerging triumphantly:

> The truly immense achievement of Schoenberg lies in the fact that his artistic career embodies and summarizes a fundamental musical crisis. More than any other composer he led the crisis to its culmination. He accomplished this by living it through to its furthest implications. But he also found technical means which could enable composers of his own and later generations to seek and find solutions. He opened up a new vein, toward which music had been tending; and the twelve-tone method is in essence the tool through which this vein can be exploited. Its discovery was a historical necessity.[32]

In detailing Schoenberg's "immense achievement," Sessions elaborated arguments that Schoenberg himself had first made in his *Harmonielehre*, that Jalowetz, had admiringly echoed, in a *festschrift* essay honoring Schoenberg's fiftieth birthday, and that Schoenberg had then elaborated in "Composition with Twelve Tones":

> Dissonance and consonance are relative concepts, not fixed for all time; the evolution of dissonance procedures are subject to the dialectic of history, the endpoint of which is the emancipation of the dissonance. In consequence, the emancipated dissonance (really a "remote consonance" to which the "musical ear" has gradually adjusted as Western musical history has unfolded) can be deployed to make music with coherent phrases, motivic development, and fluent harmonic hierarchies—in short, music that continues in the line of the Western canon.[33]

---

[31] Ibid., p. 13.

[32] "Some Notes on Schoenberg and the 'Method of Composing with Twelve Tones,'" *The Score*, May 1952, p. 9.

[33] See Arnold Schoenberg, *Harmonielehre*, and Heinrich Jalowetz, "The Harmonielehre," in "Arnold Schoenberg" (50th Birthday Festschrift), Munich, 1912, reprinted in *Schoenberg and His World*, ed. Walter Frisch (Princeton: Princeton University Press, 1999), pp. 231–237.

Sessions wrote his own first twelve-tone work, the *Sonata for Violin Solo*, a year later, in 1953. Moreover, Sessions, at Princeton, was already one of the most influential composition teachers in the country. Along with his students (and later colleagues at Princeton), Milton Babbitt and Edward T. Cone, he would play a key role in setting the agenda for advanced academic studies in music composition. The interpretation of Schoenberg's music and the extension of the twelve-tone method would come to hold a central, if controversial, place in their academic program. But the "daily comradeship" of the Black Mountain Summer Institute played a key role in forging the personal relationships underlying the professional commitments. "Those who participated in music at Black Mountain this summer will never forget the experience and will certainly do all in their power to keep it alive both there and elsewhere," he wrote in the closing paragraph of his report to the *New York Times*. If Jalowetz (as proxy to Schoenberg) was never allowed into the East Coast academic establishment, he could at least spy the promised land from the peaks of the Blue Ridge Mountains.

III. Finishing School

Regardless of his enthusiasm about the 1944 Summer Institute, Sessions did, for all intensive purposes, forget about Black Mountain College. By the end of the summer, Frederic Cohen had resigned from the college and had enlisted Sessions to join him in inaugurating a rival Summer Institute at Kenyon College. While he continued to write prolifically about musical culture in the 1940s and '50s, Sessions never mentioned the college in his copious essays. The utopia Sessions glimpsed in 1944 must have evaporated before his eyes, as Black Mountain became the "finishing school" that Buckminster Fuller joked about with John Cage and Merce Cunningham, there in the summer of 1948:

> [W]e really did have a great deal of fun because I spent that summer with them on a fun, schematic new school, and I called it "the finishing school." We would finish anything. In other words, we would really break down all of the conventional ways of approaching school . . . [W]e spent the summer trying to decide who would teach what in the finishing school. We had some devastating portfolios . . . [34]

Black Mountain itself was more or less finished as the progressive era school imagined by Rice, Dreier, and Surette; it was well on its way to becoming what Charles Olson would call his "personal college": an intensely collaborative and communal artists' colony. Cage, who had finally taken up residence in the summer of 1948 (having plotted to set up an experimental music center at Black Mountain since 1943), quickly set out to dismantle whatever remained of the Schoenberg cult. His first target was no less than Beethoven and, by extension, the conservative modernism that had prevailed through the war years. The touchstone of Cage's iconoclastic efforts was the music of Satie, the lesson plan of his finishing school course, an exhaustive series of twenty-five "amateur" performances

[34] Buckminster Fuller quoted in Harris, *The Arts at Black Mountain*, p.156.

THE RUSE OF MEDUSA, 1948: BUCKMINSTER FULLER WITH WILLIAM SCHRAUGER. PHOTOGRAPH BY CLEMENS KALISCHER. Courtesy of the artist.

THE RUSE OF MEDUSA, 1948: BUCKMINSTER FULLER. PHOTOGRAPH BY CLEMENS KALISCHER. Courtesy of the artist.

THE RUSE OF MEDUSA, 1948: MERCE CUNNINGHAM. PHOTOGRAPH BY CLEMENS KALISCHER. Courtesy of the artist.

THE RUSE OF MEDUSA, 1948: GROUP PHOTOGRAPH WITH BUCKMINSTER FULLER, JOHN CAGE, ELAINE DE KOONING AND MERCE CUNNINGHAM. PHOTOGRAPH BY CLEMENS KALISCHER. Courtesy of the artist.

JOHN CAGE AT PIANO, 1948.
PHOTOGRAPH BY CLEMENS KALISCHER.
Courtesy of the artist.

(by Cage) of Satie's piano music. The Satie series culminated happily, in a collaborative performance by Merce Cunningham, Bucky Fuller, and Elaine de Kooning
in Arthur Penn's staging of Satie's obscure play, *Le Piège de Méduse.*

The festival, as a whole, displayed Cage's sensitivity to the Black Mountain environment and his skill at subversively modifying the college's communal traditions.
With his own performances, he blurred the distinction between amateur and professional; he forged interdisciplinary partnerships with the poet, M. C. Richards,
the de Koonings, and Arthur Penn on the adaptation of the Satie play (and enlisted Fuller as a performer!); he presented engaging introductory talks before each
of his mini-recitals. But in his primary lecture, "Defense of Satie," he was vehemently confrontational: "Beethoven represents the most intense lurching of the boat
away from its natural even keel," he opined. "The derivation of musical thought
from his procedures has served not only to put us at the mercy of the waves, but
to practically shipwreck the art on an island of decadence.[35] "Such strong rheto-

[35] John Cage, "Defense of Satie," in Richard Kostelanetz, *John Cage, an Anthology* (New York: da Capo,
1970,) p. 81.

ric was interspersed with moments of mysticism and perplexing bits of absurd theater, such as the apparently solemn but entirely cryptic "analysis" near the lecture's end—a listing of the phrase lengths in two movements of Satie's music, the "Hypocritical Chorale" and the "Muscular Fantasy."[36]

The old guard of Black Mountain's music department was in disarray; Jalowetz had died; Lowinsky and Cohen had departed. Only the Prussian composer, Erwin Bodky, a student of Richard Strauss and an early music proponent, remained to lead the counterattack to Cage's polemic. Predictably, Bodky proposed a musical duel—Beethoven Quartet performances as counter-evidence. In a distinctly Black Mountain moment, the controversy itself was "dada-ized" by the current Rector, Bill Levi, who proposed a culinary duel instead—Weiner schnitzel for the Beethoven faction, crêpes suzettes for the Satie group. The proposal apparently led to genuine food fight in the dining hall.[37]

With the Satie Festival, Cage definitively inaugurated the era of the musical avant-garde at Black Mountain and offered a culminating statement of his own aesthetic development to date. "Music," he forthrightly declared, "is a problem parallel to that of the integration of the personality: which, in terms of modern psychology is the co-being of the conscious and unconscious mind, Law and Freedom, in a random world situation."[38] The "integration of the personality" would require a distancing not only from Beethoven, but from Cage's former teacher, Schoenberg, who he now considered to be atavistically attached to the expressive effects of tonal harmony—the ineluctable flow of tension and repose that admits no place for genuine silence. "(Silence cannot be heard in terms of pitch and harmony."[39]) Cage's rejection of Schoenberg and his pairing of Satie and Webern in the "Defense" were, in themselves, seditious. Satie, the ironist, had dismantled the mythology of heroic artistic subjectivity and German supremacy that Webern unswervingly advocated, however radical the implications of his music. In linking the two as his imagined forebears, Cage offered a provocative, apparently paradoxical genealogy for his own work. He famously rejoiced in such eclectic genealogies: Satie and Webern, and Huang Po and Artaud, Coomarasawamy and Thoreau, Suzuki, Duchamp, Buckminster Fuller, and so forth. Such eclectic enthusiasms marked Cage's artistic development: the break with Beethoven and the rejection of the emotional metabolism of tonality; Cage's disillusionment with the response to his own hyper-emotional piece, The Perilous Night (1943–1944); his introduction to the writing of Sri Ramakrishna through the Indian musician, Gita Sarabhai. And Chuang Tze, Huang Po, and Coomaraswamy; and a new con-

[36] Ibid., p. 83.

[37] Duberman, p. 287.

[38] Cage, "Defense of Satie," p. 84.

[39] Ibid., p. 81. Cage's rejection of the harmonic/affective structure of tonal music and his turn to Ramakrishna and Suzuki, as he grappled with personal psychic crises, has been persuasively discussed by Jonathan D. Katz in "John Cage's Queer Silence; or, How to Avoid Making Matters Worse," in Writing through John Cage's Music, Poetry, + Art, ed. Bernstein and Hatch (Chicago and London: University of Chicago Press, 2001), pp. 41–61. The question of how Cage's redefinition of compositional agency and his strategies for creating an ensemble of agents in the artistic process relates to the aesthetics of silence and to constructions of sexuality warrant extended further discussion.

ception of music "to sober and quiet the mind thus rendering it susceptible to divine influences."[40] Then Zen, "unimpededness" and "interpenetration":

> This unimpededness is seeing that in all of space each thing and each human being is at the center and furthermore that each one being at the center is most honored one of all. Interpenetration means that each one of these most honored ones of all is moving out in all directions penetrating and being penetrated by every other one no matter what the time or what the space.[41]

And hence: chance and indeterminacy. Cage's adulation of Webern, his interest in the self-referential structures of serial music and in the formalization of rhythm would provoke the avant-garde for years to come. (Boulez declared the "death" of Schoenberg, and that the ascendancy of Webern was close at hand. Stockhausen, Boulez, Babbitt, and the composers of the Cage circle would all develop new approaches to serialization of rhythm based on time points and durational proportions.) Cage had already begun to work with a scheme of durational proportions in his momentous *Sonatas and Interludes* for prepared piano, completed just before his first trip to Black Mountain and premiered there in the spring of 1948. In the ensuing years he would continue to explore fixed durations and proportions as structural elements. However, with works such as *Music of Changes* for piano, *Imaginary Landscape no. 4* for six radios, and other pieces from the early 1950s, he began to experiment with chance operations and indeterminacy in relationship to the fixing of rhythmic structures. In short, he extended the "finishing school" principle to terminate his relationship to conventions about authorship and authorial intention, while inventing a range of new ways to transform the relationship between composers, performers, and listeners.

In Cage's oeuvre, it is difficult to distinguish between influence, collaboration, and composition. For one thing, he seemed equally interested in communing with the dead as the living. And his collaborations with the living, from the time of his first visit to Black Mountain in 1948 to his return in 1952, would be key in realizing his newly-emerging mission—to place each thing and each human being at the center. The modus operandi of this re-centering project was to disperse the composer's sovereign agency—not simply by surrendering compositional choice to impersonal, aleatoric processes, but by redistributing choices traditionally associated with composition to other human beings. As early as 1941, he had engaged in an exercise in co-composition with Lou Harrison: their *Double Music*, in which they determined a number of pre-compositional parameters and then each independently wrote the music for two of the piece's four simultaneously performing percussionists.

Later, Cage would co-compose in various configurations with the other musicians in his self-proclaimed circle—Christian Wolff, Morton Feldman, Earle Brown, and

[40] Ananda K. Coomaraswamy, "The Transformation of Nature in Art," quoted in James Pritchett, *The Music of John Cage* (Cambridge: Cambridge University Press, 1993), p. 37.

[41] John Cage, "Composition as Process: Communication," in Pritchett, pp. 74–75. Pritchett notes that the text, written in 1958, is adapted from Cage's lectures in 1951–1952.

DAVID TUDOR AT HOME OF MRS. IRA JULIAN ON RETURN TRIP TO NEW YORK FROM BLACK MOUNTAIN COLLEGE, 1953. PHOTOGRAPH BY MRS. IRA JULIAN. Courtesy of North Carolina Museum of Art.

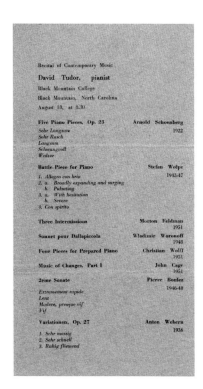

RECITAL BY DAVID TUDOR OF CONTEMPORARY MUSIC FLYER, AUGUST 18, [NO YEAR GIVEN]. PRINTED, GREY PAPER, 9 X 5 INCHES. Archives and Special Collections at the Thomas J. Dodd Research Center, University of Connecticut Libraries.

especially David Tudor. Tudor and Cage had met through Feldman in 1950, and the magisterial piano piece, *Music of Changes*, quickly materialized. Performance, composition, the work itself, became inseparable "At that time he was the Music of Changes," Cage said.[42] "David Tudor was present in everything I was doing," he recalled thirty years later.[43] John Holzaepfel has documented the way this presence worked in piano music from the late 1950s, describing Tudor's extraordinary disciplinary regiment: a vast array of measurements, translation rules, re-notations, and structural choices developed to produce fixed realizations of Cage's indeterminate notation.[44]

Tudor was the consummate partner to develop collaborative compositional procedures; Black Mountain the ideal staging ground for their innovations. It is astonishing to recall how little time John Cage actually spent at Black Mountain (a matter of a few months, mostly during the summers of 1948 and '52)—given the significance of the reciprocal relationship that developed between him and the school. Cage, who first came to Black Mountain with Merce Cunningham, also introduced Lou Harrison to the community. And Harrison introduced David Tudor, who, in turn, introduced Stefan Wolpe. Harrison and Wolpe were the two principal composers on the faculty during the 1950s, and from 1951–1953, Tudor presented a stunning series of virtuoso performances of avant-garde piano music— programs of exceptional length, complexity, and daring. Tudor's recitals focused on Cage and his circle as well as Boulez (with whom Cage was then regularly trading scores and ideas); but he also presented a broad range of otherwise largely inaccessible modern music: Schoenberg school works, Messiaen, Wolpe, Stravinsky and Debussy. Cage also proposed Willem de Kooning and the sculptor, Richard Lippold, for the faculty in the summer of 1948, and he bonded immediately with the young student artist, Robert Rauschenberg, four years later.

If Cage played a crucial role in assembling the breathtaking community of artists at the college in the early 1950s, the college provided Cage with a unique site to present his work—combining a microcosm of the artistically vital New York scene with the intimacy of summer camp. Just as daily contact with the Viennese émigré cohort helped to legitimize Sessions's claim to Schoenberg as a fellow American composer, the close quarters of Black Mountain's artistic/intellectual community provided Cage, at least briefly, with the institute for experimentation that he had imagined. An arts campus committed to the principle of integrating art and life was the ideal place to practice interpenetrability—to produce a radical synthesis of theater, experiments in noise and silence, notation, duration-based formal systems, virtuosity and chance, and the spirituality of music. And, of course, it helped that Black Mountain was ready for almost anything. As de Kooning had reputedly said, "the only thing wrong with the place is that if you go there, they want to give it to you."[45]

[42] Pritchett, p. 78.

[43] For the Birds: John Cage in Conversation with Daniel Charles (Boston: Marion Boyars, 1981), p.178.

[44] John Holzaepfel, "David Tudor and the Solo for Piano," in *Writing through John Cage's Music, Poetry + Art*, pp.137-156.

[45] Duberman, p. 283.

Although he failed in his plan to enlist Black Mountain students into helping with the production of the electronic work-in-progress, *Williams Mix*, Cage could continue to work on the graphic realization of its innovative notational system and complex score. In the summer of 1952, he developed the concept of the piece as well: refining strategies to redistribute compositional choice among sound engineers and co-composers, developing ways to link engineering and composition, devising new analog tape techniques and sound taxonomies. Perhaps most importantly, at a time when Cage's aesthetic had become highly the-oretical—and his work might have become hopelessly abstract—Black Moun-tain grounded him in a community of practice. The "Happening" (*Theater Piece no. 1*) that he and Tudor planned and executed during a single day of his brief residency in the summer of 1952, with Rauschenberg, Cunningham, M. C. Richards, among others, is, perhaps, the most fabled event in the college's his-tory. With *Theater Piece no. 1*, Cage found a perfect complement to the com-plexities of *Williams Mix*—a vivid, simple strategy for the realization of his complex ideas about chance, choice, and the dispersion of artistic agency. The "Happening" succeeded as artistic event, instant avant-garde myth, and philo-sophical text.

Martin Duberman has suggested that the pioneering collaborations of John Evarts and Alexander Schawinsky ought to be acknowledged as precursors to the appar-ently unprecedented *Theater Piece no. 1*, but Duberman's formulation may be turned on its head. That is, only with the arrival of Cage, Tudor, Cunningham, and Rauschenberg did Black Mountain redeem the potential in Evarts's collabora-tions with Schawinsky. With the arrival of Cage, the dissolution of disciplinary boundaries and the new forms of participation in the arts inchoately imagined with the founding of the college came to fruition—in forms that John Andrews Rice and Thomas Whitney Surette would never have dreamed.

IV. "A kind of rebirth . . . "

For Lou Harrison and Stefan Wolpe, the two major composers who served on the faculty during the academic terms of the 1950s, the experience of Black Mountain was arguably as formative as it was for Cage. Harrison came to the college at the age of 37—an experienced composer, who had studied with Schoenberg, Cowell, and Virgil Thomson. However, Harrison (who had also studied Indian music and philosophy with Cage) arrived with a pressing need "to sober and calm" his own mind: he was attempting to recover from a nervous breakdown. Cage had proposed Black Mountain as a refuge from New York, and he helped to arrange Harrison's appointment for the summer of 1951. At first, the experiment in rustic living seemed doomed to fail. In short order, Harrison had destroyed a painting by Joseph Fiore, tore up the score of his own work in progress, the opera *Rapunzel*, and flung a bottle through a window. Things settled down, however, and he was invited to stay on the faculty.

The college became a site of personal transformation. "I had a sudden conversion to country living of a sort when I went to Black Mountain College," he recalled. "I discovered I could never live in a city again . . . I'm a composer. My ears are

JOHN CAGE (LEFT) AND MERCE CUNNINGHAM (RIGHT) AT HOME OF MRS. IRA JULIAN ON TRIP RETURNING TO NEW YORK FROM BLACK MOUNTAIN COLLEGE, 1953. PHOTOGRAPH BY MRS. IRA JULIAN. Courtesy of North Carolina Museum of Art.

260 >

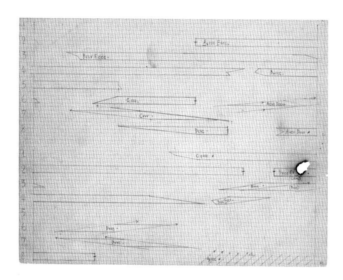

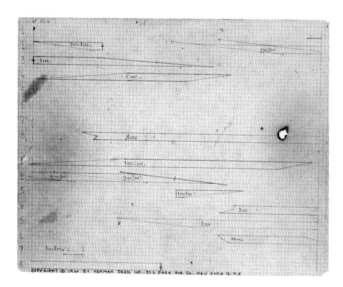

JOHN CAGE
WILLIAMS MIX, 1953.
Music score.
Music Division, The New York Public Library for the Performing Arts, Astor,
Lenox and Tilden Foundations.

LOU HARRISON
THE GLYPH, 1951–1952.
Music score.
Music Division, The New York Public Library for the
Performing Arts, Astor, Lenox and Tilden Foundations.

LOU HARRISON, BLACK MOUNTAIN COLLEGE, 1951.
PHOTOGRAPH BY JONATHAN WILLIAMS.
Collection of Jonathan Williams.

my life, and that means country living."[46] The move to Black Mountain was decisive in charting a new direction in the composer's work. "It was there that I really opted for world music. That also was a big upheaval for [me] . . . But this second upheaval was a kind of rebirth, too."[47] Like Cage, Harrison conjured an alternative to the Schoenberg ethos. And, as it was for Cage, Black Mountain would be an ideal place to invent it. Harrison had assembled an eclectic library for his sojourn in the country: Virgil's *Eclogues*, Harry Partch's *Genesis of a Music*, and A. H. Fox Strangways's *The Music of Hindostan*. The books embodied his current obsessions. Virgil's pastoral inspired his choice of a "simpler kind of music"; Partch was his guide into the world of just intonation; Fox Strangways expanded his awareness of alternative repertories to Euro-ethnic concert music.

Fortified by these texts and reborn in the country, Harrison was prolific. He completed a group of abandoned works, wrote his first piece to simulate Balinese music with western instruments ("Gamelan," from the *Suite for Violin, Piano and Small Orchestra*), and composed an exquisite study in simple transparent pitch relationships and uncommon timbres, *Praise for the Beauty of Hummingbirds*.

[46] Stuart Norman, "Interview with Lou Harrison and William Colvig," *RFD: a Journal for Gay Men Everywhere*, quoted in Heidi Von Gunden, *The Music of Lou Harrison* (Scarecrow Press Inc.: Metuchen, N.J. and London, 1995), p. 108.

[47] Virginia Rathbun and Pascal Pierini, "Ten Harrison Tapes," quoted in Von Gunden, p.111.

With a Guggenheim Fellowship for 1952, he continued to live at the college and completed an entire opera, *Rapunzel*. "I met lots of interesting people . . . Bob Rauschenberg, and Cy Twombly, and Ben Shahn, and of course, the faculty: Wes [Huss], and Charles Olson, and Mrs. Rice," he reminisced in 1972. In later years, he often expressed his appreciation for the opportunity to live among painters there; he seems to have been mesmerized by a large Franz Kline canvas that hung over the concert grand in the dining room.[48] With his extensive experience in composition for dance, he also collaborated happily with the choreographer, Katherine Litz. Harrison composed an "Adjustable Chorale" for her, the length of which could be modified to suit her own evolving conception of a particular dance piece. He also wrote *The Glyph* for Litz as part of an elaborate exchange of faculty work. Olson had had the idea for a glyph poem, inspired by Mayan glyph images; Ben Shahn responded with "A Glyph for Charles," a drawing that Olson described as a "combo of a Mayan glyph & a Chinese written character."[49] Harrison's composition, paired with Litz's dance, completed the set. Charles Oscar, Litz's husband, proposed a link between the two pairs of "Glyph gifts" by painting the Shahn design onto a backdrop for the dance performances.

KATHERINE LITZ, IN *THE GLYPH*, SUMMER 1951. PHOTOGRAPH BY TERI DICK MODLIN. BLACK MOUNTAIN COLLEGE MUSEUM AND ARTS CENTER, ASHEVILLE.

Harrison's music for *The Glyph*, in six terse movements, ranges from energetic, motor rhythms for piano (written in standard notation) to a bald, verbal instruction for movement four: "improvisation on gong or piano: follow dance." The piece, which includes a typical Black Mountain "amateur" ensemble (two bells, claves, a gong, and an optional tuning fork) in addition to a more demanding piano part, demonstrates the composer's command of dance music and the stage. But Harrison's most significant work at Black Mountain would be entirely private—his experiments with tunings. Recounting how he came to work with intonation, Harrison, like Cage, described a personal crisis followed by a change of artistic direction. In the silence of Black Mountain, Harrison could "sit and tune up things":

> [S]ince my breakdown, anyway; I had been sort of been [sic] going back through history to find out where we went wrong, or what could be preserved . . . . as you do through your own life. [What I found was] the sensuous, or the sensual actuality of intonation is true. There's just no getting around it. And once you experience it and know what it consists in, and of, and about it, and obtain some structural visualization of the whole material, the continuum of tuning and ratios, then you can't go back, and your whole musical life changes.[50]

For the most part, the compositions using just intonation would come later, after Black Mountain. (*Four Strict Songs* for eight baritones and orchestra, which calls for just tunings, was begun there in 1951.) But his new course was set, and it would take Harrison away from Cage as much as Schoenberg. For Harrison, the twelve-tone universe was predicated on equal-temperament, and hence might be

[48] Mary Emma Harris, "Interview of Lou Harrison," January 5, 1972, Aptos, California," ms.

[49] Harris, *The Arts at Black Mountain College*, p. 221.

[50] Harris, "Interview of Lou Harrison".

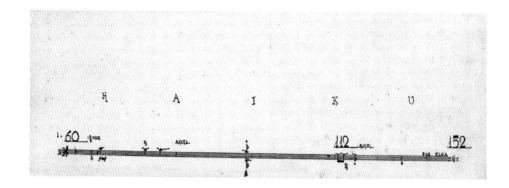

JOHN CAGE
HAIKU, 1952.
Music score, 4¹⁵⁄₁₆ x 12⅘ inches.
The Poetry/Rare Books Collection,
State University of New York, Buffalo.

part of the history of "where we went wrong"; but he also began to disavow Cage's involvement with aleatoric processes. Precision tuning was the means to "preserve [a] relation to art or skill"[51]—an alternative to the emotional turbulence of German music, but a link to traditional notions of compositional control, in contradiction to Cage's evolving ideas about unimpededness, chance, the "un-aesthetic choice."[52]

However unsettled his compositional ideas were during his sojourn at Black Mountain, Harrison appears to have been happy teaching traditional musical skills to a handful of students. He listed harmony, 16th century counterpoint, and composition, an entirely mainstream academic program, as his course offerings in 1952. His break with Cage was, for the time, inchoate. When he set out to launch the Black Mountain College Music Press, with funds he had solicited from Charles Ives, the first (and only) piece to be published was Cage's *Haiku*, a sample of his friend's stunning calligraphy and supremely spare music. Harrison planned a series of beautiful editions of small-scale pieces; works by Ives and Wolpe were scheduled for the series. But *Haiku* was destined to be the sole work in the catalogue. Stefan Wolpe joined the summer faculty in 1952 at the suggestion of Tudor and with the support of Cage. Wolpe quickly befriended Charles Olson. He was asked to stay on, and Harrison reluctantly left Black Mountain in 1953.

V. "The will to connect"

Wolpe, who Theodor Adorno had described as "an outsider in the best sense of the word," a composer who was "impossible to subsume," was a perennial exile.[53] Born in Berlin in 1902, he was driven out of Germany in 1933. He fled to Vienna, where he studied briefly with Webern (and met Jalowetz) before immigrating to Jerusalem (1934–1938) and then the United States. As a young composer, Wolpe had embraced dadaism and leftist politics, joined the Novembergruppe in 1923, and went on, later in the decade to write hundreds of songs and anthems for the

[51] Ibid., p. 18.

[52] The phrase comes from a letter to Pierre Boulez, January 1950: "All this brings me closer to a 'chance' or if you like to an un-aesthetic choice." Jean-Jacques Nattiez, ed., *The Boulez-Cage Correspondence*, (Cambridge: Cambridge University Press, 1993), p.48.

[53] Adorno's comments come from a radio broadcast in 1940; they are quoted in Austin Clarkson, "Stefan Wolpe, 25 August 1902-4, April 1972," in *Stefan Wolpe, A Centenary Celebration, 2002* (Stefan Wolpe Society), p.7.

STEFAN WOLPE, 1953. PHOTOGRAPH BY CLEMENS KALISCHER. Courtesy of the artist.

labor movement and agit-prop theaters along side the radical composer, Hans Eisler. Between 1920 and 1923, he had also returned repeatedly to the Weimar Bauhaus. "[W]e all traveled there like pilgrims to Jerusalem or Mecca," he recalled, thirty years later, listing the faculty artists who had influenced him, among them: Klee, Kandinsky, Schlemmer, Johannes Itten, and Lionel Feininger.[54] As Austin Clarkson has noted, Bauhaus concepts permeate Wolpe's later thinking: "the principles of opposites, proportions, and multidimensional space; the nature of intervals and motions as elements of music . . . the importance of found objects; the synesthetic and vitalistic (even spiritual) nature of the image. . ."[55] As Wolpe recalled, "I remember the experience of the adjacencies of opposites. That was a new concept . . . that all things are in the reach of the human mind, and that to connect is

[54] Stefan Wolpe, "Lecture on Dada," *Musical Quarterly*, 72/2 (1986), p. 204.

[55] "Stefan Wolpe in Conversation with Eric Salzman, Edited and with a Preface by Austin E. Clarkson" *Musical Quarterly*, Fall 1999, 83/3, p. 381.

STEFAN WOLPE

ENACTMENTS FOR THREE PIANOS. MOVEMENT I ("CHANT"), 1953.

Musical score.

a mental act depending on the will to connect."[56] Throughout his life, Wolpe demonstrated a tireless will to connect. He had not only assimilated avant-garde techniques and proletarian music in Berlin but found vivid musical analogs to the visual arts concepts at the Bauhaus; in Vienna, he incorporated the methods of twelve-tone music; in Palestine, he had absorbed the modal systems of classical Arabic music. And in New York, he worked with, and learned from, a stunning range of younger Americans—jazz and pop musicians such as George Russell, John Carisi (an arranger for Miles Davis), Elmer Bernstein and Mike Stoller; and the avant-gardists: Feldman, Tudor, Herbert Brün and Ralph Shapey. By 1950, Wolpe, like Cage, had become a vocal participant in the Eighth Street Club scene. There, he and his wife, the poet Hilda Morley, befriended a number of the artists who would frequent Black Mountain—Willem and Elaine de Kooning, Franz Kline, Estéban Vicente.

And so, when the fifty-year-old émigré composer came to Black Mountain, the college of Albers and Feininger, of David Tudor, Franz Kline, and Willem de Kooning, it was as much a homecoming as a new beginning. Wolpe later recalled the disorientation of his first decade in the U.S., a time of "fragments, failures, minor achievements and enormous amount [sic] of theoretical stuff." "[I]t took me a long, long time to discover and rediscover my unity."[57] In the new but familiar environment of Black Mountain, he would indeed rediscover his unity, devising a breathtaking integration of everything he had experienced as a composer. Employing unordered collections of pitch classes (what he more picturesquely called "any bunch of notes"), Wolpe began to write music comprised of highly contrasting musical gestures, gestures which erupted fitfully and with apparent spontaneity, even though they had been constructed in relation to an elaborate system of spatial proportions. For Wolpe, *Enactments for Three Pianos*, the first Black Mountain work, "announced and indicated a new world that was bound to be delivered."[58] In it, he realized his dream of a music in which events of highly contrasting character and complexity could overlap or occur in close proximity—"where the ideas live within a multidimensional space and behave that way, behave discontinuous [sic], behave abrupt, behave collapsing, behave cohering, coalescing."[59] Wolpe was just as explicitly animistic but even more poetic, in another description of the piece: "Grand Chant, Stones Sing, flowers, throats, the chlorophyll, the dead leaves, the traces, the history with chemical reactions, the pulses of cells, of what is in the making and in the changing phase."[60]

In each of the major Black Mountain works, Wolpe linked his ideas about the projection of proportional relationships in musical space to his deep, intuitive sense of music's animistic nature. The conceptual base of this project was his evolving concept of the "organic modes." He produced a catalogue of these modes, which

[56] Wolpe, "Lecture on Dada," p. 205.

[57] "Stefan Wolpe in Conversation with Eric Salzman," p. 398.

[58] Ibid., p.399.

[59] Ibid., p. 400.

[60] Harris, *The Arts at Black Mountain*, p. 206.

each defines a network of correspondences between aspects of experience, in his 1959 essay, "Thinking Twice." In each organic mode, Wolpe associates a class of intervals or a spatial arrangement with: 1) an "organic, structural phenomenon" (e.g., "an interplay of curves, a simultaneous release of impulses"), 2) "pictorial sensations" (e.g., "birds' flight, movements of waves"), and 3) "expressive sensations" (e.g., "extension on all sides, giving and being given").[61] In Wolpe's hands, the organic modes yielded music of great density, explosiveness, and mutability. In his *Symphony*, the culminating work of his three years at Black Mountain, he sought "a very mobile polyphony in which the partials of the sound behave like river currents and a greater orbit-spreadout [sic] is guaranteed to the sound, a greater circulatory agility (a greater momentum too)."[62] The *Symphony*, commissioned by the New York Philharmonic, proved to be so dense in its gestures, complicated in its rhythmic structure, and technically demanding, that its premiere had to be cancelled—and few performances have ensued.

Although Wolpe composed music of unprecedented complexity during his time at Black Mountain, he also participated voraciously in the community life and maintained the tradition of composing for its theatrical productions. He wrote music for four plays, including Brecht's *Good Woman of Setzuan*. As the writer, Fielding Dawson, describes in a vignette of life at Black Mountain ("How Stefan Got Me to Sing"), the ever-excitable composer was an animated teacher and coach:

> I crossed the room to him, who rose from his piano (grand), and greeted me. Typical: effusive, head tilted, eyes bright, big grin. Arms out, fingers spread, seeing I was nervous, assumed a look of amusement, and slight reproach. Said I was nervous and I was nervous, said not to worry and I was worried, said he'd help me to learn to sing—we, together. We would do it together. "Sit."

What follows is a more or less predictable, though touching, session—Wolpe coaching the non-singer Dawson into being able to project something for a singing stage role. The conclusion:

> JA JA he laughed as I cut loose, THAT'S IT!—a force, a call I never knew came out of my throat, I saw his face shine, as he played, and I sang, until the song was over, and we fell silent. He began again and I sang along, loud and strong GOOD GOOD he cheered, and finished he began again and I sang with him, clear through, I loved it, and after I'd finished, Stefan sat back, looked at me, expression warm tender triumphant. "Good! See? What a good voice you have!"[63]

STEFAN WOLPE, BLACK MOUNTAIN COLLEGE, 1954.
PHOTOGRAPH BY JONATHAN WILLIAMS.
Black Mountain College Museum and Arts Center, Asheville.

[61] The organic modes, as they relate to Wolpe's Black Mountain works, are discussed in Anne C. Shreffler, "Wolpe and Black Mountain College," in *Driven into Paradise: the Musical Migration from Nazi Germany to the United States*, ed. R. Brinkmann and C. Wolff, (Berkeley and Los Angeles: University of California Press, 1999), pp. 279–297. See also, Stefan Wolpe, "Thinking Twice," in *Contemporary Composers on Contemporary Music*, ed. B. Childs and E. Schwartz (New York: da Capo Press, 1978), pp. 304–305.

[62] Clarkson, "Stefan Wolpe," p. 9.

[63] Fielding Dawson, "How Stefan Got Me to Sing," *The Black Mountain Book* (North Carolina: Wesleyan College Press, 1991), pp. 34-36.

For a composer so sensitive to the relationship between musical shapes and gestures, tactility, and visual phenomena, the Black Mountain community must have been thrilling. The gestures of Wolpe's Black Mountain music—so fierce, teetering so precariously between symmetry and asymmetry—bear an especially strong relationship to the paintings of his close friend, Franz Kline. His other great artistic confrere was Olson. As Anne Shreffler has suggested, Wolpe's organic modes are kin, both in concept and spirit, to Olson's "composition by field," his conjuring of "the split second act" and of the "push"—the inner energy that animates the substance of art.[64] In Olson, Wolpe found an artistic fellow traveler as committed to extreme innovation as himself—and as unrepentantly enigmatic and prolix.

Wolpe stayed at Black Mountain through the lowest point, the winter of 1954–1955, when only eight to ten people remained on campus, and, with no money for heat, classes were suspended.[65] Things were so bad that he almost wished to be exiled again. "[I]n Switzerland we used to have parties and everybody used to sit around on lovely iron chairs and people came to serve us beautiful things to eat," he recalled, adding sardonically: "and look at us now, we're on the garbage heap of the world."[66] Soon, however, the college would be gone, and its waning community dispersed. Wolpe would deeply mourn its loss and yearn for the time he spent there with Olson "when both of us felt/lonely in the wilderniss [sic]of so much/unforgotten/unredeemable BMC bliss."[67]

But the bliss of BMC was redeemed in its heterogeneous and heterodox legacy. It was expressed in Wolpe's music, and Cage's and Harrison's, and it affected the Americanization of Schoenberg, the bond between Edward Lowinsky and Roland Hayes, the optimism of John Evarts. Wolpe might have been speaking for all of them, when he wrote to Olson, as the school was slowly closing down, in the spring of 1957: "I wished BMC stood there forever ever and my longing for it sits deep." But he continued with especially intimate words, aimed at the heart of his dear friend: "I hold with a smiling eye the place in my hand."[68]

M. B.

---

[64] See Shreffler, "Wolpe and Black Mountain College," p. 290.

[65] Duberman, p. 401.

[66] Shreffler, p. 284.

[67] Letter to Charles Olson, November 1, 1958, quoted in Shreffler, p.285.

[68] Letter to Charles Olson, May 2, 1957, Shreffler, p.285.

Kevin Power

IN, AROUND, AND ABOUT THE BLACK
MOUNTAIN REVIEW: *ROBERT CREELEY
AND COMPANY*

It was he, the figure of outward.
He was there. And the chopped seas, the crowd
of things
had head.
                              He gave them
that, he was so much
acknowledgement

When it is he the figure of outward
when he is there, the postcard sea
is written on, all things, and time,
are glass.
                    There is an evidence
the intimate
is an exactitude.

He has to come once
the figure of outward, and when he does
when he is there
there is. Suddenly
all things stand by him, and all the others
are the better known
                              In the instant
he emerges,
and tips his hat

CHARLES OLSON
The Maximus Poems[1]

Mallorca: Divers Press, *The Black Mountain Review*, the Island

IN MAY 1951, the poet Robert Creeley moved from the United States to France. The impulse for this move was the result of conversations with Denise Levertov and Mitchell Goodman, who had set themselves up in Aix en Provence. For an American, this was

[1] Charles Olson, "Early Unpublished Maximus Poems," noted as "Charles Olson, for R.C.," published in *Olson: The Journal of the Charles Olson Archives*, University of Connecticut, Storrs, no. 6, fall 1976, p. 3. This unpublished section of *Maximus* contains the phrase "the figure of outward," which appears on the dedication page of *The Maximus Poems*, under the words "for Robert Creeley." Further down the same page, one reads "All my life I've heard/one makes many." Rutherford Witthus provides us with this additional information: "[The phrase "the figure of outward"] also appears in one of Olson's notebooks (unpublished) in May 1969 as he recounts the dream in which the phrase first occured to him. He mentions how he wrote the epithet 'waking up & writing it on the white wall of South Lodge? in the night? And it is probably still there under new coats of paint like new coats . . .' In a 16 January 1953 letter to Creeley, Olson reports how 'the first senses of it got written in the dark on the white, and scratched-on, wall.'" (E-mail to Vincent Katz, dated 30 May 2002, from Rutherford W. Witthus, Curator of Literary and Natural History Collections, Thomas J. Dodd Research Center, University of Connecticut Libraries, Storrs).

ROBERT CREELEY, SAILING OFF OF BAÑALBUFAR,
MALLORCA, 1952. PHOTOGRAPH BY JONATHAN
WILLIAMS. Collection of Jonathan Williams.

Europe steeped in all its culture, though for Creeley there were more prosaic reasons for coming: to find a place he and his family could live on his wife's small allowance.

Unfortunately, he ran into a period of inflation in France, and it proved to be far from easy to survive cheaply. Creeley was already engaged in what would prove to be a marathon correspondence with critic and poet Charles Olson and actively attempting to find effective outlets for their work. In 1952, Creeley published his first chapbook, *Le Fou*, with Golden Goose Press. He also published in *New Mexico Quarterly*, *Montevallo Review*, *Contact*, and in Rainer Gerhardt's[2] *Fragmente*.

Creeley decided it was time to move in search of a greater economic stability, and Spain fit the bill. Locked into its Franquist introversion, it could guarantee low cost living, and the Baleares provided, as well as their own natural beauties, a certain veneer of internationalism. Martin Seymour-Smith—a young poet already living in Mallorca, who had published a poem attracting Creeley's attention—served as the linch pin for this new venture. Seymour-Smith worked as tutor to Robert Graves's son (a post W.S. Merwin had occupied before him), and he nursed a publishing project that would prove to be the origin of Divers Press.

Creeley left Marseille by boat with his family for Mallorca in 1953, initially living in Bañalbufar in the northwest of the island, later moving to Bonanova, closer to Palma de

---

[2] Gerhardt was the first European translator of Olson and Creeley.

Mallorca. Bañalbufar is a little village at the end of what was then a dirt track road, disappearing downwards through pines towards the sea from a curve in the road that leads to Soler. Paul Blackburn went to see him there. He rented a house in the village and during his stay wrote a poem as clear as the light, hewed tight into the particularities of his own voice, despite the rather unwieldy title, which however sets the scene:

BAÑALBUFAR, A BRAZIER, RELATIVITY, CLOUD FORMATIONS & THE KINDNESS & RELENTLESSNESS OF TIME, ALL SEEN THROUGH A WINDOW WHILE KEEPING THE FEET WARM AT THE SAME TIME AS:

Southwind
        and lines of clouds walk across the mountains, straight
        across the sea; the land, the mountains at angle.
                Between the cloudbanks
                        sun Falls.
                    Lemon trees
            outside the window under sun
             making a sweet quadrangle:
        parallel lines of sun straight,
                    trees bent
             under the double weight,
                    wind
                    fruit.
                How prevent
        the clouds from moving, now that sun . . . . Sunlight on

        pear blossom, apple blossom, the red wall,
        roofs' tile, red and yellow, yellow!
                lemons under sun.
            The mountain now in one
                    shadow, huge;
        the colors in old wood, the door, sun,
        dark green of pines, dark blue of rock, more
                cloud, the
                wing of a cloud
                        passes.
                            Alas!
        Alles, ala, the wing, everything,
                            goes.

            No,
        Always is always all ways.
                No, not so.
        My love says to me, — Not so.
        I am humble under this wind
        but stupid, and hopeful even.

    "Come
        into this cold room.
            The smell of wildflowers is

in every corner.
                    The mind
        is filled with flower smell and sun
                    even when sun is not."[3]

THE DISSOLVING FABRIC BY PAUL BLACKBURN, DIVERS, 1955. COVER BY DAN RICE.
Collection of Ann van de Wiele.

THIS BY CHARLES OLSON, 1952, COVER BY NICHOLAS CERNOVICH, PRINTED BY NICHOLAS CERNOVICH AT BLACK MOUNTAIN COLLEGE GRAPHICS WORKSHOP. The Poetry/Rare Books Collection, State University of New York, Buffalo.

Here is the power of music flowing from the world through him into the poem. The self is here, as Duncan so consistently insisted, a center that gathers and filters emotions, impressions, and ideas. It is this music that becomes the form, the shaping of self in the world. Work and life here intertwine: the interaction of the thing seen with the man seeing. Blackburn complies perfectly to Olson's idea that *la forme c'est l'homme*. "The test is the intensity of the position, which is the man. But it will be marked by the substance of the stuff to which he gives his attention . . . and the worked quality of language."[4] He has understood Olson's first principle that the poem register exact fulfilment of thought in a moment of breath, or as Blackburn himself observes: "What goes into the poem . . . is very much a matter of speech rhythms and of natural, rather than forced rhythms. That is why a poem very often seems to have no obvious structure whatsoever—in terms of what is conventionally thought of as form. It just doesn't work out that simply, because the rhythms that you start with and you have to resolve are very often irregular in themselves, or are more highly charged, simply because they are the way we speak. The thing is to speak carefully."[5]

Blackburn was to become the New York distributor for *The Black Mountain Review*, and he would be contributing editor to one of its issues. What is already clear from this early poem is that in Blackburn one of the most skilled practitioners of punctuation, line breaks, and text alignments had been located. In other words, here was a poet clearly engaged in the practice of composition by field as outlined by Olson in his "Projective Verse" essay.[6]

Poet Robert Duncan and his companion, the artist Jess Collins (often referred to by first name only) also came to see Creeley on the island. They stayed in Bañalbufar, from where Duncan continued his own round of correspondence with Olson, at a less hectic pace than Creeley's but equally engaged with the entire activity of writing. Duncan seems to have written some of these letters from Mallorca while Creeley was teaching at Black Mountain.

Yet, the two men did spend time on the island together, and Creeley recalls Duncan's telling him on a crowded bus that he (Creeley) apparently had little interest in history. What comes across is the way in which all three of them—Creeley, Duncan, and Olson—were all involved in a joint process of finding, applying, and positioning an emerging poetics centered on a new and necessary definition of the particularity of American experience. It is also clear that Duncan and Creeley (and a little later, Michael McClure would apply these same recognitions) were becoming increasingly aware that intuitions of these same preoccupations were already fully present in the gestural language of Abstract Expressionism.

[3] Paul Blackburn, *The Selected Poems of Paul Blackburn* (New York: Persea, 1989), pp.18–19.

[4] Charles Olson, *Olson Journals*, no. 5, University of Connecticut, 1976, p.44.

[5] Paul Blackburn, *The Sullen Art* (New York: Corinth Books, 1963), p.24.

[6] Charles Olson, "Projective Verse," first published in *Poetry New York*, no. 3, 1950.

ROBERT DUNCAN, CALIFORNIA, 1954. PHOTOGRAPH BY JONATHAN WILLIAMS. Collection of Jonathan Williams.

Duncan was interested in the artists in San Francisco, both those associated with the Assemblage Movement and the Abstract Expressionists. He even ran a gallery for time. He has acknowledged the impact of Elmer Bischoff and Hassel Smith on his writing, the way they opened up certain compositional possibilities, and the fact that they manifested the difference between energy as something referred to (seen) and energy embodied (felt) in the work.

Duncan writes to Olson from Mallorca, taking up a phrase from Olson's *Maximus Poems* ("there are no hierarchies") where the insistence—literally, or physiologically—falls on the eye:

> There are no hierarchies, no infinite, no such many as mass, there are only
> eyes in all heads,
> to be looked out of[7]

THE IMMORAL PROPOSITION BY ROBERT CREELEY, AUTUMN 1953, JARGON 8. DRAWINGS BY RENÉ LAUBIÈS, EDITION OF 200, PRINTED IN GERMANY. The Poetry/Rare Books Collection, State University of New York, Buffalo.

This preference for a lack of hierarchies and a trust in the efficacy and directness of seeing might equally be applied to Pollock's work with its multifocal tensions and lack of center. Duncan, however, is evidently reading the phrase from a different angle: "But

[7] Charles Olson, "Letter 6," *The Maximus Poems*, (New York: Jargon/Corinth Books, 1960), p. 29.

CHARLES OLSON. BLACK MOUNTAIN COLLEGE, 1949.
PHOTOGRAPH BY DIANA WOELFFER.

THE SONG OF THE BORDER-GUARD, POEM BY ROBERT
DUNCAN, COVER BY CY TWOMBLY, UNDATED.
NICHOLAS CERNOVICH PRINTER AND PUBLISHER,
BLACK MOUNTAIN GRAPHICS WORKSHOP, BLACK
MOUNTAIN COLLEGE. Archives and Special
Collections at the Thomas J. Dodd Research Center,
University of Connecticut Libraries.

what I've got in mind in conversation with you is a note to my enthusiasm for the hierar-
chically arranged thing, I don't get to it in the notes so far on *Maximus* but I heartedly,
by heart agree with you that 'There are no hierarchies' or it could come as an agonized
cry from this man glamorized, in love with the great wheels of cultures 'There are only
hierarchies!' . . . the dynamics of making needs as much incoherence (incorporation of
natural inability, corrupt flesh etc) as it needs coherence (a genius, skeleton etc)."[8]

Duncan is already recognizing that incoherence is part of any event and that it has its
own coherence because it is of the man who makes it. Both Duncan and Creeley
want a writing that can lead on following the sounds. Both men also share the sense
that you can begin anywhere and that almost anything can enter the compositional
field if it does so with enough intensity, literally earns its place. It is worth stressing that
Duncan sees the word as autonomous and apocalyptic and the image as a natural
emergence from the poetic organism, "something actually seen in the process of the
poem, not something pretended or made up."[9]

Creeley had been drawn to the island because he knew that printing costs were low
and he would be able to publish things that interested him. He was fully aware that

[8] Robert Duncan, "Some Letters to Charles Olson," *Maps*, Shippensberg, Pennsylvania, 1974, p. 59.

[9] Robert Duncan, "Rites of Paticipation—11," *Caterpillar* no. 2, 1967, p. 152.

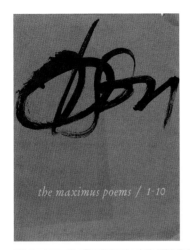

there was a growing urgency to create the necessary platform for a community of voices. He wanted to publish writers that were breaking free of academic molds, specific voices including his own and those of Blackburn, Duncan, Irving Layton, and Olson.

The much-needed cheap printing was to be found at the Mossén Alcover Press, just behind the ramparts, overlooking the sea and not far from the splendid cathedral that dominates the entrance to Palma de Mallorca. Graves and Laura Riding had published two magazines in the 1930s, *Epilogue* and *Focus,* under the imprint of the Seizen Press in Deia, using a hand-lever Albion press, that, after the war, reappeared in the hands of workers in the Mossén Alcover Press, where Creeley published both the Divers Press books and *The Black Mountain Review.*

Creeley and Seymour-Smith started out on their printing venture with the Roebuck Press. They published one book, also printed at the Alcover Press—the work of Seymour-Smith's mother, Elena Fearn. Despite their friendship, disagreements arose concerning literary taste, especially the significance of William Carlos Williams. The disagreements came to a head when Seymour-Smith wished to publish Donald Hall, who had attacked Williams, Olson, and Creeley in *The World Review* in December 1952. Creeley decided to work on his own, using the Divers Press imprint—a name in fact suggested by Seymour-Smith, who continued to maintain contact with Creeley and contribute to *The Black Mountain Review,* as both critic and poet. Over a short

THE MAXIMUS POEMS 1–10 BY CHARLES OLSON, 1953, JARGON 7, JONATHAN WILLIAMS PUBLISHER, STUTTGART, EDITION OF 350. Archives and Special Collections at the Thomas J. Dodd Research Center, University of Connecticut Libraries.

CHARLES OLSON: *I, MAXIMUS,* MAY 17, 1950. Paper, typescript with black ink notations in hand, 11 x 8 ½ inches. Archives and Special Collections at the Thomas J. Dodd Research Center, University of Connecticut Libraries.

CHARLES OLSON: *EPIGRAPH TO THE MAXIMUS POEMS,* UNDATED. Paper, typescript with pencil notation, 11 x 8 ½ inches. Archives and Special Collections at the Thomas J. Dodd Research Center, University of Connecticut Libraries.

IN COLD HELL, IN THICKET BY CHARLES OLSON, WINTER 1953, DIVERS PRESS. EDITED BY ROBERT CREELEY AND ISSUED AS ORIGIN 8. PRINTED BY MOSSÉN ALCOVER IN PALMA DE MALLORCA. The Poetry/Rare Books Collection, State University of New York, Buffalo.

THE GOLD DIGGERS BY ROBERT CREELEY, 1954, DIVERS PRESS. PRINTED BY MOSSÉN ALCOVER IN PALMA DE MALLORCA. COVER BY RENÉ LAUBIÉS. The Poetry/Rare Books Collection, State University of New York, Buffalo.

CAESAR'S GATE: POEMS 1949–50 BY ROBERT
DUNCAN, 1955, DIVERS PRESS. COVER BY JESS
COLLINS. Archives and Special Collections at the
Thomas J. Dodd Research Center, University of
Connecticut Libraries.

span of three years, Creeley's Divers Press published many remarkable books (see list on page 163). Creeley also began to edit *The Black Mountain Review*, all seven issues of which were printed by Mossén Alcover.

The Black Mountain Review

Although Olson and Creeley had been corresponding for years, they had never met when, in 1954, Olson suggested that Creeley start a magazine, using the inexpensive yet high-quality printing of Mossén Alcover, to promote Black Mountain. Creeley was in touch, by letters, with many of the writers he wanted to publish, and he cites Cid Corman's journal *Origin* as a starting point from which to conceive a literary company.[10]

The ostensible reason for launching the magazine was that Black Mountain College was in deep financial trouble and needed to attract students. The survival of the institution depended upon increased enrollment. Charles Olson, by then rector of the college, suggested a magazine might serve as a promotional vehicle to bring in more students, or at least more than a mere listing of the programs would do. The cost of producing the magazine for a year was, according to Creeley, approximately two thousand dollars. At that point in time, and for an institution as short of cash as was Black Mountain, that implied a serious commitment.

There were inevitably other, more substantial, grounds of interest for Creeley and Olson in such a venture, including publishing their own work and creating a forum for energies and dictions that questioned the strangle-hold of New Criticism as the legitimizing agent of American poetry. The Black Mountain School of poetry, as a movement of poets sharing ideas and agreeing on certain intentions for their work, came about through Olson's early efforts to establish a theoretical program, especially through the publication of "Projective Verse."

MOSSÉN ALCOVER PRESS, PALMA DE MALLORCA.

Olson was larger than life, and his energies became fully projective with the appearance of Corman's journal, *Origin*, where his work was prominently and regularly represented. Olson also made it his task to act as though personally responsible for every aspect of that journal's editing, insisting it should declare in print the ideals of the new poetry. When Corman became less inclined to conform to the increasingly authoritarian role Olson had assumed, the logical answer was to create a new space and a new journal: *The Black Mountain Review*. Olson urgently needed this vehicle, as it would allow him to fulfill a range of possibilities, especially with Creeley as editor.

The first issue of *The Black Mountain Review* arrived just before Creeley left Mallorca for the United States in the Spring of 1954. Three more issues appeared—corresponding to Summer, Fall, and Winter, 1954—shortly after his return in July to spend the Summer with his family. Then, as that pace must have been difficult to sustain, there were three annual issues with a change in format and size, in 1955, 1956, and 1957. Five to seven hundred fifty copies were printed for each issue of the magazine.[11]

---

[10] Robert Creeley, *Contexts of Poetry: Interviews 1961–71* (Bolinas: Four Seasons Foundation, 1973), p. 4.

[11] Only about two hundred were distributed.

Creeley knew that contributing editors would be key for the success or failure of the magazine: Olson, who was a key point of reference; Blackburn, who helped with distibution and was constantly present during numerous critical moments; the energetic figure of Irving Layton, whom Creeley had come to know through a Canadian mimeographed magazine, *Contact,* where many of the writers associated with *The Black Mountain Review* had also been published; and Allen Ginsberg, whose influence was pivotal in the crucial final issue.[12]

Creeley also approached Paul Goodman, who expressed sympathy but did not wish to become directly involved. Kenneth Rexroth did agree but right away became offended when, in its first issue, the magazine produced negative reviews of Dylan Thomas and Theodore Roethke. Rexroth failed to understand what was at stake, failed miserably to catch the pulse of a changing time. Creeley was placing under question the elitist modernist vision of a world that was changing in front of their eyes, and his attacks against certain figures of the 1930s and 1940s were not simply the challenge of the next generation but a fundamental questioning of their reading of the world.

Another seminal figure was Duncan who, although he was never on the editorial board, had a constant impact. Creeley had suggested printing an excerpt of the first contribution Duncan sent, to which Duncan responded that if he had wanted a section of a poem printed he would have sent it. Duncan was to provide another of the polemical moments when his poem "For A Muse Meant" was published in the Fall 1954 issue.[13] Both Olson and Levertov felt it was a veiled attack and parody on their writing, whereas Creeley saw it as an "an extraordinary summary and exemplum of contemporary possibilities in poetry."[14]

Creeley picks out four groups of contributors to the magazine: those associated with *Origin;* the occasional contributors; those who had been students; and those who were still at the college. It is a constellation that consistently opens itself up to writing that shares its affinities and commitments. Zukofsky and Edward Dahlberg are two writers associated with the editorial commitments of *Origin,* whereas Goodman and James Purdy would be two of the occasional contributors.

Three former students who benefited from the impact of Olson's writing and teaching are significant: Fielding Dawson, Joel Oppenheimer, and Jonathan Williams who was already engaged in his own publishing venture, *Jargon.* Then there are those there at the college—student-friends who shared not only Creeley's incisive mind but the breaking chaos of his life: Edward Dorn, Tom Field, and Michael Rumaker. It is a list to which one should add the name of Dan Rice, who did the cover drawing for issue number six. Dorn's "C. B. & Q" and Rumaker's "The Pipe" were their first stories in print.

FIELDING DAWSON. BLACK MOUNTAIN COLLEGE, CA. 1950. PHOTOGRAPH BY HAZEL F. LARSEN.

JOEL OPPENHEIMER, BLACK MOUNTAIN COLLEGE. PHOTOGRAPH BY RENA OPPENHEIMER.

ALL THAT IS LOVELY IN MEN BY ROBERT CREELEY, 1955, JARGON 10. DRAWINGS BY DAN RICE, COVER PHOTOGRAPH BY JONATHAN WILLIAMS. The Poetry/Rare Books Collection, State University of New York, Buffalo.

[12] See Creeley, *"The Black Mountain Review," The Collected Essays of Robert Creeley* (Berkeley and Los Angeles: University of California Press, 1989), pp. 505–514. [Various observations in the current essay derive from this crucial account.–*Ed.*]

[13] In *Black Mountain Review* no. 3, Fall 1954, the poem is titled "Letters For Denise Levertov: An A Muse Ment." [In Duncan's *Selected Poems,* New Directions, New York, 1993, it is titled "For A Muse Meant," a softening of the spelling, perhaps in deference to Levertov, poet-muse.–*Ed.*]

[14] Creeley, *Collected Essays,* p. 511.

Creeley was the mainstay, soliciting contributions, organizing the printer, writing reviews and poems, occasionally under different pseudonyms—Mauritius Estaban, Thomas White, W.C. and A.M. The last issue is an appropriately fitting closure, since it symbolizes the inclusive spirit that drives Creeley, gathering the Beats into this wider community of voices after his contact with them in San Francisco in 1957.

The last issue of *The Black Mountain Review* in 1957 is emblematic of the climate of openness and inclusion that was part of Creeley's spirit. It signs on the San Francisco Renaissance poets and the Beats, equally expansive types of underground writing. This was not only a natural but a strategic opening that threw the arc wide open, in tune with the proliferation of City Lights, Grove Press, New Directions, and numerous small presses, as well as *Evergreen Review, Yugen, Big Table, Measure* and a whole flock of little magazines.

It provides one more rung in the ladder that finally materializes in Donald Allen's *The New American Poetry: 1945–60*. This anthology sets out the major alternatives for poetics in the 1960s. In retrospect, one would have to say *almost* sets them out, since the absence of the Deep Image poets or the Subjective Verse poets would now be questioned. Allen probably left them out at the time because of their obvious debt to European poetry—to Char, Ekelof, Lorca, or Ungaretti, as well as to the classic poets of the European avant-gardes—but in retrospect Bly, Kelly, and Rothenberg might easily and comfortably have been included.

Creeley also insists that there was a real need for a magazine with a regular wide-ranging critical and essay section that *Origin* did not have and where he himself would often have to write under pseudonyms that Blackburn has identified for us.[15] Creeley states exactly what it was he was looking for and ultimately found: "critical writing that would break down habits of 'subject' and gain a new experience of context generally."[16] *The Black Mountain Review* provided this forum with a series of essays and critical readings that range from Jung's 57-page "The Mass and the Individuation Process" to Duncan's "From a Notebook" (no. 5); from Borges's "Three Versions of Judas" (no. 2), that Creeley says he read without even realizing it was a fiction, to Louis Zukofsky's "Bottom on Shakespeare" (no. 6); from Olson's "Against Wisdom as Such" (no. 1) to Creeley's "By God, Pomeroy, You Here!" (no. 4).

The languages of poetry and painting that Creeley recognized as significant were outside the cultural mainstream, and the artists involved were putting the dominant cultural forms under question, pushing towards what Olson had already called a "postmodern"[17] man with a more defined stance towards reality and engaged in the search for an alternative to the ego-structure.

The Black Mountain Review placed emphasis on the direct manifestation of energy and on the quest (continued from Williams, who had shown Creeley there is a place for

[15] Paul Blackburn, "The Grinding Down", *Kulchur* 3, no. 10 (summer 1963).

[16] Creeley, *Collected Essays*, p. 510.

[17] Charles Olson, letter to Louis Martz, readdressed to Robert Creeley, dated August 8, 1951, published in *Charles Olson and Robert Creeley: The Complete Correspondence* (Santa Rosa: Black Sparrow Press, 1987), vol. 7, p. 75.

everything in the poem and that "the province of the poem is the world"[18] for an American speech that corresponded to a people whose formative experience was space rather than history. Particular attention was accorded to the physiological, specifically to breath as the natural measure of line, which opened up new possibilities for poetics.

Olson wanted to push beyond the egocentric bind of Modernism and called for an "alternative to the ego-structure." He wanted knowledge to be active, to literally produce a change in those who were making use of it. He thus insisted that each man had to discover his own bibliography, to find whatever it was he needed when he needed it. *The Black Mountain Review* undoubtedly provides an opposition front to the dominant poetics. It appears as intensive, reductive, and sharp, in terms of its span of interests. Creeley's editing and design turns it into an effective vehicle for his and Olson's post-modern agenda.

The Black Mountain Review no. 1[19]

The first issue contains one of the best 1953 *Maximus* pieces, "On First Looking out of Juan De La Cosa's Eyes," a projective summoning of a geomythic New World that amounts to a new mapping of the American literary landscape—an attempt to define a locus for Olson's search for post-modern man, emerging as both a continuity of and a rupture with the tenets of Modernism. Olson also contributed "Against Wisdom as Such," in which he dismisses, with his characteristic expansive rhetoric, the San Francisco Renaissance poets as softheaded mystics. The Zen and transcendental push that marked the work of Gary Snyder, Lew Welch, and Philip Whalen apparently appeared to Olson mushy, exotic, and alienating. In the case of Duncan, he seemed either to miss or to hit the fact Duncan's work drew extensively from the English Romantics and that his excesses were the result of his heritage and writing tradition. Olson also held reservations about the nature-driven energy that marked William Everson and Thomas Merton.

This issue also contains Creeley's note on René Laubiès, a painter who also happened to be Pound's first translator into French. William Bronk, Creeley, Larry Eigner, and Layton provided the poems. There were also two pieces by Seymour-Smith criticizing Roethke and Thomas that led, as I have mentioned, to Rexroth's withdrawal from his post as contributing editor. Creeley, naturally and vehemently, supported the gist of Seymour-Smith's argument, seeing Roethke as representing a kind of critical writing that consists of "diffusion, generality, and a completely adolescent address to the world in which he finds himself."[20]

The Black Mountain Review no. 2

In the second issue, we find an article by Ronald Mason on the poems of Herman Melville, a selection from Artaud's last poems translated by Kenneth Rexroth, "The

THE BLACK MOUNTAIN REVIEW. VOLUME 1. COVER BY KATUE KITASONO. Archives and Special Collections at the Thomas J. Dodd Research Center, University of Connecticut Libraries.

THE BLACK MOUNTAIN REVIEW. VOLUME 2. COVER BY KATUE KITASONO. Archives and Special Collections at the Thomas J. Dodd Research Center, University of Connecticut Libraries.

[18] William Carlos Williams, *Paterson*, collected edition (New York: New Directions, 1963), p. 121.

[19] The first four numbers of *The Black Mountain Review*, all published in 1954, were grouped as Volume 1. For no. 5, summer 1955, no. 6, spring 1956 and no. 7, autumn 1957, no volume numbers were used. Therefore, for ease of reference, we use only issue numbers 1–7, leaving out the volume number.

[20] Robert Creeley, "Comment," *The Black Mountain Review* no. 3, fall 1954, p. 64.

Devil's House," a story by Toda Tomoya, as well as Olson's piece on "Mayan Heads." In other words, a mixed bag suggesting Creeley is still looking for the real presence of American diction he wishes to stamp upon the magazine. The Artaud translations are a literary flourish, in tune with Rexroth's interests. The dark angel of surrealism, uncontrolled and apocryphal, representing the initial pessimism and revolt of the group—the man who, as Breton said, went right through the mirror—would have had a special appeal for certain Beat poets, especially Michael McClure, but he remains outside the arc that Creeley ultimately wished to draw.

Melville does, in fact, seem to carry the sense and preoccupations of writing that would become integral to Black Mountain poetics. Their concern for the sentence as a field of force and not as a completed thought, recognizing that completion is impossible when the real is perceived as literally what is happening. Olson notes that it was Melville who had understood the real as "the apprehension of the absolute condition of present things."[21]

Olson knew that in Creeley he had found "the figure of outward" and that he had a vehicle for the actual. The magazine was as immediate, as "event-full" as the newspapers that Olson used in one of his Black Mountain courses. Here was a launching pad into the real. For students such as Rumaker and Dorn, it quickly became a standard for writing. Olson must be included among the most influential teachers of the last part of the 20th century, to the extent that he made knowledge into an active principle. Olson realized that the magazine gave the students a chance to be engaged in witnessing the process of editorial decision and design, that it could serve as one of the vehicles of his teaching.

The Black Mountain Review no. 3

The third issue marks Duncan's first appearance with "Letters For Denise Levertov: An A Muse Ment," although as a writer he already had ample outlets in the San Francisco small press world. There are also poems by Creeley, Field, Layton, and Levertov that share a climate of affinities. A prose piece by Creeley, entitled "A Dilemma," juxtaposed with photographs by Peter Mitchum, can easily be read as an emotional graph of the poet's state of mind at the time: "I am sorry myself not to care anymore, or not care for much beyond one or two things. That, say, to love anyone becomes more impossible. 'I did love . . . ', one says, etc. I still want to, etc. Perhaps against the distortion, lying, deceit, viciousness, horror, cruelty, and all that, it will still be possible to make the most minimal of defenses—at least the knowledge that there might be others likewise confronted."[22]

The critical sharpness of the review section is maintained on this occasion through Cid Corman's radical questioning of Karl Shapiro's work: "Shapiro and the Auden-American gang have evidently run dry. They now and then still flex their muscles, as though they were young men still fooling with rusty dumb-bells. These poets have

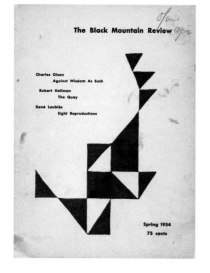

THE BLACK MOUNTAIN REVIEW. VOLUME 3. COVER BY KATUE KITASONO. Archives and Special Collections at the Thomas J. Dodd Research Center, University of Connecticut Libraries.

[21] Herman Melville, from a letter to Nathaniel Hawthorne, April 16, 1851, quoted by Charles Olson in his essay "Equal, That Is, to the Real Itself," *Collected Prose*, (Berkeley and Los Angeles: University of California Press, 1997), p. 121.

[22] Robert Creeley, *The Black Mountain Review* no. 3, fall 1954, p. 28.

done nothing but maintain the English succession on the American literary scene. All the gorgeous dilapidation of these poems, all the old purple rags, cannot draw the alert attention from the truer, if rougher, ground."[23]

THE BLACK MOUNTAIN REVIEW. VOLUME 4. COVER BY KATUE KITASONO. Archives and Special Collections at the Thomas J. Dodd Research Center, University of Connecticut Libraries.

The Black Mountain Review no. 4

The fourth issue, published in the winter of 1954, includes Olson's "I, Mencius, Pupil of the Master . . ."and poems by Paul Carroll, Layton, Levertov, and Oppenheimer. Levertov was the only woman to penetrate the male Black Mountain bastion, and she did so not only because she had been at university with Creeley and was thus a known and respected quantity but above all because of her capacity to lay it down straight and uncover the workings of desire and the mind in tight, direct rhythms. She had been influenced by Williams, whose work—with its insistence on an American speech and unembellished perceptions—had helped her break away from her roots in English Romanticism. Levertov looked for the rhythms of life, though without falling into what she considered to be the slackness and sloppiness of the Beats.

There are two essays by Creeley, a short piece on Kline, painter par excellence as far as the Black Mountaineers were concerned (see Fielding Dawson's *An Emotional Memoir of Franz Kline*) and a longer note on Francis Parkman, "By God, Pomeroy, You Here!" in which Creeley recognizes Parkman's sense of history as bringing it into the present through his "countless anecdotes and (finally) flavors of a place I of course am too 'old' to know as he must have, because *The Oregon Trail* was written from a journal no man can ever keep again. For me, he returns 'history' to the only place which it has, in an actual continuity—hardly ours because we are its issue, but because we can perhaps recognize that we are."[24] Parkman was one of the American writers Olson suggested to Dorn in the *A Bibliography on America for Ed Dorn*, which he delivered to Dorn's room at Black Mountain one midnight in January, 1955.[25] By giving Dorn—and then publishing—this list of texts, Olson stressed the need for a bibliography that is active in changing our perception of things, that is specifically of *use* to us and thus each one of us has to find on his own.

The Black Mountain Review no. 5

The fifth issue shows a change of both format and of size. It has turned into an annual. The covers now become the work of artists with Abstract Expressionist leanings. For the fifth issue, it is the work of John Altoon, to whom Creeley had been introduced in part through the agency of Fielding Dawson. There are poems by Duncan, Layton, Levertov, and Oppenheimer, as well as Creeley's "A Wicker Basket," Olson's "O'Ryan (2)" and Zukofsky's "A-12" and the following lyrical but philosophically terse lines by William Bronk, "For an Early Italian Musician":

THE BLACK MOUNTAIN REVIEW. VOLUME 5. COVER BY JOHN ALTOON. Archives and Special Collections at the Thomas J. Dodd Research Center, University of Connecticut Libraries.

[23] Cid Corman, ibid., p. 57.

[24] Robert Creeley, *The Black Mountain Review* no. 4, winter 1954, p. 46.

[25] Olson also refers to Parkman in his Melville study, *Call Me Ishmael*, first published (New York: Reynal & Hitchcock, 1947), reprinted (Baltimore: The Johns Hopkins University Press, 1997). [This demonstrates Olson's impact on Creeley.—*Ed.*]

And there is also this:
that one wishes to last, that one needs to make
a world for survival, which cannot be done
simply, or soon, but by a slow
crystal on crystal accretion of a made
world, a world made to last.

One is nothing with no world.[26]

As had been the case with Olson, Creeley's friendship with Irving Layton had been a result of their correspondence that reached its point of maximum contact between 1953 and 1955. The two men did not meet each other face to face until 1962. The fact that Layton was engaged in running his own small magazine made him a natural choice as a contributing editor for the *The Black Mountain Review*. He was offered a teaching post at Black Mountain, but his role as a political activist had led to a prohibition on his physical movements. Along with Creeley and Blackburn, he was also much involved in trying to get Ezra Pound released from prison. Creeley maintained a profound respect for him as a man as is evidenced in the following poem:

At seventeen women were strange & forbidding phenomenons.
Today they leer at me from street corners. Yet

who is to say it,
that we have come to an agreement.

Aging, aging, even so there is some song, some
remote pulse,

an argument still visible, an
excuse for it.[27]

The magazine has now expanded and yet the editing is tighter. The fifth issue includes Jung's "The Mass and the Individuation Process," Paul Carroll's discussion of "Pound's Propertius," Rumaker's "The Truck," Aaron Siskind's photos, and Duncan's answer to Olson's charges against him in "Against Wisdom as Such." Rumaker was still a student at the time. He had been recruited to Black Mountain by Ben Shahn, on the occasion of a talk he had given at the Philadelphia Museum in 1952. Rumaker talks about his encounter with Olson and his complex sense of him as a person: "I was very drawn to Olson, and very repelled by him. I think so many people have that feeling. He's a very large man, and he's very dynamic; he's ruthlessly honest and great about detecting any kind of fraud or dishonesty in another person . . . Charles would always say, '*You* are interesting, as a person, and you may have a feeling that what you have to say is not interesting, but this is not true. You as an individual are interesting.'"[28]

---

[26] William Bronk, *The Black Mountain Review* no. 5, Summer, 1955, p. 166.

[27] Robert Creeley, "For Irving," first published in *The Charm* (San Francisco: Four Seasons Foundation, 1979), p. 63, reprinted in *The Collected Poems of Robert Creeley* (Berkeley and Los Angeles: University of California Press, 1982), p. 64.

[28] Michael Rumaker in Martin Duberman, *Black Mountain: An Exploration in Community* (New York: Dutton, 1972), pp. 401–402.

Duncan's answers to Olson's charges are affirmative. In an essay entitled "From a Notebook," he confesses guilt and admits that he does indeed intend to revive the romantic spirit: "This is of course the radical disagreement that Olson has with me. In a sense he is so keen upon the virtu of reality that he rejects my 'wisdom' not as it might seem at first glance because 'wisdom' is a vice; but because my wisdom is not real wisdom." He then goes on to define his concerns as a poet: "He suspects, and rightly, that I indulge myself in pretentious fictions. I, however, at this point take enuf delight in the available glamor that I do not stop to trouble the cheapness of such stuff. I mean that it is, for a man of rigor, an inexpensive irony to play with puns on pretending and pretension. I like rigor and even clarity as a quality of a work—that is, as I like muddle and floaty vagaries. It is the intensity of the conception that moves me. This intensity may be that it is all of a fervent marshmallow dandy lion fluff."[29] Duncan, despite Olson's objections, believes that his attraction to English Romanticism can push him into what he sees as a mythic reality, a spiritual romance able to bring love and lust together.

The Black Mountain Review no. 6

In issue six, with its Dan Rice cover, Fielding Dawson appears for the first time with a short story, "A Tragic Story," and a drawing. The major contribution to the issue is Zukofsky's essay "Bottom: On Shakespeare—Part Two," in which he points to two things that must directly have impacted on Creeley: firstly, his observation that "Love needs no tongue of reason if love and the eyes are *1*—an identity. The good reasons of the mind's right judgment are but superfluities for saying: *Love sees*—if it needs saying at all in a text which is always hovering towards *The rest is silence*"[30]; and secondly, his quoting of Wittgenstein's "The world is everything that is the case,"[31] which could almost stand as a tenet for Creeley.

There are poems on this occasion by Creeley, Duncan, Layton, Levertov, Hilda Morley, Lorine Niedecker, Olson, Oppenheimer, and Williams. Jess's collage pieces and his translations of Christian Morgenstern's poems assert Duncan's presence and editorial influence. The opening to Levertov's poem, "The Way Through," provides us with the sense of the poem listening to itself as sound and focusing intently on its emergence as event that was a common impulse for the majority of these poets:

> Let the rain plunge radiant
> through sulky thunder,
> rage on rooftops
>
> let it scissor and bounce its denials
> on concrete slabs and black
> roadways.[32]

---

[29] Robert Duncan, *The Black Mountain Review* no. 5, 1955, p. 210.

[30] Louis Zukofsky, *The Black Mountain Review* no. 6, spring 1956, p. 132.

[31] Ibid., p. 146. Zukofsky is quoting from Ludwig Wittgenstein's *Tractatus Logico-Philosophicus* (1918).

[32] Denise Levertov, *The Black Mountain Review* no. 6, spring 1956, p. 38.

The two short stories have the clean sharp edges of Black Mountain writing, carefully hewing to the contours of the author's own voice. Michael Rumaker's "The Pipe" is exemplary democratic prose, held tight in on its own activity. It is sparse, brutal, and shaped according to Rumaker's registering of his own feelings. Dawson's "A Tragic Story" is also the result of the particular rhythms of a particular speech, more idiosyncratic, intentionally less macho.

The issue also contains Duncan's "Notes on Poetics Regarding Olson's *Maximus*," where he sets out the following argument, relative not only to his own work but to Olson's poetics. Duncan asserts that Olson's writing introduces a new dimension of the self into poetry, namely "internal sensation." According to Duncan, a mastery of ear and eye had already been realized in the poetic tradition, but a final mastery of this other function, where the "inner voice" resides, still remained to be gained, and this had been Olson's achievement. His *Maximus Poems* succeeds in both the articulation of the neural and muscular responsiveness of the poet and in the precise expression of what eye and ear perceive. In conclusion, Duncan writes: "On the level of reference, the gain from Whitman's address to his cosmic body to Olson's address to 'The waist of a lion/for a man to move properly' is immense."[33]

He reaffirms his belief in romance and his sense of collage as the major language of the twentieth century and reveals his desire to unite the voluptuous lyricism of Romantic poetry with an American Imagist reductiveness that would allow the immediate world to become the central referent. He takes off from a quote from Dewey: "Order rhythm and balance means that energies significant for experience are acting at their best." And notes: "I point to Emerson or to Dewey to show that in American Philosophy there are foreshadowings or forelightings of *Maximus*. In this aesthetic, 'conception cannot be abstracted from doing,' beauty is related to the beauty of an archer hitting the mark. Referrd [sic] to its source in the act, the intellect actually manifest as energy, as presence in doing, is the measure of our *arete* (as vision, *claritas*, light, illumination, was the measure of Medieval *arete*)."[34]

Creeley's note for this number is on painter Philip Guston, and he seems to pick up on the same notions of care and accident that Zukofsky mentions regarding Aristotle in his essay on Shakespeare: "For a sense of it, say—I tried to be careful, but the form would not have it. My care was the form I had given it. How to care, that one does care?"[35]

The Black Mountain Review no. 7

For the final issue, with its cover by Ed Corbett, Allen Ginsberg appears as contributing editor, gathering and assembling into a wider alternative poetics more of the key figures from the 1950s. Here, set about before our eyes, is the preparatory ground and the naming of the figures to inhabit Don Allen's *New American Poetry*. The number includes Ginsberg's poem "America," with its dramatic and bitter declaration of intent:

[33] Robert Duncan, *The Black Mountain Review* no. 6, 1956, p. 211, referring to Charles Olson, "Tyrian Businesses," *The Maximus Poems* (New York: Jargon/Corinth Books, 1960), p. 35.

[34] Duncan, *The Black Mountain Review*, p. 202.

[35] Creeley, *The Black Mountain Review* no. 6, 1956, p. 170.

America I've given you all and now I'm nothing.
America two dollars and twentyseven cents January 17, 1956.
I can't stand my own mind.
America when will we end the human war?[36]

Kerouac contributes "October in the Railroad Earth," with its emotive identifications of the Beat agenda of night, jazz, Negroes, bums on 3rd Street, San Francisco, and the rituals of getting high, as well as his influential "Spontaneous Prose" essay. There are poems by McClure, Snyder, and Whalen, as well as sections from Burroughs's *Naked Lunch,* with its stark opening in the form of a letter to Ginsberg: "Last night I took last of Yage mixture I brought back from Pucallpa. No use transporting to U.S. It doesn't keep more than a few days. This morning, still high. This is what occurred to me. Yage is space time travel. The room seems to shake and vibrate with motion. The blood and substance of many races . . . Migrations, incredible journeys through deserts and jungles and mountains . . . "[37]

We find Dorn's precise understanding of the way that landscape forms and informs those who inhabit it ("C. B. & Q."), together with passages from what would become Hubert Selby Jr.'s *Last Exit to Brooklyn,* with its breathless, forward driven, gay-confessional prose:

> Georgette was a—hep—queer. She (he) didn/t try to disguise or conceal it with marriage and—man/s talk—; satisfying her homosexuality with the keeping of a secret scrapbook of pictures of favorite male actors or athletes; or by supervising the activities of young boys; or visiting Turkish baths or men/s locker rooms, leering sidely while seeking protection behind a carefully guarded guise of virility (fearing the moment at a cocktail party or in a bar when this—front—may start crumbling from alcohol and be completely disintegrated with an attempted kiss or groping of an attractive young man and being repelled with a punch and—rotten fairy—, followed with hysterical, and incoherent apologies and excuses and running from the room) . . .[38]

This issue makes a conscious attempt to signal Modernist roots and precursors: an exchange of correspondence between Edward Dahlberg and Herbert Read, a piece by William Carlos Williams on Marsden Hartley and Ford Madox Ford, as well as a poem by Alfred Kreymborg. Creeley and Olson are themselves present—the first through a note on the work of the photographer Harry Callahan (also at Black Mountain), where the clarity of the eye to register an instant and capture images of isolation are picked out as key qualities; and the second through a review of Cyrus H. Gordon's *Homer and the Bible,* calling attention to the etymological and archaeological concerns in the East Mediterranean that were so central to his own writing.

[36] Allen Ginsberg, *The Black Mountain Review* no. 7, autumn 1957, p. 25.

[37] William Burroughs (as "William Lee"), *The Black Mountain Review* no. 7, p. 144.

[38] Hubert Selby, Jr., "Love/s Labour/s Lost," *The Black Mountain Review* no. 7, autumn 1957, p. 169.

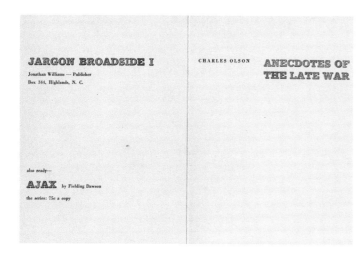
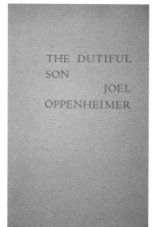

To round things off, and to maintain the customary critical spirit, there is a surprisingly critical review of *Howl* by Rumaker that Creeley feels is one of the most balanced pieces of writing to have been written on this emblematic text:

> The poem does not contain itself.
>
> A listing of horrors described with inaccurate adjectives sheared would have produced greater shock—the cumulative adjectives exhaust whatever fine tension of feeling the poet may have had in the concept—but it is reduced to hysteria and the force of the poem loses by waywardness, thrashing about. The right words (found, culled) and not overloaded with adjectives for fear the point will be missed if too spare. It's spareness that's needed here, to let the poem emerge from its adjectival obfuscation.
>
> The poem builds to hysteria. The last section is chaos, the logical conclusion to the build-up. The poem scatters itself, finally, on its own pitiful frenzy. A way has not been found.[39]

Rumaker's review is tempered by William Carlos Williams's contribution, written as a preface for Ginsberg's as yet unpublished volume of poems, *Empty Mirror*. Given its function, the tone is inevitably more positive. He centers on the fated, Dantesque line of Ginsberg's poems, written as if it were prose but "prose among whose words the terror of their truth has been discovered."[40]

Jonathan Williams, in Highlands, North Carolina, published the final number of the *Review*. Potentially, there still remained material for another number, including essays by Dahlberg and photos by Frederick Sommer, but Creeley had by then left Black Mountain, which had closed, and was in New Mexico. The work in a certain sense had been done. The seeds had been sown, and there were new magazines spring-

[39] Michael Rumaker, "Allen Ginsberg's *Howl*," *The Black Mountain Review* no. 7, autumn 1957, p. 230.

[40] William Carlos Williams, *The Black Mountain Review* no. 7, autumn 1957, p. 240.

ing up all over the place. San Francisco was a hive of activity, with Duncan blithely proclaiming it the New Venice. Jonathan Williams, as he had already been doing with *Jargon*, paralleled and continued the lines of interest of the review, in terms of both Modernist and Postmodernist writers, publishing Bob Brown, Creeley, Dawson, Duncan, Eigner, Russel Edson, Paul Goodman, Levertov, Mina Loy, Paul Metcalf, Olson, Oppenheimer, and Kenneth Patchen.

Black Mountain College: Creeley and Olson

Not referential, but inner inherence
Not learning, but applicableness

CHARLES OLSON
Last lecture at Connecticut[41]

Those associated with the Black Mountain School of writing have different approaches to and distinctive manners of writing, but, says Creeley, there is a common ground: "That is, we each feel that writing is something we're given to do rather than choose to do; that the form an actual writing takes is very intimate to the circumstance and impulses of its literal time of writing . . . that the modality conceived and the occasion conceived, is a very similar one."[42]

Joel Oppenheimer is specific about the formative weight Olson exercised on the emerging poetics. He argues that the Black Mountain poets are more interested in the formal use of the line than the Beats or the New York School poets, that they share a certain texture and emerge from the same general attack on language. He insists they share a common concern for finding their voice in the sound of the poem and that the poem on the page should reflect the intimacies of the individual voice: ". . . the poem should read on the page as I myself read it to you aloud. It should have my breath in it . . . I tend toward a very loose, flat control of my line and Creeley has an incredibly tight control of his line . . . "[43] His own writing displays these preoccupations and places a clear emphasis on natural physiological rhythms, making the poem correspond, as it were, to the tightened shape of the man. Oppenheimer's poem "An Answer" pulls together into a natural tension:

> what mercy is not
> strained, what justice
> not bought, what
> love not used come thru.
> my lady asks me
> not without reason
> where is pleasure in it. where sense.

[41] Charles Olson, *Charles Olson in Connecticut: Last Lectures,* quoted by J. Cech, O. Ford, and P. Rittner (Iowa City: The Windhover Press, University of Iowa, 1974), unpaginated.

[42] Robert Creeley in Martin Duberman, *Black Mountain: An Exploration in Community* (New York: Dutton, 1972), p. 414

[43] Joel Oppenheimer in Duberman, *Black Mountain* (New York: W.W. Norton, 1993), p. 414.

BEAUTY AND THE BEAST (JOEL OPPENHEIMER AND FRANCINE DU PLESSIX), BLACK MOUNTAIN COLLEGE, 1951. PHOTOGRAPH BY JONATHAN WILLIAMS. Collection of Jonathan Williams.

my ear is not worth much
in these matters, tho it be
shelllike, and acute.
offer beyond a dedication?
and a particular care.[44]

What was it that Creeley found at Black Mountain that so attracted him? Creeley convincingly suggests that the answer may well be a group of "highly volatile and articulate people in rather extraordinary circumstances of isolation,"[45] people who matched and echoed his own personal extremity. Rumaker addresses the man and his work, the significant evidences of his writing: "His is a scrupulous and highly exact examination of conscious processes. His own clearances, then as now, are in areas of excruciating wakefulness. If his demons are 'conscious' ones, they are, paradoxically, no less real and terrifying than those lurking in the dark under-roots of the unconscious. Yet much of his writing has the quality of dreams, in definitions of consciousness so newly realized that they have an other worldly aura, so foreign are they, seen from the prospect of his unique and stripped-down acute angle of vision . . ."[46]

[44] Joel Oppenheimer, *The Dutiful Son*, Jargon 16/Jonathan Williams, 1956, unpaginated.

[45] Robert Creeley, quoted in Duberman, p. 419.

[46] Michael Rumaker, in *Robert Creeley's Life and Work* (Ann Arbor: University of Michigan Press, 1987), p. 65.

This pushing hard into the corners of self comes through in "Chasing the Bird," where the careful listening to the complex ordering of sound and syntax lies at the centre of the writing. Creeley seems here to be engaged with the substance of an emotion, with a very distinct content of feeling. It is a question of moving along, even stumbling painfully, with the writing, with the feelings as felt. There is a direct, unbroken connection between means (content) and end (form):

> The sun sets unevenly and the people
> go to bed.
>
> The night has a thousand eyes.
> The clouds are low, overhead.
>
> Every night it is a little bit
> more difficult, a little
>
> harder. My mind
> to me a mangle is.[47]

What Creeley is doing is to evidence emotion and intelligence, turning language into an active principle.

The staff at Black Mountain College chose their own teaching hours. Duncan taught early in the morning and Olson late at night. Dorn recalls Olson's classes as beginning in the evening and going on until they finished, sometimes all night. Dorn makes the mind as sharp as the eye, building on Olson's sense of the horizon being what the eye literally takes in with a single glance. Dorn's poem "Geranium" opens:

> I know that peace is soon coming, and love of common object,
> and of woman and all the natural things I groom, in my mind, of
> faint rememberable patterns, the great geography of my lunacy.[48]

or as he writes in "A Fate of Unannounced Years": "I am American finding myself in America."[49] Dorn is a writer who considers the American southwest: issues of ownership and histories of ruthless speculation, the rape of the land. In his influential essay "What I See in *The Maximus Poems*"[50] he contrasts his own landscape with that of Olson in *The Maximus Poems*, so deeply rooted in the rich, central and complex history of New England. His own residence in Santa Fe, New Mexico, offers little to match Olson's vital aesthetic; it is incapable, he feels, of such immensities of reality.

---

[47] Robert Creeley, "Chasing the Bird," first published in *The Charm* (San Francisco: Four Seasons Foundation, 1979), p. 59, reprinted in *The Collected Poems of Robert Creeley* (Berkeley and Los Angeles: University of California Press, Berkeley, 1982), p. 60.

[48] Ed Dorn, "Geranium," *The Newly Fallen* (New York, Totem, 1961), p. 4, cover drawing by Fielding Dawson.

[49] Ed Dorn, *Hands Up* (New York: Totem/Corinth Books, 1964), unpaginated.

[50] First published (Ventura/Worcester: Migrant Press, reprinted in Ed Dorn, *Views* (San Francisco: Four Seasons, 1980).

Dawson's recollections are often hyperbolic, excited, and myth-making, told in a charged, yet vulnerable, rhetoric: "It was real; we felt it. Charley gave it everything he had; in his humanity he was occasionally inhuman; the Ahab in him. His generosity with his perceptions and deductions was selfish in that sometimes he left us out, not because we couldn't understand it, but because it was too intensely Charley-Black-Mountain. The kind of man that suddenly realized maximum power, he became a whirling wind of himself realized, and in a man, a big man, a huge man, Charley turned into the very thing he foresaw, with him receiving like a fine computer. Charley isn't a genius, Charley is the prototype of his genius and in 1950, 51, 52, 53 he went into high, seeing a form of education in sense, it was like a dream. We were there with him."[51]

The Painters

Creeley and Olson wanted a poetry at the center of a larger movement among the arts toward less-structured forms of self-expression. Jazz, orchestral composition, abstract expressionist painting, theater-in-the-round, ballet, architecture, and design had already abandoned traditional structural principles. Except for jazz, leading figures in each of these fields congregated at Black Mountain College to teach new techniques to their students. Franz Kline, Willem de Kooning, Robert Motherwell, Esteban Vicente, all came to teach summer courses. Their work, if not a direct model to the writers, provided key parallels in the ways in which they engaged process or explored the concept of the painting as an inclusive field.

Creeley, in discussing the impulses and influences behind his early work, pinpoints the fact that he tended to work with a small focus and an intensive kind of address. These short lyric poems from the 1950s appear as pared-down blocks in tersely worded lines. One can find analogies with the emotional process that underlies Abstract Expressionist painting from this same time—even more so when Creeley affirms his need for a more various emotional state and a more inclusive space within which to work.

Duncan had acknowledged that painters had given insights into new compositional organizations, where anything could come into the field, including trivia, as long as it did so with a real insistence. Duncan was thinking specifically of collage and assemblage as providing a language, but it is also clear that Elmer Bischoff, De Kooning, Pollock, or Hassel Smith were engaged in a similar practice.

Fielding Dawson wrote *An Emotional Memoir of Franz Kline*, its endpapers bearing the image of Kline's *Shenandoah Wall*. This memoir immortalizes De Kooning, Kline, Pollock, the atmosphere of the Cedar Bar, the parties, the women, artists' lofts, the bustle of the streets, comings and goings. Kline was Dawson's role model, larger than life, a counter-balance to Olson, built of the same kind of massive energy that guaranteed the two personalities could only clash. Why? Perhaps, as Dawson notes, "Because Charley, in his perception and deduction had included Franz even before Franz had arrived. It makes sense. Two includers with big egos who stressed attitude . . . so inherently it was a personal philosophy, almost an orientally potent combination of

ROBERT MOTHERWELL TEACHING. BLACK MOUNTAIN COLLEGE, SUMMER, 1945. PHOTOGRAPH BY MARGARET WILLIAMSON.

BUCKMINSTER FULLER'S ARCHITECTURE CLASS (WITH WILLEM DE KOONING AND ALBERT LANIER). BLACK MOUNTAIN COLLEGE, SUMMER, 1948. PHOTOGRAPH BY KENNETH SNELSON.

[51] Fielding Dawson, *The Black Mountain Book* (New York: Croton Press, 1970), p. 88.

guilt and ego. Visible in strong American men: an almost feminine sensitivity to the felt formal gesture, from which emanates a charm so beguiling in its humanness it kills the men who possess it."[52]

Creeley's contacts with artists have been constant across his life from the 1950s up to the present, and they demonstrate a range of concerns, a pulse-taking of our times, from Laubiès to Baselitz, from Kitaj to Sultan, from Indiana to Clemente. The contributions of artists and photographers to *The Black Mountain Review* had been to freshen things up when everything seemed to be becoming too dense. John Altoon, Harry Callahan, Edward Corbett, Philip Guston, Franz Kline, René Laubiès, Dan Rice, and Aaron Siskind brought new ways of seeing to the review's readers.

Creeley, recognizing that painters had taken a lead on the writers in many ways, drew on them to give shape to a poetics that was in the air: "They had . . . already begun to move away from the insistently pictorial, whether figurative or non-figurative, to a direct manifestation . . . of the energy inherent in the materials, literally, and their physical manipulation in the act of painting itself. Process, in the sense that Olson found it in Whitehead, was clearly much in their minds."[53]

Meanwhile, Creeley sees a common base for painters and poets in that Americans come without history and can therefore live the moment without complication:

> But all I want to do is to say this has been seen in the world and this is my experience of it. Not as argument but as invitation to come. You can see the relevance. We were making things. Not only of our own imagination, which was after all finally the point, but we were making things in the materials particular to our own experience of things, just as John Chamberlain was experiencing the particular facts of materials in his world, e.g. those car parts, and seeing how the imagination might articulate that experience. I was trying to

HARRY CALLAHAN: *ASHEVILLE, NORTH CAROLINA*, 1951, PRINTED 1971.
Gelatin silver print, 9 x 12 inches.
San Francisco Museum of Modern Art. Purchase, sale of Edward Westons Fund. © The Estate of Harry Callahan. Photograph by Ben Blackwell.

HARRY CALLAHAN: *ELEANOR*, 1951, PRINTED 1971.
Gelatin silver print, 10 ⅜ x 11 ¹⁵⁄₁₆ inches.
San Francisco Museum of Modern Art. Purchase, sale of Edward Weston Funds. © The Estate of Harry Callahan. Photograph by Ben Blackwell.

[52] Dawson, p. 105.

[53] Robert Creeley, *Poets and Painters of the Cities* (New York: Dutton, 1974), p. 58.

AARON SISKIND
NC 29.
Vintage silver print, 10 x 8 inches.
Robert Mann Gallery. © Aaron Siskind.

AARON SISKIND: *NORTH CAROLINA*, 1951.
Gelatin silver print, 19 ½ x 13 ½ inches.
Gift of Richard L. Menschel, 1977.668.
Image © The Art Institute of Chicago.
© Aaron Siskind.

make do with the vocabulary in terms of experience in my world. And neither one of us had history. Neither one of us had articulate experience of history, as something we'd come through as persons the issue of.[54]

And to conclude, should I have to look for a phrase that holds so much of the intent, the desire, the energy, perhaps I'd select that remark of Duncan's "conception cannot be abstracted from doing." It serves as the quintessence of an American aesthetic, allowing the poet to catch the energy pulsing in a single word, the painter in a single brushstroke. Black Mountain, like a poem or a painting, came to an end when it had nothing else to say, or when the energy ran out, or when there was no more money. But then again, at another level, it clearly didn't end. The pulse continues until we stop. This is the place wherever we are: "All that would matter to me, finally, as a writer, is that the scale and the place of our common living be recognized, that the mundane in that simple emphasis be acknowledged."[55] We keep on moving till it stops and the movement goes on alone. Here is a man and here are his words, and in paying attention to the latter the former takes shape.

K. P.

[54] Robert Creeley, *Contexts of Poetry: Interviews 1961–71* (Bolinas: Four Seasons Foundation, 1973), p. 156.

[55] Robert Creeley, *Autobiography* (New York, Hanuman Books, 1990), p. 55.

DIVERS PRESS PUBLICATIONS,
EDITED BY ROBERT CREELEY,
PRINTED BY MOSSÉN ALCOVER,
PALMA DE MALLORCA

All Devils Fading, by Martin Seymour-Smith, 1953.

From the Sustaining Air, by Larry Eigner, 1953.

In Cold Hell, In Thicket, by Charles Olson, edited by Robert Creeley, issued as *Origin* 8, winter 1953.

The Kind of Act of, by Robert Creeley, cover René Laubiès, 1953.

Proensa, by Paul Blackburn, translations of Provençal poets, cover Ann Mackinnon, 1953.

The Gold Diggers, by Robert Creeley, cover René Laubiès, 1954.

Mayan Letters, by Charles Olson, edited by Robert Creeley, cover Ann Mackinnon, 1954.

Black Rain, poems and drawings by Katue Kitasono, cover by Katue Kitasono, 1954.

In the Midst of My Fever, by Irving Layton, cover design by Jonathan Williams, 1954.

Caesar's Gate: Poems 1949–50, by Robert Duncan, with collages by Jess Collins, cover Jess Collins, 1955.

The Dissolving Fabric, by Paul Blackburn, cover by Dan Rice, silkscreen reproductions by Arthur Okamura, 1955

The Hypocritic Days, by Douglas Woolf, cover by Katue Kitasono, 1955

Robert Creeley

OLSON AND BLACK MOUNTAIN COLLEGE

THE PAINTER Jack Tworkov tells a great story about meeting Charles Olson by accident one day in Washington, D.C. It is the proverbial moment. Both are about to cross the street in opposite directions. But for whatever reason or impulse, Olson begins to sketch out for Tworkov his sense of the frames of Western art, from the primordial caves on out. Tworkov recalls it was a fascinating and unexpected survey, given he had no sense even of Olson's interest in the subject. Yet here Olson was, in the street, qualifying brilliantly the genesis of forms, the determining character of materials, the transformation of gesture into substance—a demonstration of conception and example such as Tworkov had never previously witnessed. So not very long after Tworkov contrived to have Olson invited to give a talk in a series otherwise committed to art historians and the like. Tworkov assured all that they would hear a synthesis of art's origins from Olson, the like of which they would never have chance to hear again. But the afternoon proved an extraordinary disappointment. Olson seemed uninterested, his talk rambled and proved almost evasive. People grumbled and left thoroughly disappointed. Tworkov mused, how could this be the same man he had listened to on the street corner with such enchantment and respect?

Be it said, there were many Olsons, or, better, there were many ways in which this protean person took hold of the world and all that he found in it. It's as if he were, as he puts it in Maximus, his great epic poem, "testing and missing some proof," conjecturing endlessly, trying on for defining size all the manifests of the apparent, the real of each day's event. It was hard not to come under his spell and he was finally bored by those who did. He hated the "father" people at times wanted to make him and threatened Fielding Dawson that he would come after him, if ever Dawson were to publish his Black Mountain Book, which, of course, to his credit, Dawson did. One evening in his company I remember him holding entranced a room full of people from something like eleven in the evening till just before dawn. When at last we were out on the street, he said to me with a shrug, "I thought those people would never stop talking!"

At Black Mountain, a class of his which met at seven in the evening one time ended at one the next afternoon. Olson had been the active protagonist throughout. As a talker he had few peers indeed—only the poet Robert Duncan could match him, and Duncan said his own solution to the unintended contest was that they should both talk at once. I wondered if he were aware of his effect on people in that way. A trained student orator and a great poet to boot, he must have known the power of his own speech? Yet he was shy often in beginning, would shift, repeat, hesitate, until the wind filled his sails and he was off. I think it was the wonder of thinking he delighted in, the way things came together and then opened to unexpected prospects, endlessly "projective"—to use a term with which he was much identified. That the world experienced could be thought, could be recognized without a distracting translation, could be entered particularly, was the abiding wonder he insistently returned to.

My own relation with Charles Olson began in the spring of 1950. His Gloucester, Massachusetts friend, Vincent Ferrini, sent some of Olson's poems to me for a "little

Portrait of the Artist (Robert Creeley) as a Spanish Assassin, 1954. Photograph by Jonathan Williams. Black Mountain College Museum and Arts Center, Asheville.

magazine" I was trying to get started. My quick response to Vincent was simply that the poems were "looking for a language." I was twenty-four. Olson was thirty-nine. Although we wrote to one another almost obsessively in the years before we met in person—ten volumes of the correspondence are now in print, covering only the dates from April 21, 1950 to July 12, 1952—I was not prepared for his actual presence. So following the college's having given me a journal to edit and to publish in 1954 (*The Black Mountain Review*, 1954–1957), on Olson and the faculty's invitation I went there to teach that same spring. I had never taught before and learned as I went. So, curiously, began a life I had never thought possible—a world with others as myself that both recognized and included me.

I had heard that Charles Olson was a tall man but then there are many tall people, and many short ones, and all those in between. I don't know quite what I expected but, when I finally got to the college in my old truck, the person who answered the door of the small house to which I'd been directed was no one I'd thought to see. It wasn't his height simply—some six foot eight—or his bulk. He was barrel-chested but his waist seemed trim and his legs as well. He was not heavy, in the usual sense. The scale and compactness of his head were impressive, if that's the word. He was bald for the most part and had great, bushy eyebrows, snub nose, broad forehead. His head was solid, round. I think of Picasso and, to some extent, Williams. He wore thick-lensed glasses, which concentrated his eyes and their look, intent, direct. His voice was extraordinary and that I had heard before—a taped reading of his poems

CHARLES OLSON, BLACK MOUNTAIN COLLEGE, 1951, WRITING *THE MAXIMUS POEMS*. PHOTOGRAPH BY JONATHAN WILLIAMS. Collection of Jonathan Williams.

which he had done for Richard Wirtz Emerson, who in turn had loaned it to Cid Corman for use on the latter's late 40s Boston radio program, This is Poetry. Finally, there was an attractiveness he had that was a bit uncanny. I have never known anyone, before or since, who could so engage the attention and response of people, so bring them to his common need and interest.

However, what I first saw was this very big man, clothed only with a towel, still wet from the shower, saying and gesturing, come in, come in! In I went and moments later, it seemed, we were altogether engaged with talking of all that our letters had touched on and worked to locate—writing, magazine, person, history, presence, conjecture—how to enter most particularly the literal world. Then I do remember he said, "But you will want to get right to work! I have arranged for your first class to meet this afternoon at two." The time—given all the years past—may have been earlier or later, but I remember absolutely that it was to be that very day. I was still groggy from having driven all the night before, and now, with this intensity and scale of friend suddenly in front of me, I realized that all my preparation, call it, such as it had ever been, was ridiculous. I was there and I was there to teach—and now, as Olson rightly insisted, was the time to begin. In fact, it took some weeks for me to learn to speak loudly enough so that all the patient students might finally hear what I was saying? But it never occurred to me to say then that it was too soon to start, that I needed a day to settle, to catch my breath. Olson was not simply overbearing, but curiously including—one found oneself settled in his terms without question.

DAN RICE AND ROBERT CREELEY, BLACK MOUNTAIN COLLEGE, 1955. PHOTOGRAPH BY JONATHAN WILLIAMS. Collection of Jonathan Williams.

No doubt his initial background, first as a student orator and then his work in politics, gave him a unique training for this exceptional capability. I remember his saying once, "I need a college to think with" It seemed very true. He depended on multiple reference, relevant density, context particular, an occasion for the "testing some proof" he speaks of in Maximus. Given that Black Mountain was a place "where people were more interested in what they didn't know than in what they did," as the sculptor John Chamberlain later said, Olson's was the perfect intelligence and intellectual habit for its use and coherence. He was immensely bored with the static, the talking about talking, which he dubbed "the universe of discourse," as opposed to that initial place, the literal and transforming world into which one was born, and then lived and died. He wanted to regain a way through to the primary, to have the human be again a freshness, not merely an echo of whatever it might once have been. The Lacandone Indians of Mexico fascinated him. They were all that was left of their great people, the Mayans, and again and again in his time at Black Mountain he pushed himself, his colleagues and students to attempt that crucial passage to the radical or root by whatever means that they could find. He spoke of the American as "the last first people" and himself as an "archaeologist of morning."

Perhaps most relevant for the situation of our present world is the moving elegy he wrote for the young German poet Rainer M. Gerhardt, whose early and despairing death in 1954—two years before the college was to close—came to us, his fellow poets, as a painful and final death knell for all the old European patterns. But it was not "Europe vs. America" that engaged either Olson or myself then. America was also lost in the same gray emptiness, bled out in congealing dollars, and was the equal victim of its own static habits and abstracting humanism.

> O my collapsed brother,
> the body
> does bring us
> down
>   The images
> have to be
> contradicted
>   The metamorphoses
> are to be
> undone

(from "The Death of Europe," August 1954)

Had Olson had his way, Black Mountain College might well have continued as an itinerant complex, a kind of wandering band of artist and scholar fellows. He considered the possibility of an urban "weekend" college, for example, thinking it might get use of space in some office building that the week's end otherwise emptied out. New York would have been its ideal setting and its faculty would be both that "happy few" who were still there after the college's collapse in North Carolina and then the fortuitously present transients, met with by accident—who had always been, in one way or another, a very real part of the college from the outset. Still for Olson the heyday must have been the early fifties just before I came, when the painters, composers and dancers were there in some real number, not to mention those as Buckminster Fuller and Paul Goodman. It was a denser, more various company. I know, for example, that he took some dance classes with Merce Cunningham. Years later I asked Merce what Olson had been like and he answered, "A very serious elephant!"

True enough that the college did echo in shards and pieces for years and years after its closing—and continues to do so, even to this day. Fledgling schools and artists alike still long for some possible replica—to found a new "Black Mountain," to teach without an overseeing and absent "board," to be ostensibly free in one's inquiry and production. Yet what Bill de Kooning said about it all still makes sense. "The only problem with Black Mountain is that if you go there, they want to give it to you." No doubt that's the other side of "freedom". There are few colleges whose president, bursar and professors might be found on a Sunday morning, pulling classic gunk out of a clogged up main drain so as to allow the student toilets to continue to function. But we did it, Olson, Wes Huss and I and I don't remember us finding it exceptional.

Charles Olson was the last of Black Mountain's defining persons, its great and concluding rector, and though he taught sporadically at other institutions (the University at Buffalo and the University of Connecticut among them), it was never to be the same, either for him or for those who looked to him for guidance. Perhaps the best he could tell them was that "limits are what any of us are inside of . . ." Yet how one recognized these "limits," and how one then responded, were finally the crux of what he had to say. At last the point must be made as he had it, that "art is the only true twin life has." Willy-nilly these go together into whatever human world can now be the case.

A last sense of him, then, might well be an evening we went together to meet a younger friend of Hazel-Frieda Larsen, a retired teacher of photography at the college who continued to live in the town of Black Mountain. Her friend had just come down from some job in the art industry, which he had unfortunately lost. Hazel thought there might be something for him to do at the college. We sat in her small living room, the candidate, appropriately dressed, across from us, while Olson sat more or less facing him. My own part was to be company for Olson, and to witness. As the fellow talked of his background, what he had done, what he hoped to do, Olson began to wrap the shawl he characteristically had with him around his large head, so that finally only his eyes with their glasses, his nose, and his mouth were visible. As the man continued, a bit distracted, Olson's hand began to stroke at his mouth, making a curious mewing sound as he did, pulling at his lips. Hazel, her friend and I were transfixed. Olson seemed not to be conscious of his acts and looked to the man to continue. Finally it all faltered and ended, and Olson and I said good night and left. Not for us, Olson said, or words to that effect, just another art hustler, cheap mind. I realized he had been "reading" the sad person, as it were, miming his state, his defensiveness, his confusion. Nothing hostile—unless the very fact of such an ability to perceive another is in itself contesting. As it was, Olson had no consciousness of either his act or its effect. Whether artist or teacher, or both, it matters that one read the world, one's life, like a book, Olson said—a Tantrist. Black Mountain and Olson were a consummate company for one another, and for all who were there with them.

R. C.

3 Black Mountain Poems

Charles Olson
A GLYPH

Robert Creeley
AN ODE (FOR BLACK MT. COLLEGE)

John Wieners
THE BLACK MOUNTAIN BLUES

Charles Olson

A GLYPH

Romans, my contrymen [sic]
your daemons
are neglected, abundance
is what you have, all
that you produce

so you should be surprised

what is left to us, except
to shut us up in our houses
like fattening birds and gorge
our bellies in the dark until
we burst with fat

Previously unpublished poem.
Charles Olson Papers,
University of Connecticut, Storrs.

Robert Creeley

AN ODE

(for Black Mt. College)

There is this side of it.
                    And two weeks ago I was
reading
of it — a book, and a long poem:
                    Simon Bolivar.

And why not. One is much too
repentant. The secrets are
to be shared.

Why go to college. Or, as a man said, it
is too far away.

Why go.

If I don't get there, — I did
once

If I don't get there, this year
anyhow I know some of the names, I know
what it might have been like, say, or

you say. (The creeleys
are all comediente.)

The sky here, dark enough, tonight
the moon is
is not to any other
insistence,
            is mute in
itself.

Tonight, fire. The race
of fire. And what the hell else to say but
run.

Previously unpublished poem.
Robert Creeley Papers,
Stanford University.

John Wieners

THE BLACK MOUNTAIN BLUES

I want to go back to old black mountain this morning,
I want to sing old songs with Dorn and Charlie O,
I want to take my bleeding heart,
I wanta break my bleeding heart
all over this city's asphalt floor,
I want to swish a mountain shadow,
hear tree frogs say good morning, mister,
and the red clay roads will deep my feet in mud,
I want to sleep in the same pants every night
I want to eat spaghetti every night
with the ladies who play gay guitars
and the boys who lie down
in rain to see the stars,
I want the copperheads, the roses and the streams,
I want the mountains, and Lake Eden in my dreams
I want to go back to Black Mountain in the morning
and play ping pong in the cellar,
hear Billie Holliday through the woods
drink half a dollar wine till I'm drunk for good,
I want to leave the neon and the cement towers,
I want to spend my life in loneliness,
without a cheap lover to wash my face,
a lover who will fill my place when I turn my back,
I want to go back so fast
I want to be lonely,
I want only the shadow of those black mountains,
and kiss the rain, that's my roman fountains,
I want to catch lunar moths,
and pee on the chairs.
I want to walk down mornings,
and pick up the mail,
I want to see the men in grey come from the
county jails to clean our fields,
to wash our faces,
I want to go back to those empty rooms,
and taste the dirty delight of lonely nights,
I want to cry in bed again,
and sleep under windows that have no glass,
drink my beer with ten outcasts that make up
the people, make up for lovers
I leave behind me when I take for cover
under the warm and black hills of black mountain.
I want to roll my cigarettes again, and play piano,
with one finger, I want to walk down pathways and linger
by roses and japanese vines,
I want to hear Miles Davis sing again,
and old Bessie do swing again,
I want to hear the husbands and wives throw ink again

on each other's sink again,
those old tree frogs are calling me, the mountains,
are growing tall for me,
oh take me back, carry me back,
on the morning train, the tuesday train,
I shall go by the lumber yards,
and wait in the stations, the colored pardners,
I left behind, at Peek's, at all the
old familiar roads I bicyled,
I will ride again by the rapids,
and see the dogs catch lizards in the dawn,
oh those old grey mountains are calling,
those pink mountains are calling,
so it takes my lover away from me,
it brings me to a lonely country,
I go there, I run there, to see Charlie O,
and Connie O, with the dogs and babies who swear and wear no clothes,
I will give up my heart I will go in the dark to go back
to them someday, and take the beautiful bends, the road
that shows me my end, alone, alone, is the road I see,
but still I'll go there and I'll kiss the hornets and bees,
I'll hear foxes under my window,
I'll be afraid to go out in the dark, and I'll
whisper into my pillow, your light's gone out,
your light is up in the city, in bed with somebody else,
but it doesn't matter, in the mountains,
it doesn't matter in the hills, cuz there I'll be,
and there I'll wander from room to room,
from fellow to fonder, I'll take my
chances in the hills again,
I'll go and take my chances in the hills, again,
so mister man, buy a one-way ticket, I'm going back
dad I'm leaving this circuit, I'm cutting my space, I'm leaving
this time, I'm going on mountain, eastern mountain saving time,
so take your ticket for me, I'll kiss you goodbye,
I'll have nobody now, to kiss me and cry
I'll have no lips to keep mine dry,
I'll be alone, there,
I'll be alone with nobody to care
for me,
but still I'm taking that trip,
and it's the end of the road,
but the end shall be high up
and I'll die with gold
clothes on,
in the black mountains of northern carolina,
I'll die and my face will have a silver-lining.

Previously unpublished poem.
Printed with permission of the poet.

Appendix

SELECTED BIBLIOGRAPHY

BOOKS AND ARTICLES BY FACULTY AND STUDENTS OF BLACK MOUNTAIN COLLEGE

Anni Albers. "Work With Material," *Black Mountain College Bulletin*, no. 5, November 1938, reprinted in Anni Albers, *Selected Writings on Design*, edited and with an introduction by Brenda Danilowitz. Middletown: Wesleyan University Press, 2000.

Anni Albers. "One Aspect of Art Work," first published as "We Need the Crafts for Their Contact with Materials," *Design*, 1944, re-titled and reprinted in Anni Albers, *Selected Writings on Design*, edited and with an introduction by Brenda Danilowitz. Middletown: Wesleyan University Press, 2000.

Josef Albers. "Concerning Fundamental Design," from "Werklicher Formunterricht," published in *bauhaus. zeitschrift für gestaltung*, nos. 2/3. Dessau, 1928.

Josef Albers. "Concerning Art Instruction," published as *Black Mountain College Bulletin*, no. 2. Black Mountain College, June 1934.

Josef Albers. "Present and/or Past," in *design 47*, no. 8 (April 1946).

John Cage. "To Describe the Process of Composition Used in *Music of Changes* and *Imaginary Landscape no. 4*," originally published in *trans/formation*, vol. 1, no. 3, New York, 1952. Reprinted in John Cage, *Silence*. Middletown: Wesleyan University Press, 1961.

John Cage. *Conversing With Cage*, edited by Richard Kostelanetz. New York: Limelight Editions, 1988.

Robert Creeley. *The Island*. New York: Charles Scribner's Sons, 1963.

Robert Creeley. *The Gold Diggers And Other Stories*. New York: Charles Scribner's Sons, 1965.

Robert Creeley. *The Collected Poems*. Berkley and Los Angeles: University of California Press, 1982.

Robert Creeley. *The Collected Essays*. Berkeley and Los Angeles: University of California Press, 1989.

Robert Creeley. *Autobiography*. Madras and New York: Hanuman Books, 1990.

Robert Creeley. *Tales Out of School: Selected Interviews*. Ann Arbor: University of Michigan Press, 1993.

Fielding Dawson. *An Emotional Memoir of Franz Kline*. New York: Pantheon Books, 1967.

Fielding Dawson. *The Black Mountain Book: A New Edition*. Rocky Mount: North Carolina Wesleyan College Press, 1991.

Fielding Dawson. *The Sun Rises into the Sky and Other Stories 1952–1966*. Los Angeles: Black Sparrow Press, 1974.

Robert Duncan. *Fictive Certainties: Essays*. New York: New Directions Books, 1985.

Robert Duncan. *Selected Poems*, edited by Robert J. Bertholf. New York: New Directions Books, 1997.

R. Buckminster Fuller and Robert Marks. *The Dymaxion World Of Buckminster Fuller*. New York: Anchor Books, 1973.

Clement Greenberg. *Art And Culture: Critical Essay*. Boston: Beacon Press, 1961.

Walter Gropius. *The Theory and Organization of the Bauhaus*, originally published as *Idee und Aufbau des Staatlichen Bauhauses Weimar*, Bauhausverlag, Munich, 1923, translation in *Bauhaus 1919–1928*, edited by Herbert Bayer, Walter Gropius, and Ilse Gropius. New York: Museum of Modern Art, 1938.

Walter Gropius. *The New Architecture and the Bauhaus*. Cambridge: MIT Press, 1965, (first published in 1936).

Walter Gropius. "Living Architecture or 'International Style'?" in *design 47*, no. 8 (1946).

Franz Kline. Interview with Frank O'Hara, 1958, published in Frank O'Hara, *Art Chronicles 1954–1966*. New York: George Braziller, 1975.

Elaine de Kooning. "Albers Paints A Picture," *Artnews*. November 1950.

Elaine de Kooning. *The Spirit Of Abstract Expressionism: Selected Writings*. New York: George Braziller, 1994.

Willem de Kooning. *Collected Writings*. Madras and New York: Hanuman Books, 1988.

Robert Motherwell. *The Collected Writings*, edited by Stephanie Terenzio. Berkeley and Los Angeles: University of California Press, 1999.

Charles Olson. *The Maximus Poems*. New York: Jargon/Corinth Books, 1960.

Charles Olson. *The Distances/Poems*. New York: Grove Press, 1960.

Charles Olson. *Mayan Letters*. London: Grossman Publishers/Cape Editions, 1968.

Charles Olson. *Muthologos: The Collected Lectures And Interviews*, Volume 1, edited by George F. Butterick. Bolinas: Four Seasons Foundation, 1978.

Charles Olson. *Charles Olson and Ezra Pound: An Encounter at St. Elizabeth's*, edited by Catherine Seelye. New York: Paragon House, 1991.

Charles Olson. *The Collected Poems (Excluding the Maximus Poems)*. Berkeley and Los Angeles: University of California Press, 1997.

Charles Olson. *Collected Prose*, edited by Donald Allen and Benjamin Friedlander. Berkeley and Los Angeles: University of California Press, 1997.

John Andrew Rice. "Fundamentalism and the Higher Learning," *Harper's Magazine*, May 1937.

Michael Rumaker. *Gringos And Other Stories*. New York: Grove Press, 1966.

Michael Rumaker. *Robert Duncan in San Francisco*. San Francisco: Grey Fox Press, 1996.

Xanti Schawinsky. "Spectodrama" in *Form*, no. 8. September 1968.

John Wieners. *Selected Poems 1958–1984*, edited by Raymond Foye. Santa Barbara: Black Sparrow Press, 1986.

John Wieners. *Cultural Affairs In Boston: Poetry And Prose 1956–1985*, edited by Raymond Foye. Santa Barbara: Black Sparrow Press, 1988.

BOOKS AND MAGAZINES ABOUT BLACK MOUNTAIN COLLEGE, ITS FACULTY AND STUDENTS

Louis Adamic. "Education On A Mountain," *Harper's Magazine*, April, 1936, p. 520, reprinted in *My America 1928–1938*. New York: Harper and Brothers, 1938.

Tom Clark. *Charles Olson: The Allegory of a Poet's Life*. Berkeley: North Atlantic Books, 2000.

Edwin Denby. *Willem de Kooning*. Madras and New York: Hanuman Books, 1988.

Martin Duberman. *Black Mountain: An Exploration in Community*. New York: Dutton, 1972.

Mary Emma Harris. *The Arts at Black Mountain College*. Cambridge: MIT Press, 1987; reprinted 2002.

Mervin Lane, ed. *Black Mountain College: Sprouted Seeds (An Anthology Of Personal Accounts)*. Knoxville: University of Tennessee Press, 1990.

Kevin Power. "Black Mountain College, 1933–1956," *Poesía*, no. 38. Madrid: Ministerio de Cultura, 1992.

Black Mountain College Dossiers, published by Black Mountain College Museum And Arts Center, Asheville, 1995-present. No. 1 Joseph Fiore by James Thompson, No. 2 Fannie Hillsmith by James Thompson, No. 3 Lore Kadden Lindenfeld by Sigrid Wortmann Weltge, No. 4 Ray Johnson by William S. Wilson, No. 5 Susan Weil by Donna Stein, No. 6 Michael Rumaker by Leverett T. Smith, Jr., No. 7 Gwendolyn Knight by Glenis Redmond.

INDEX

O'Keefe, Georgia, 119

Okamura, Arthur, 295

Olitski, Jules, 66

Olson, Charles, 11, 93, 115, 128,
139, 141, 170, 177, 182–187, 192,
196–202, 205, 210, 211, 215–217,
234, 235, 251, 261, 262, 267, 271,
274–289, 291–293, 295, 299–304

Olson, Connie, 215

Oppenheimer, Joel, 177, 199–201,
279, 283, 285, 288–290

Oppenheimer, Rena, 279

Orozco, José Clemente, 76, 84

Oscar, Charles, 261

Ovid, 197

Ozenfant, Amédée, 11, 46, 55,
76–78, 81

P
Page, Don, 25

Page, Franklin, 121, 124

Panofsky, Irwin, 182

Parkman, Francis, 283

Parsons, Betty, 15, 119, 121, 210

Partch, Harry, 260

Passlof, Pat, 115, 116, 227, 230, 234

Patchen, Kenneth, 289

Pearlman, Judith, 71

Pearman, Charles, 152

Penn, Arthur, 136, 239, 253

Pessi, Yella, 249

Plato, 34, 35

Piaf, Edith, 139

Picasso, Pablo, 77, 124, 300

Pierini, Pascal, 260

Plessix Gray, Francine du, 139, 177,
290

Pollock, Jackson, 58, 66, 105, 159,
275, 292

Porter, Fairfield, 128

Poser, Mimi, 60

Pound, Ezra, 183, 198, 281, 284

Power, Kevin, 11, 14

Prather, Marla, 105

Preger-Simon, Marianne, 140, 141

Prestini, James, 76

Pritchett, James, 255

Purdy, James, 279

Q
Querol, Agustín, 77

R
Ramakrishna, Sri, 254

Rathburn, Virginia, 260

Rauschenberg, Robert, 11, 114, 137,
139, 144, 145, 152, 153, 155,
157–159, 162, 177, 188, 196, 199,
200, 217, 219–222, 239, 256, 257,
261

Read, Herbert, 91, 94, 287

Redmond, Glenis, 85

Reed, Alexander, 21, 25

Reinhardt, Ad, 94

Rembrandt, 159, 200

Rexroth, Kenneth, 279, 281, 282

Rice, Dan, 196, 199, 210, 231, 234,
279, 285, 293, 295, 302

Rice, John Andrew, 15–19, 32, 75,
182, 216, 240, 241, 251, 257

Rice, June, 141

Rice, Mrs, 261

Richards, M. C., 136, 138, 139, 182,
253, 257

Riding, Laura, 277

Rimbaud, Arthur, 165, 197

Río, Carmen del, 14

Roberts, Joseph J., 162

Rockburne, Dorothea, 11, 159, 188,
191, 227, 232, 234

Roethke, Theodore, 279, 281

Rodin, Auguste, 77

Roosevelt, Franklin D., 183

Roscio, Nicola del, 14

Rosen, Kenneth, 14

Rosenberg, Harold, 94

Rothenberg, Jerome, 280

Rothko, Mark, 100, 119, 227

THE PRINTING OF THIS BOOK WAS COMPLETED ON 18 OCTOBER 2002